The Lost Cinema of Mexico

*Reframing Media, Technology, and Culture in Latin/o America*

# THE LOST CINEMA OF MEXICO

From Lucha Libre to Cine Familiar and Other Churros

Edited by Olivia Cosentino and Brian Price

Héctor Fernández L'Hoeste and Juan Carlos Rodríguez, Series Editors

UNIVERSITY OF FLORIDA PRESS
Gainesville

Publication of this work is made possible by a Sustaining the Humanities through the American Rescue Plan grant from the National Endowment for the Humanities.

Copyright 2022 by Olivia Cosentino and Brian Price
All rights reserved
Published in the United States of America

27 26 25 24 23 22   6 5 4 3 2 1

Library of Congress Cataloging-in-Publication Data
Names: Cosentino, Olivia, editor. | Price, Brian L., 1975– editor.
Title: The lost cinema of Mexico : from lucha libre to cine familiar and other churros / edited by Olivia Cosentino and Brian Price.
Other titles: Reframing Media, Technology, and Culture in Latin/o America.
Description: 1. | Gainesville : University of Florida Press, 2022. | Series: Reframing media, technology, and culture in Latin/o America | Includes bibliographical references and index.
Identifiers: LCCN 2021027214 (print) | LCCN 2021027215 (ebook) | ISBN 9781683402534 (hardback) | ISBN 9781683403050 (paperback) | ISBN 9781683403210 (pdf) | ISBN 9781683403395 (ebook)
Subjects: LCSH: Motion picture industry—Mexico—History. | Motion pictures—Mexico—History. | Motion pictures—Social aspects—Mexico. | BISAC: PERFORMING ARTS / Film / History & Criticism | SOCIAL SCIENCE / Media Studies
Classification: LCC PN1993.5.M4 L58 2022 (print) | LCC PN1993.5.M4 (ebook) | DDC 791.430972—dc23
LC record available at https://lccn.loc.gov/2021027214
LC ebook record available at https://lccn.loc.gov/2021027215

University of Florida Press
2046 NE Waldo Road
Suite 2100
Gainesville, FL 32609
http://upress.ufl.edu

# CONTENTS

LIST OF FIGURES  vii
ACKNOWLEDGMENTS  ix

Introduction: El Santo versus the Cineteca Nacional de México; Rethinking the Lost Cinema of Mexico  1
*Olivia Cosentino and Brian Price*

1. I Know It's Only Rock and Roll, but I Like It: Popular Music and the Advent of the *Churro*  34
*Brian Price*

2. On Virgins, Malinches, and *Chicas Modernas*: The Star Power of Lorena Velázquez in *Lucha Libre* Cinema  62
*David S. Dalton*

3. The Mexican *Superochero* Moment: Countercultural Nations and Utopian Assemblages in Small Format  88
*Iván Eusebio Aguirre Darancou*

4. The Mexican Chili Western and Crisis Masculinity  116
*Christopher Conway*

5. Blackness and Racial Melodrama in 1970s Mexican Cinema  142
*Carolyn Fornoff*

6. *Un cine familiar*: Recovering the 1980s Mexican Family Film  166
*Olivia Cosentino*

7. Felipe Cazals: The Question of the Film Auteur in the Age of Cinematic Crisis   192
   *Ignacio M. Sánchez Prado*

8. Finding the Lost Cinema of Mexico: Critical Recovery, Rescue, and Reconceptualization   220
   *Dolores Tierney*

LIST OF CONTRIBUTORS   233
INDEX   237

## FIGURES

3.1. Low-angle shot from *La fórmula secreta*  94
3.2. *Mi casa de altos techos*  95
3.3. *Víctor Ibarra Cruz*  97
3.4. *Otro país*  100
3.5. *Otro país*  101
3.6. *El fin*  105
3.7. Still from *Ah, verdá . . . ?*  107
3.8. *Chuchulucos y arrumacos para burgueses*  108
3.9. *Un toke de roc*  111
4.1. Still from *La venganza del Charro Negro* (1942)  119
4.2. Still from *El rayo justiciero* (1955) with Antonio Aguilar as the cowboy avenger  121
4.3. Title panel from *El solitario* (1965)  122
4.4. Julio Alemán in *El tunco Maclovio* (1970)  125
4.5. Still from *La mula de Cullen Baker* (1971)  128
4.6. The gigolo and fugitive characters in *Las víboras cambian de piel* (1974)  134
6.1. An (approximate) Galindo family tree  172

## ACKNOWLEDGMENTS

There are many individuals and institutions who made *The Lost Cinema of Mexico* possible. We are indebted to the staff of the Centro de Documentación at the Cineteca Nacional and the Filmoteca UNAM for their assistance in gathering materials and information surrounding this lost cinema. We are especially grateful to archivist extraordinaire Raúl Miranda López for offering his support and expertise. We would also like to thank the College of Humanities at Brigham Young University for its crucial financial backing of this volume. We are so appreciative of the enthusiasm and encouragement that our editor, Stephanye Hunter, and our series editors, Héctor Fernández L'Hoeste and Juan Carlos Rodríguez, have shown for *The Lost Cinema of Mexico*. And finally, this volume would not exist without our contributors. Thank you for sticking out this process with us and for finishing this up amid a global pandemic.

Olivia would like to express gratitude to her partner, Spencer, and her writing companion, Ziti, for their patience, support, and love during the six long years it took to make this dream a reality.

Brian would like to thank his wife, Janine, and their children, Cora and Sam, for listening to him drone on about movies they have never seen and for providing much needed moral support, good humor, and encouragement throughout this project.

# INTRODUCTION: EL SANTO VERSUS THE CINETECA NACIONAL DE MÉXICO

Rethinking the Lost Cinema of Mexico

OLIVIA COSENTINO AND BRIAN PRICE

The conventional wisdom about Mexican film history follows a tight birth, boom, death, and rebirth narrative. As the story goes, the industry was born in the Porfiriato, produced its first features during the first two decades of the twentieth century, matured during the Golden Age of the 1930s–1940s, and declined in the 1950s to the point of a true "crisis" in the 1960s. The fallow years of the 1970s and 1980s were followed by an overly exulted "renaissance" in the mid-1990s that led to international success and recognition of contemporary auteurs. Existing scholarly work tends to focus on two subject areas: first, the consolidation of the national industry in the Golden Age; and second, the rebirth of Mexican cinema in the twenty-first century.[1] Very little work has been done, however, on the intervening decades—namely the 1960s, 1970s, and 1980s—because films from this period are generally disdained by critics, in- and outside of Mexico, for their perceived low production values, poor sound quality, shabby scripts, and surprising popularity among viewers. Scholars like Sergio de la Mora and Seraina Rohrer suggest that this era has been "widely overlooked" and even "deliberately ignored."[2] This gap in the field is especially curious given that the first English-language monograph on Mexican cinema, Charles

Ramírez Berg's foundational *Cinema of Solitude* from 1992, covers precisely the era of 1967–1983.³

Many commercial films from the 1960s–1980s have fallen victim to cultural and academic elitism, which results in their erasure from scholarly work today. Volumes like Christian Wehr's *Clásicos del cine mexicano: 31 películas emblemáticas desde la época de oro hasta el presente* [Classics of Mexican Cinema: 31 Emblematic Films from the Golden Age to the Present] demonstrate this generally accepted history. In mapping the scope of the volume, Wehr notes that *Clásicos del cine mexicano* "va desde la llamada Edad de Oro, pasando por las décadas de los setenta y ochenta—marcadas por una profunda crisis económica y artística—y los inicios de un nuevo cine independiente en los años noventa, hasta llegar, finalmente, a los éxitos internacionales a partir del 2000" [goes from the so-called Golden Age, passes through the 1970s and 1980s—which were marked by a profound economic and artistic crisis—and the beginnings of the new independent cinema in the 1990s, until arriving, finally, at the international successes beginning in 2000].⁴ Out of the thirty-one emblematic films, Wehr includes only three from the period of 1960–1989, all of which are directed by well-respected auteurs: Julio Bracho's *La sombra del caudillo* (1960), Paul Leduc's *Reed: México Insurgente* (1970), and Arturo Ripstein's *El lugar sin límites* (1977). To be fair, every volume has gaps, but it is significant that not a single film from the 1980s is examined, as if that decade of production never existed.

### The 2017 FICM Showdown: Commercial Cinema and Institutional Bias

This underlying narrative came to a head in 2017 when Alejandro Pelayo, director of the Cineteca Nacional de México, offered some off-the-cuff disparaging remarks about commercial cinema. At the Festival Internacional de Cine de Morelia (FICM), a journalist from the digital cultural magazine *Revés Online* asked Pelayo if the institute would sponsor a film series to celebrate the centennial of Rodolfo Guzmán Huerta, better known to the world as the silver-masked *luchador* El Santo. Guzmán became the most beloved figure in the pantheon of Mexican *lucha libre* and one of the country's most enduring film and cultural icons in a wresting career that spanned five decades. Between 1961 and 1982, El Santo starred in more than fifty feature-length films where, time and time again, he battled mummies, vampires, mad scientists, international terrorists, monsters, aliens, and criminals. Mexican moviegoers flocked to theaters to watch their hero prevail in his never-ending battle against evil. However, as Heather Levi points out, despite the fact that El Santo movies are "among the most popular films in the history of Mexican cinema and gained an extremely wide audience," a legion of detractors, namely film critics seeking to bolster the credentials of national film production on the global stage, have discarded *luchador* films as lowbrow, cheap entertainment for the masses.[5]

Pelayo immediately rejected the possibility of showing El Santo films at the Cineteca because, in his words, "no es un buen cine, es kitsch. No es un cine que nosotros queramos pasar, fue muy comercial, muy popular. Pero no son buenas películas" [it is not good cinema: it's kitsch. It's not cinema that we want to show. It was very commercial, very popular. But they're not good films]. He based his refusal on the principle that the Cineteca Nacional, as the nation's premiere film institute, should be dedicated to promoting "cine de calidad" [quality cinema], echoing discourse from 1980s film critics who lamented the disappearance of "quality" cinema amid the "crisis."[6] Pelayo further discards these films because of their low production value: "Es un cine comercial que tuvo mucho éxito nacional e internacionalmente pero no deja de ser un cine comercial. Además, no bien hecho. Es decir, eran de lo peor. Podemos ver los alambritos y todo. O sea, no se pueden tomar en serio las películas de El Santo" [This is commercial cinema that had great national and international success but it's still commercial cinema. Moreover, it was poorly made. That is to say, it's some of the worst. We can see the wires and everything. I mean, you can't take El Santo films seriously]. Pelayo's appeals to quality cinema and aesthetic value serves as a thin veil for an entrenched anti-popular sentiment. Frankly, the lack of technical expertise has never dissuaded popular viewership. On the contrary, one could even argue that these mistakes add to the humorous-by-accident viewing experience of El Santo cinema. Despite recognizing the *luchador* films as a "fenómeno comercial" [commercial phenomenon] linked to Mexican popular culture, Pelayo believes that the Cineteca's role is to preserve and promote "quality" Mexican cinema, which he defines strictly in terms of style and technique.[7]

Missing from these discussions is a more in-depth contextualization of Pelayo's position, which also serves to situate this volume in its re-understanding of "crisis." Pelayo was an up-and-coming director himself in the early 1980s, an era in which state funding under President José López Portillo (1976–1982) was almost entirely unavailable, and the fact that he made *any* films was a remarkable achievement. His firsthand experience influences his views of "cine de calidad" and certainly explains the bitterness that seems to color his assessment of commercial cinema. Pelayo's monograph, *La generación de la crisis,* underscores the changing economic dynamics of the Mexican industry, but more importantly, pays homage to a generation (*his* generation) of independent filmmakers who refused to be stomped out despite unthinkable economic conditions.

Pelayo's resentment about finances are part and parcel of a broader disdain for commercial films, which often operate on a shoestring budget and generate significant revenue and which he considers unworthy of critical attention or institutional celebration.[8] He reminds his interviewer that: "la Cineteca es parte de la Secretaría de Cultura, no de Comercio o Economía; es como cuando curas una exposición en una galería, en un museo, así nosotros tratamos de rescatar solo lo mejor del cine mexicano. Si se tratara de lo comercial, también tendríamos que homenajear al cine de ficheras, ¡imagínate!" [the Cineteca is part of the Secretariat of Culture, not Commerce or Economy; it's like when you curate an exhibition at a gallery, in a museum, so we only try to preserve the best of Mexican cinema. If this were about commercial film, we would have to pay tribute to *fichera* films as well. Imagine that!]. In broad strokes, the director establishes parity between all genres of commercial film—wrestler movies are equally as bad as sex comedies—and all are unworthy of preserving and showcasing, despite the fact that the two stated missions of the Cineteca include, first, "Preservar la memoria fílmica tanto nacional como mundial" [Preserving national and world film history] and, second, "Promover la cultura cinematográfica en nuestro país" [Promoting cinematographic culture in our country].[9]

Shortly after a video of the interview aired on the internet, several small online magazines (*Revés Online, Reporte Cínico,* and *Tomatazos*) as well as established national publications (*El Universal* and *El Economista*) picked up the story and ran with it.[10] Featuring clever headlines like "En esta esquina ... El Santo. Y en la otra ... Pelayo" [In this corner ... El Santo. And the other ... Pelayo] that attest to El Santo's prominence in the popular imaginary, the media published the director's remarks, which were met with such backlash on social media that the Cineteca was forced to intervene.[11] In a press release entitled "El Santo contra la Cineteca Nacional" [El Santo versus the Cineteca Nacional], the Cineteca distanced itself from Pelayo's interview, stating that it represented the director's personal feelings but not the position of the Cineteca.

> Alejandro Pelayo, como cineasta, académico y especialista en cine mexicano, reconoce el valor del personaje y su cine como parte de la cultura popular, no obstante mantiene su postura personal sobre la calidad estética de los filmes mencionados. La Cineteca Nacional reitera la importancia y el legado cultural que evidentemente aportó 'El enmascarado de plata' [sic], dando cabida a ésta y otras filmografías, siempre organizadas bajo un contexto histórico y cultural específicos. Muestra de ello es la presencia que el cine de luchadores, así como maneras cinematográficas populares como el *videohome* o el cine de ficheras, han tenido en la institución con la exposición *¿Actuamos como caballeros o como lo que somos? El humor en el cine mexicano*, así como en diversas exhibiciones de películas protagonizadas por El Santo.
> 
> [As a filmmaker, academic, and specialist in Mexican cinema, Alejandro Pelayo recognizes the value of this character and his films within the realm of popular culture; nevertheless, he has his own opinions about the aesthetic quality of the mentioned films. The Cineteca Nacional reaffirms the importance and the cultural legacy of the *Enmascarado de Plata*, as well as other film genres within their specific historical and cultural contexts. To wit, *luchador* movies, *videohome* films, and *fichera* films have been shown by our institution in the series *¿Actuamos como caballeros o como lo que somos? El humor en el cine mexicano* (Do We Behave Like Gentlemen or Like What We Are?: Humor in Mexican Cinema), as well as in numerous screenings of films starring El Santo.][12]

The press release then listed a handful of occasions when the Cineteca screened El Santo films, falling back on the bureaucratic excuse that its programming team "no ha recibido una propuesta oficial para exhibir la filmografía de El Santo" [has not received an official proposal to screen El Santo's filmography]. The Cineteca ultimately never dedicated a film series to the wrestling icon at the center of the kerfuffle, but rather, the Filmoteca of the UNAM seized the opportunity to screen a cycle of El Santo films in December 2017, which *Reforma* claims was met with great success and public interest.[13]

At the same FICM where *Revés Online* interviewed Pelayo, the magazine also spoke with filmmaker Viviana García-Besné, founder of Permanencia Voluntaria and champion of popular Mexican cinema.[14] The resulting article, entitled "Basta de menospreciar al cine popular" [Stop Disparaging Popular Cinema], discussed the effect of the September 2017 earthquake on Permanencia Voluntaria, Mexico's only independent archive and a repository for original copies of films, promotional materials, articles, and other documents kept by García-Besné, whose family owned the production company Cinematografía Calderón.[15] Permanencia Voluntaria seeks to restore and preserve "las películas que lograron que la gente fuera masivamente al cine" [movies that drew large crowds to the theaters], countering the work of public institutions that García-Besné says focuses only on "un cine que se considera digno: el cine apreciado por la crítica" [films that are considered worthy: films that are appreciated by critics]. García-Besné also discussed with *Revés Online* the challenges she faced in attempting to screen El Santo cinema at the Cineteca Nacional. Despite having restored one of Permanencia Voluntaria's holdings, *Santo en la venganza de la momia* [*Santo in the Vengeance of the Mummy*] (René Cardona, 1971), and having proposed the screening months in advance, García-Besné "solo encontró el rechazo de sus directivos" [only encountered rejection from the directors] for unspecified reasons. The restoration eventually screened at the Macabro XVI: Festival Internacional de Cine de Horror de la Ciudad de México in August 2017. But the Cineteca's unwillingness to show the film demonstrates the lingering elitist bias against commercial cinema evidenced in Pelayo's interview. Ironically, as Pelayo spoke with *Revés Online*, FICM screened García-Besné's 35mm restoration of *Santo contra los hombres infernales* [*Santo vs. Infernal Men*] (Joselito Rodríguez, 1961), which was attended by an enormous crowd.[16] Despite rejection from the Cineteca, the embrace of El Santo by the public at FICM left García-Besné optimistic about the future: "No creo que la puerta esté cerrada, será cuestión de convencerlos, de mostrarles una foto de Morelia y cómo reaccionó la audiencia" [I don't think the door is closed; it's a matter of convincing them, of showing them a picture of (the crowd at) Morelia and how the audience reacted].[17]

*Revés Online*'s FICM interviews with Pelayo and García-Besné brought to light a long-standing tension between filmmakers, critics, cultural and academic institutions, and spectators about the value of popular, commercial cinema. The anti-populist bias inherent in Pelayo's comments tie to a long history of disdain for popular movies in Mexico that, ultimately, has relegated a substantial portion of national film history to the dustbin. At the same time, figures like García-Besné demonstrate how the field is changing and point to new possibilities and spaces for reclaiming commercial cinema. Just as García-Besné's goal has been to "'reconciliar los públicos' para que el cine popular pueda convivir con el llamado cine de arte o de autor" ['reconcile the publics' so that popular cinema can coexist with so-called art or auteur film], this volume seeks to shine light on this "lost" cinema.[18]

One of our goals in *The Lost Cinema of Mexico* is to pivot away from the dismissive and disdainful tone, the haughty aesthetic critiques, and the shame and/or embarrassment that this cinema seems to cause. While Mexican film historians have recently signaled a desire to expand beyond traditionally studied films in the two-volume set *Miradas al cine mexicano* from 2016, lingering biases are layered into the diction of this call to action:

> El estudioso debe explicar y comprender cualquier tipo de producción, sea de calidad o basura de narcos, albures, ficheras, charros, chinas, vecindades o melodramas en casas de lujo, porque todas nos historian, bien o mal, y entre los migrantes a los Estados Unidos suelen constituir un elemento de identidad. Esa basura refleja bajos índices de escolaridad y de cultura de un sector mayoritario de la población mexicana; lamentablemente, y muy a pesar de posiciones intelectuales, debemos estudiar esas películas en todos sus aspectos.
>
> [The scholar should explain and comprehend every type of production, whether it be quality filmmaking or the kind of trash that includes narcos, double entendres, *ficheras, charros, chinas,* shantytowns or melodramas in luxury homes, because all of these films tell our story, for better or worse, and they are frequently used by immigrants to the United States as a constitutive element of their identity. This garbage reflects the low education and cultural levels of the majority of the Mexican population; unfortunately, and against all intellectual inclinations, we should study these films from every angle.][19]

*The Lost Cinema of Mexico* and its contributors advocate for critical evaluation without the use of such disparaging judgments of taste. Likewise, we seek to avoid facile labels like "good" or "bad," and to take the study of 1960s–1980s films seriously and without shame or self-loathing.

## The Lost Cinema

Films treated in *The Lost Cinema of Mexico* can be characterized as humorous (by design or by accident), fun, thrilling, melo/dramatic, and, at times, wacky, providing entertainment and enjoyment through pleasurable viewing experiences. The corpus is doused with popular appeals: beloved, outlandish, and desirable stars; faddish music and dance trends; and references to prominent transnational genres. These movies were and are widely consumed audience favorites, and many later became cult classics. By and large, films of *The Lost Cinema of Mexico* tend to oppose the sentiment that cinema is, or must be, a high art form. Most of the films treated here could be termed "commercial," that is, not art cinema, experimental cinema, or independent cinema, but industrial products usually funded by private, profit-seeking sources. (This, of course, excludes the extra-industrial, small-format *superocheros*.) This corpus shares some other significant qualities: all are directed by men, filmed in Mexico (except for some Chili Westerns), (co)produced by Mexican companies, and employ fictional narratives usually featuring phenotypically light-skinned Mexican actors (with the notable exception of Black melodramas with Afro-Mexican and foreign Black leads). While progressive moments that question norms of gender, (hetero)sexuality, capitalism, and modernization appear across *The Lost Cinema*, the dominant ideological stance is conservative, heteropatriarchal, and supportive of the state apparatus. In other words, they are not entirely dissimilar to films produced during the Golden Age. Beyond narrative content, *The Lost Cinema* corpus indicates how the film industry responded to economic and socio-political change in the 1960s–1980s and provided new visions of modernity.

*The Lost Cinema* is a result of the loosening of the link between cinema and national identity. Golden Age cinema provided the basis for nationalism, teaching Mexicans how to be Mexican and forming them into necessary social roles. Cannes winners like *María Candelaria* (Emilio Fernández, 1944) displayed *mexicanidad*—a term employed throughout this book to signify the discourses about Mexican national identity—to the world in strategic, controlled ways. Unlike Golden Age film, most of *The Lost Cinema of Mexico* corpus was not distributed globally nor screened at festivals. Critics often frame this as another reason to discard this "lost" cinema, but it is rarely discussed in terms of the freedom and creative liberty afforded to these films and filmmakers. Instead of a hyper focus on the pursuit of critical acclaim, festival recognition, or the perfect representation of *mexicanidad* to send abroad, this cinema sought audience appeal (or, in the case of *superocheros*, the creation of alternative nations). The lost cinema was not bound to the rigid norms of "quality" aesthetics nor even the confines of reality, given the boom in science fiction, horror, and monster films that these years witnessed.

As a result, films explored in *The Lost Cinema of Mexico* offer new ways of imagining a modern Mexican identity that were beyond the reach of the national political establishment. Unlike the films of the post-revolutionary period, which contributed to stabilizing a cohesive national narrative and supported the newly instituted government, films made from the 1960s–1980s responded to the national social imaginary but were no longer directly tied to officially sponsored revolutionary nationalism. *The Lost Cinema* articulates being modern in numerous ways: the recognition of youth as a social subject (and a new way to discuss the generational divide, Chapter 1); the foregrounding of the *chica moderna* and emergent, conflictive gender roles for women (Chapter 2); the circulation of anarchist, alter-capitalist, and countercultural ideas (Chapter 3); the dialogue with global and transnational film trends (Chapters 1, 3, 4, 5, 6, and 7) and vogue theories like psychoanalysis (Chapter 4); the engagement with difference, namely ethnic and racial diversity, yet not quite *mestizaje* (Chapter 5); the jouissance and pleasure of the consumption of excess, both in terms of sexuality and melodrama (*ficheras, sexycomedias*); and the incorporation of new forms of media, like television, and popular music genres (Chapters 1, 6, and 7). The lost cinema frequently envisioned a cosmopolitan modernity in which Mexico functions as a site of negotiation between the national and the global.

## Reframing Crisis in Mexican Film History and Historiography

This volume takes issue with the discourse of "crisis" precisely because of the way it allows critics to group together and discard a rich era of filmmaking that is not easily assimilable to a singular narrative nor obeys the sacrosanct aesthetic precepts of art film. *The Lost Cinema of Mexico* counters this narrative of "death" and "crisis" by offering the first critically comprehensive study of the very-much-alive cinematic production during the 1960s, 1970s, and 1980s in Mexico. This positioning allows us to question what the term "crisis" glosses over and hides. Through a revisionist lens, the authors of this volume offer new approaches to this largely forgotten historical era while seeking to make an overall historiographic intervention.

This is not to say that the Mexican film industry did not face crises during the ambiguous "end" of the Golden Age, but rather that the idea of "crisis" has become historiographically problematic and leads critics to teleological flaws. The notion of crisis is so embedded in Mexican film history that scholars tend to create narratives around it as an inevitable decline.[20] Thus, films from the end of the Golden Age *must* signal the beginnings of crisis and decline, and the late 1990s–early 2000s *must* be preceded by "death" in order for cinema to be "reborn" in Mexican cinema's "renaissance," a phoenix born from the ashes. Rather than explore the vast, complex filmography, certain movies (art, auteur, independent, and political) are often cherry-picked to exemplify and/or simplify existing narratives of Mexican film history. The idea of "decline" in itself is a bit of a misnomer and is often exaggerated, given that levels of production did not, in fact, significantly change from the late 1930s to the end of the 1980s. In many years of the "crisis," the number of Mexican films produced each year held steady. It was only in the 1990s that this number plummeted to historic lows. As such, we re-frame our approach to ask: what changes *did* occur in the Mexican film industry during this period?

Drawing from Andrew Paxman's "holistic, business-conscious history of the Golden Age fade-out," which he dates 1946–1960, the following section traces the effects of economic, (geo)political, and institutional transformations on the Mexican film industry from the post-war era through the 1980s.[21] Like Paxman, most film historians point to the year 1947 as the first signs of crisis, with a notable drop in nationwide and overall production rates. This correlates to the "resurgence of Hollywood film production" in addition to the removal of "financial and technological support" lent to the Mexican film industry during the WWII era.[22] The return of competition from other film industries, especially Hollywood, exposed some of the major issues and fault lines within Mexico's movie-making enterprises. The same year, the Mexican state founded the distribution agency Películas Nacionales, S.A., to compete with Mexico-based US businessman William Jenkins's monopoly of theaters.[23] Jenkins frequently privileged the exhibition of Hollywood films, which "offered safer returns" than low-budget Mexican films.[24] This preferential treatment of Hollywood led to an issue of *enlatamiento* [canning], or the process of withholding a new film from circulation, for Mexican productions that "made it more difficult for producers to recover their investments."[25] Producers grew increasingly dependent on the Banco Nacional Cinematográfico, a state-sponsored investment institution founded in 1942 and designed to support national cinematographic production; as they waited for their films to screen and earn profits, the interest on their loans accrued.

In 1953, Eduardo Garduño, director of the Banco Nacional Cinematográfico, attempted to solve some of these industrial problems by proposing a plan that would restrict the annual number of imported films to 150, increase the Banco Cinematográfico's total contribution to a film's budget from 50–60 percent to 85 percent, and "loosen the rules on what a movie could depict."[26] Paxman describes what came to be known as the Plan Garduño's failure to change the industry, noting that producers continued "making the cheap fare that appealed to lower-income audiences," receiving state subsidies as they inflated budgets and lined their own pockets, often investing profits outside of the film industry.[27] In 1960, under Adolfo López Mateos, the Banco Cinematográfico bought out Jenkin's Operadora de Teatros theater chain and became the major stockholder in Estudios Churubusco. Yet, as Mora laments, "the same commercialist-minded elements still dominated decision making throughout."[28]

With regard to the bleak economic situation surrounding Mexican cinema in the 1950s–1960s, producers, unions, and the state played the blame game, pointing fingers at one another. Producers blamed the Sindicato de Trabajadores de la Producción Cinematográfica (STPC) union for "artificially high production costs," the STPC looked to the state to regulate and nationalize the industry, and the state believed the producers' lack of "quality" cinema made it un-distributable outside of national circuits.[29] While these "disintegrating" markets for Mexican film could be attributed subjectively to "a general rejection by the publics of the steadily worsening Mexican product," Mora offers the more convincing argument that "economic and political problems in the various countries, [plus] stricter currency controls" made it more difficult to distribute Mexican cinema.[30] Two major industrial changes resulted from these high costs. First, from 1956 to 1960, there was a huge increase in films that were made as "series" by the Sindicato de Trabajadores de la Industria Cinematográfica (STIC), a cheaper alternative that were made episodically in "condiciones bastante rudimentarias" [quite rudimentary conditions] with less crew members than required by the STPC's traditional, more costly methods of filmmaking.[31] Second, the industry witnessed a rise in coproductions made with Mexican directors and casts with technicians and sets outside of Mexico. Neither strategy provided a long-term solution.

The era's economic pressures to ensure returns on films only increased the Mexican industry's reliance on the formulaic execution of films: x director + y genre + z star = profitable movie. Carl Mora argues that the successes of the Golden Age became the industry's downfall, claiming that "producers became wedded to audience-tested genre pictures not only because such movies were popular with the public but also because the Banco Cinematográfico would only back projects with the greatest possibility of commercial success."[32] Movies depended heavily on the presence of particular stars and "consequently the director and the script became of secondary concern."[33] Thus, critics often point to the untimely passing of popular singer-actors Pedro Infante (1957) and Jorge Negrete (1953) as both evidence and cause of the "death" of the Golden Age and the film industry. Building on Seraina Rohrer's work on La India María (María Elena Velasco) and Sergio de la Mora's assertion that "Latin American exploitation produces its own stars," our volume underscores the emergence of a new system of stars, like Lorena Velázquez (see Dalton, Chapter 2) or youth singing sensations (see Price, Chapter 1, and Cosentino, Chapter 6), who indeed continued to draw audiences in the era of "crisis."[34]

State intervention and involvement in the film industry influenced the types of films that were made, often seeking to please the middle classes and to avoid political repression. Mora notes that in 1954, over half of Mexico's output of films consisted of "melodramas dealing with middle-class tribulations," and more than thirty comedies "based on the new dance craze, the cha-cha."[35] Genre films were considered safer investments as they were usually understood to be politically benign.[36] In the 1950s, producers wanted to avoid the harsh censorship they witnessed after Miguel Alemán legislated the "Autorización obligatoria para la exhibición de películas," run jointly by the Secretaría de Gobernación and the Dirección General de Cinematografía in 1951 as part of the Reglamento de la Ley de la Industria Cinematográfica.[37]

Another major cause of 1950s filmic stagnancy was the lack of turnover in directors and film crews in "an aging, inbred industry," as Charles Ramírez Berg puts it.[38] The director's union "closed-door policy" made it difficult for newcomers (not to mention, women) to enter the film industry, a problem exacerbated by the absence of a school for filmmakers in Mexico. Between 1951 and 1955, 70 percent of the films produced were made by only twenty-three directors, all men.[39] The old-school directors who could churn out pictures quickly with low budgets were favored and constantly re-hired by producers. Grupo Nuevo Cine, an all-male contingent of independent filmmakers and intellectuals, took great issue with the "establishment," publishing damning appraisals of the Mexican industry in their eponymous magazine *Nuevo Cine* from 1961 to 1962.

Another important consideration for the "decline" of the Golden Age is the changing mediascape, beginning in 1950 with the introduction of television to Mexico. Mexican society "warmed" to television from 1958 to 1964: in 1955, fewer than 5 percent of homes had a TV, but by 1968, close to half of Mexican households owned a television set.[40] The competition and threat that TV posed to cinema spurred the film industry to innovate in costly ways through the use of color and Cinemascope, as well as to opt for more nudity and eroticism, content un-airable on television.[41] *Ficheras, sexycomedias,* and other body-centric "sex-Mexploitation" films can thus be read as part of the way that cinema distinguished itself from television.[42]

Ironically, just as the increased state involvement via the Banco Cinematográfico led to more commercial, formulaic, genre films in the 1950s and 1960s, the second half of the 1970s witnessed the opposite process. The election of José López Portillo in 1976 saw the near elimination of state support for Mexican cinema. This created space for the rise of private producers who focused largely on commercial cinema as a way to garner profits (described more in depth in Chapters 6 and 7).[43]

## The Lost Cinema in Mexican and Latin American Film Studies

Our field's inattentiveness to the Mexican cinema treated within this volume can be attributed to a series of factors, including the organizing paradigm of *mexicanidad*; the privileging of auteur, art, and independent cinema ("exceptional" films and prize-winners on the festival circuit); and the incompatibility of popular and commercial film with the politics and aesthetics of New Latin American Cinema (NLAC) despite their temporal overlap. The following sections delve into why this Mexican cinema has been forgotten, neglected, or "deliberately ignored," in part by considering how the select few visible films from the 1960s–1980s shed light on the implicit biases of the field.

Mexican film studies are often driven (and limited) by the idea of national cinema and national identity, but scholars like Ignacio M. Sánchez Prado have begun to lay the groundwork for moving away from *mexicanidad* as an organizing paradigm. Sánchez Prado pushes forward a model that "strategically underplays the role of Mexican national identity and that considers modernization as the core signifier" in 1940s–1950s production.[44] He shows how the wide variety of topics and genres in non-canonical films—"unjustly exclude[d] from critical attention (and even from commercial reissue)"— have been displaced by the often-cited and studied figures of Ismael Rodríguez, Emilio Fernández, Gabriel Figueroa, Pedro Infante, and Cantinflas.[45] Dolores Tierney likewise advances this project vis-à-vis the past few decades in her recent book, *New Transnationalisms in Contemporary Latin American Cinemas*.[46] Although Sánchez Prado offers this framework for the Golden Age, his rethinking of *mexicanidad* and the canon shape the theoretical push of this volume. Indeed, the popular "crisis" cinema that has received some critical attention to date, like the El Santo *luchador* filmography or La India María, can fit neatly within the paradigm of Mexican national identity. In other words, while it may not be "quality" cinema, it also does not threaten existing narratives.

The critical prioritization of auteur and art cinema as well as independent production in Mexico marginalizes popular, commercial, and mainstream cinema, films made for "entertainment," and private production, unnecessarily creating a divide of worthy/unworthy objects of study.[47] *The Lost Cinema of Mexico* opposes the tendency to privilege "exceptional" films, a term that Charles Ramírez Berg uses to distinguish "Classical Mexican Cinema" from "the run-of-the-mill industrial product."[48] Ramírez Berg's neoauteurist approach provides a basis to reject the study of mainstream, industrial films in the Golden Age with a romantic vision of the elevated aesthetics and "poetics" of the "ideologically oppositional" Classical Mexican Cinema.[49] This preference for auteurism is also evident in the Cineteca Nacional's course "Diplomado en historia del cine mexicano" [Diploma in the History of Mexican Cinema], where the 1960–1990 unit is entitled, "La generación del cine de autor" [The Generation of Auteur Cinema]. Instructors for this 2018 class were none other than Alejandro Pelayo and Juan Antonio de la Riva. The course's curriculum is of historiographic significance because this framing influences the way that younger generations of filmmakers and critics in Mexico conceptualize an era for which many do not have firsthand memories.

Mexican films from our era of interest that are deemed "worthy" of recovery are nearly always auteur, art, or independent cinema and often "legitimized" by national or international prizes. Take, for example, the collaboration between Instituto Mexicano de Cinematografía [Mexican Cinematographic Institute] (IMCINE) and Academia Mexicana de Artes y Ciencias Cinematográficas [Mexican Academy of Film Arts and Sciences] (AMACC) with the objective to "rescatar y difundir nuestro cine mexicano" [recover and promote our Mexican cinema] via the release of past Ariel winners in sleek, special edition DVDs with commentary by Mexican film critics.[50] Mexico's version of the Academy Awards, the Ariel Awards first began in 1947 (a year that Emilio García Riera identifies as the first sign of "crisis" with a drop in production), were briefly suspended from 1958 to 1972 when the AMACC was dissolved and were later revived when the Academy was reinstated in 1971.[51] The name of the prize itself is based on José Enrique Rodó's *Ariel* (1900) that seems to reflect the value of cinema as high culture, as IMCINE describes it, "El premio Ariel ... es una apuesta por el cine como expresión del espíritu, como séptimo arte, por encima de las limitaciones materiales o las presiones del mercado" [The Ariel prize ... advocates for film as an expression of the spirit, as the seventh art, above and beyond material limitations and market pressures].[52] The first Ariel collection, released in 2014–2015, included *Las puertas del paraíso* (Salomón Laiter, 1971), *Mecánica nacional* (Luis Alcoriza, 1972), *El principio* (Gonzalo Martínez, 1973), *La otra virginidad* (Juan Manuel Torres, 1974), *Naufragio* (Jaime Humberto Hermosillo, 1977), *Veneno para las hadas* (Carlos Enrique Taboada, 1985), and *Mariana, Mariana* (Alberto Isaac, 1987).[53] The series was met with significant popular embrace as Octavio Alfaro from *SensaCine* cites that 2,300 copies of *Veneno para las hadas* were sold.[54] Given the success of the first set of DVDs, the AMACC released its second collection in 2018, comprised of more auteur-centric works: Arturo Ripstein's *El castillo de la pureza* (1973), *El lugar sin límites* (1978), and *Cadena perpetua* (1979); Emilio Fernández's *La choca* (1974); Diego López Rivera's *Goitia, un dios para sí mismo* (1989); and Sergio Olhovich's *Esperanza* (1988).[55] Also part of this collection was Felipe Cazals's *Bajo la metralla* (1983), treated by Sánchez Prado in Chapter 7 as exemplar of an auteur in cinematic crisis. The final DVD released, *Actas de Marusia* (1975) by Chilean cineaste Miguel Littín, had been nominated for a US Academy Award and entered in the Cannes Film Festival.

The prestige of the Ariel Awards and other prizes from festivals has led to the exultation of certain (now canonical) films and the unjust exclusion of an enormous corpus of Mexican cinema. Seraina Rohrer affirms that "only a handful of Mexican films premiered in renowned international film festivals" in the late 1960s to the late 1980s.[56] Missing from the Ariel DVD collection are the vast majority of the commercial films explored in the chapters of *The Lost Cinema of Mexico*, especially because of the prize's fifteen-year suspension that spanned the entirety of the 1960s and the beginning of the 1970s.[57]

With the term "lost" in this volume's title, we not only affirm the existence of 1960s–1980s films, but also imply that this abhorred commercial cinema is also worthy of recovery, preservation, and analysis. Though lost in criticism and scholarship and almost entirely absent from institutionalized memory (special edition DVDs, homages at the Cineteca Nacional, etc.), these films are certainly present in the alternative cultural imaginary. They are shown on Mexican free-to-air television and Spanish-language cable channels in the US, available for streaming on Televisa subsidiary Pantelion's Pantaya, sold as pirated DVDs in video shops and informal markets, and uploaded illegally to YouTube. Thus, we assert that this cinema has been "lost" within plain sight.

Zooming out further, we see that this era of Mexican film production has also been invisibilized because it does not fit well into existing narratives from Latin American film and cultural studies surrounding the NLAC of the late 1950s–1970s.[58] NLAC typically encompasses a series of manifestoes that propose new models of "revolutionary" filmmaking, including Brazilian Glauber Rocha's "Uma estética da fome" [An Aesthetics of Hunger] (1965), Argentina's Grupo Cine Liberación's (Octavio Getino and Fernando E. Solanas) "Hacia un tercer cine" [Towards a Third Cinema] (1969), and Cuban Julio García Espinosa's "Por un cine imperfecto" [For an Imperfect Cinema] (1969).[59] This highly political, revolutionary formalism that sought disruption and reflexivity with a purposeful use of aesthetics are particularly unhelpful for understanding these decades of filmmaking in Mexico. While cinema created by Mexico's Grupo Nuevo Cine fits most closely with what Getino and Solanas call "second cinema," the vast majority of Mexican films were operating within the Hollywood-like system of "first cinema" without goals of liberation or revolution.[60] The films in our volume are not explicitly concerned with politics and many, likely, are depoliticized in order to circulate among the "dictablanda" [soft dictatorship] of the Partido Revolucionario Institucional (PRI).[61] Mexican directors were forced to navigate state censorship that, after 1951, legally required the review and approval of all scripts.[62]

We are not the first scholars to note the limitations of the categorization of NLAC. In *The Routledge Companion to Latin American Cinema*, editors Martin D'Lugo, Ana M. López, and Laura Podalsky gesture toward "the standard periodization of Latin American film history" (i.e., silent era, studio era, NLAC, contemporary cinema) as a subject "ripe for interrogation."[63] Specifically, they argue that associating the period of NLAC with political filmmaking "frequently overlooks the substantive commercial output during those same decades, from youth films to crime thrillers and sexycomedias."[64] While D'Lugo et al.'s volume focuses on a continental phenomenon, *The Lost Cinema of Mexico* takes a decidedly more national approach by reconsidering a wide variety of commercial cinema within the Mexican context.

Overall, it is surprising that 1960s–1980s Mexican cinema remains relatively untouched given recent trends in Mexican and Latin American film scholarship. Scholars like Fredrick Luis Aldama, Misha MacLaird, Ignacio M. Sánchez Prado, and Paul Julian Smith have all argued for the importance of studying films that Mexicans actually watch.[65] Their monographs take up contemporary Mexican film (with the exception of Sánchez Prado, who traces the neoliberalization of the industry back to 1988), focusing namely on the 1990s–2010s, without significant discussion of prior decades. *The Lost Cinema of Mexico* also builds upon the de-hierarchizing gesture of Victoria Ruétalo and Dolores Tierney's *Latsploitation, Exploitation Cinemas, and Latin America* and Seraina Rohrer's groundbreaking *La India María*. A few not-quite-academic texts written for cult film enthusiasts in the mid-2000s—like Doyle Greene's *Mexploitation Cinema: A Critical History of Mexican Vampire, Wrestler, Ape-Man and Similar Films, 1957-77* and *The Mexican Cinema of Darkness: A Critical Study of Six Landmark Horror and Exploitation Films, 1969-1988* or Robert Michael "Bobb" Cotter's *The Mexican Masked Wrestler and Monster Filmography*—demonstrate a general interest in these films beyond the academy.

*The Lost Cinema of Mexico* likewise builds upon a wealth of recent *sexenio* and decade-based studies of this era, many of which put politics at the forefront, as well as genre-centric criticism.[66] This includes essays on the 1960s and the period of 1971 to 1982 in the unofficially published *El Estado y la imagen en movimiento,* Sánchez Prado's reflections on "el cine echeverrista," Eduardo de la Vega's monograph on censorship during the Mexican Miracle, and the chapters on Mexican cinema during the Cold War and the Echeverría and López Portillo regimes in *A la sombra de los caudillos: El presidencialismo en el cine mexicano,* edited by Álvaro A. Fernández and Ángel Román Gutiérrez.[67] Fabián de la Cruz Polanco's *Cine mexicano del 70: La década prodigiosa* contains a series of interviews and conversations with industry members from the 1970s. The 2010s have witnessed an uptick in scholarship on particular modes or genres of filmmaking in Mexico during the post–Golden Age era. This is exemplified by Álvaro Vázquez Mantecón's monograph *El cine súper 8 en México, 1970–1989,* readings of *fichera* films from the 1970s and 1980s, and Carolyn Fornoff's work on 1960s Mexican melodramas.[68] Olivia Cosentino's star studies scholarship proposes a reconsideration of youth films/stars from these "lost" years as a way to see Mexico's twentieth-century mediatic transformations.[69]

Even earlier, scholars of Mexican-American, Chicanx, Fronterizo, and/or border cinema signaled the need to take low-budget, critically-disdained films seriously by centering film publics. Norma Iglesias published *Entre yerba, polvo y plomo: Lo fronterizo visto por el cine mexicano* in the early 1990s, one year prior to Ramírez Berg's *Cinema of Solitude*.[70] Iglesias's follow-up chapter in *Mexico's Cinema* analyzed "border cinema" with regard to audiences, cinematic pleasure, and taste.[71] While some bias against this "low quality" cinema lingers in Iglesias's work, scholars like María S. Arbeláez and Adán Ávalos seek to counter this narrative by re-valorizing "naco" cinema from the 1970s, 1980s, and 1990s that was screened in the US or available on VHS at video stores.[72] Arbeláez and Ávalos lay the groundwork for Rohrer's deeper dive into the importance of La India María's films to Mexican migrant communities in the US and the dependence of the Mexican industry on US exhibition profits. Touched upon by Cosentino's chapter on 1980s Mexican family films in the present volume and exemplified by Laura Isabel Serna's work on pre–Golden Age Mexican film consumption in the US, overall, this area of study merits further critical attention.[73]

## Approaches to the Lost Cinema

Our volume's revival of "lost" cinema relies on contributions from a variety of film and cultural studies scholars who share the belief that popular, widely consumed commercial cinema merits critical attention. The essays directly engage the discursive modes that thrived and thrilled in those decades: the dirty, the cheesy, the overtly sexual, the countercultural, the weepy, and the horrific. Part of the value of this "lost" cinema is that it was widely seen by Mexico's working classes—both in country and abroad—who found ways to engage with the rapidly changing realities and values connected to Mexico's modernization through the act of moviegoing.[74] In this prioritization of the audience and the reception of these films, the essays consider the ways in which these films shaped discourses on race, class, and gender.

As noted earlier, while there are singular projects on this era, *The Lost Cinema of Mexico*'s utility resides in its comprehensive format, which allows for a broader understanding of the development of the Mexican film industry. This "lost" cinema reflects larger cultural, economic, and social processes in the makings of a "modern" Mexico. The essays highlight that the development of Mexican identities can go beyond facile clichés of nationalism. In many of the essays, a sense of transnationalism emerges in which Mexico figures as the site of negotiation between national and global, tracing connections to both Latin American and Hollywood cinema at large. On the whole, Mexican cinema from the 1960s, 1970s, and 1980s reveals paradigmatic shifts in national film culture, marking major institutional transformations that are unfairly equated to crisis.

The chapters that follow are arranged in a loose chronological order as a means of recognizing that the films, tendencies, stars, and directors described here often cross the arbitrary boundaries of decades. We take cues from Mexican historian Jaime Pensado, who advocates for a "long sixties" historiographic model in *Rebel Mexico*, tracing student political culture from 1956 to 1971 as a means of decentering the watershed moment of Tlatelolco in 1968.[75] In this reappraisal of Mexican cinema from the 1960s–1980s, the chapters inevitably dip into the 1950s and the 1990s in order to trace the trajectory of processes like modernization, *mestizaje*, or the entrance of new cultural forms like rock and roll, and the consequences of institutional, economic, and political transformations over time. To better follow the natural developments of industry history and to allow readers to recognize trends flowing from one chapter to the next, we have chosen to organize the chapters via a chronology rather than methodology.

*The Lost Cinema of Mexico* opens with two reflections on commercial cinema in the late 1950s and 1960s. As the Golden Age model of filmmaking began to fail, studios turned to an assembly-line style of genre filmmaking that relied heavily on shoestring budgets, formulaic production, and quick turnaround. As Carl Mora observes, "quality plummeted but production increased."[76] In Chapter 1, Brian Price explores one of the first popular genres to emerge during this period: rock and roll movies that, beginning at the end of the 1950s, came to replace the cowboy musicals that had been such an integral part of the national film industry's overall production throughout the 1930s, 1940s, and 1950s. He argues that, as modern sounds from the US and Britain grew in popularity with middle- and upper-class audiences, films depicting new dance trends, fashion, and music displaced traditional folkloric musicals and offered Mexican youth an alternative to rigid nationalism. While concerns about the social and cultural dangers of rock and roll shaped some early films, Price suggests that rock films simultaneously promoted local rock bands and domesticated many of the perceived subversive elements of cosmopolitan counterculture. Chapter 2, written by David S. Dalton, studies the career and films of Lorena Velázquez, who made her name as one of the country's most popular actors by starring in the *lucha libre* films that heavily favored masculine actors like El Santo, Blue Demon, and Mil Máscaras. Unlike the male actors of *lucha libre* cinema, however, Velázquez was never a professional wrestler and, as such, was initially cast in roles that emphasized sex appeal in order to draw audiences to theaters. As her star power increased, however, Velázquez was able to negotiate better and more complex roles for herself and other female actors.

The next essays demonstrate how, as the 1960s gave way to the 1970s, pressures on filmmakers—both in the form of censorship and decreased federal funding—pitted political and social commitment against box office viability. Iván Eusebio Aguirre Darancou demonstrates how activism became a central feature of the independent Super-8 film movement that emerged in the aftermath of Tlatelolco and other oppressive actions in Chapter 3. Aguirre Darancou conceptualizes small format, independent filmmaking as a direct response to government interventions, one which sought to change forms of political engagement in line with anti-colonial and anti-capitalist thought from the Global South. The central figure that emerges in this movement is Sergio García Michel, who not only directed important countercultural short and feature-length films but also documented the history of the format, established artistic collectives, founded an important cultural center, and taught filmmaking at local and national levels. However, despite the difficulty of accessing García Michel and other *superochero*'s works, Aguirre Darancou makes a compelling argument that the movement offers a model for creating alternative spaces. In Chapter 4, Christopher Conway demonstrates how Westerns—and specifically the variant known as Chili Westerns—grapple with deeply entrenched notions about masculinity in Mexican society and how these engagements are, essentially, political. Arguably one of the most popular and influential commercial genres of the decade, Chili Westerns recreate a lawless and corrupt space that mirrors the collapse of the legitimacy of the Mexican state after 1968. The films then proceed to exact brutal vigilante justice in its place. In this way, Chili Westerns are a kind of political critique, although dressed up in the trappings of gunslinging US cowboys. Carolyn Fornoff rounds out this selection of chapters with a meditation on Blackness in Mexican cinema in Chapter 5. Following the Mexican Revolution (1910–1917), intellectuals and artists engaged in a series of debates about how to constitute the new national body. The official paradigm focused on *mestizaje* as a way to bring together the European and indigenous, the city and province, and the civilized and barbarous. However, this emphasis on *mestizo* citizens oftentimes overlooked citizens of African descent. Fornoff's chapter considers trajectories in the representation of Afro-Mexicans on film, from blackface performances by white actors in early films to the casting of Black foreigners—largely from the US and the Caribbean—in the 1970s. Fornoff suggests that, by analyzing a broad sampling of these films in conjunction, we can better understand the way in which the influx of Black protagonists reflected the rise in popularity of Hollywood's Blaxploitation genre, as well as how the incorporation of diversity allowed these films to better appeal to transnational audiences.

The last three chapters point toward new approaches for reading commercial cinema. The first two, written by Olivia Cosentino and Ignacio M. Sánchez Prado, consider films made during the 1980s, albeit for radically different audiences. In Chapter 6, Cosentino proposes the term *cine familiar* to categorize a body of films with narratives about families and whose advertising and marketing materials suggest that it was intended for family audiences. *Cine familiar* likewise addresses the shift in 1980s industrial production structures to chart the rise of private, family-run filmmaking companies. She argues that *cine familiar*, with its use of popular youth stars and veteran actors, was not only extremely popular with audiences (then and now, via YouTube uploads), but it also allegorizes ideal citizen-nation relationships through the microcosm of the Mexican family. Cosentino suggests that these narratives function as escapist fantasies in response to Mexico's economic and political crises (the 1982 debt crisis and the 1985 earthquake, respectively), often absolving state failures by turning the emphasis to demonstrations of collective solidarity. Sánchez Prado takes a much narrower track in Chapter 7, focusing on the understudied films of one of Mexico's most revered auteurs, Felipe Cazals, who is most often regarded for his political films like *Las poquianchis* (1976), *El apando* (1976), and *Rojo amanecer* (1989). Without disregarding the importance of these movies, Sánchez Prado invites us to consider the director's films from the same period about *cumbia* stars and sexploitation as complements and alternatives to his political work. Instead of breaking Cazals's oeuvre down into discrete genres, the chapter presents them together so that we can fully appreciate the scope of an auteurial trajectory shaped by crisis and the marks of cinematic form and ideology that appear across his work. This approach allows Sánchez Prado to recuperate the "cinema of crisis" as an articulation point from which we can think more productively about precarity in national film industries. *The Lost Cinema of Mexico* closes with a brief essay by film historian and critic Dolores Tierney. Tierney's foundational work on Latin American exploitation film and commercial cinema serves as one of the cardinal points for this book. Here she reflects upon changes in the field of film studies since the publication of *Latsploitation* and discusses how the essays in *The Lost Cinema of Mexico* respond to some of these trends.

We recognize that our attempt to recover three decades' worth of filmmaking will fall short of universal inclusivity. The sheer volume of genres, directors, actors, and trends makes such an undertaking quixotic at best. That said, we feel that these chapters are as significant for what they explicitly accomplish as for the areas of research that their gaps suggest. For instance, Price, Conway, Fornoff, and Cosentino explore the implications of some important commercial genres, but there is still much to be said about gothic horror films, *sexycomedias,* punk films, children's media, and border or "naco" cinema. Dalton's chapter constitutes an important excursion into star studies, signaling an imperative need to expand the field of star studies to include figures like Angélica Chaín and other vedettes or the iconic *Lola la Trailera* played by Rosa Gloria Chagoyán. Aguirre Darancou's work on the ideological innovations of *superochero* films underscores the need for more work on smaller formats and their directors as well as independent student and feminist filmmaking in the era.[77] Sánchez Prado's chapter points to the kinds of innovative scholarship that can be done on Mexican, Latin American, and Global South auteurs working in uneven industrial conditions. Additionally, there are few, if any, studies on Mexican commercial directors like José Díaz Morales, René Cardona, Benito Alazraki, Carlos Enrique Taboada, and others who shaped the industry through their often decades-long careers. This also brings up one of the major shortcomings of this volume: every film discussed in *The Lost Cinema of Mexico* was directed by a man, which requires us to reconsider the trajectories and legacies of women directors like Matilde Landeta, María del Carmen Lara, Marcela Fernández Violante, and Busi Cortés.[78] At the time of writing, a special issue on "Forgotten Cinemas: The Institutional Uses of Documentary in Twentieth-Century Mexico (1930–80)" was published in *Studies in Spanish & Latin American Cinemas.*[79] This issue lays the groundwork for studies of ethnographic, educational, non-theatrical, home videos, and non-fiction cinema from the 1960s–1980s that, while falling outside of our selected corpus, have been just as "lost" as the cinema treated here. We view these topics as opportunities for future research that can build upon the revisionist thrust our volume offers to Mexican film studies at large and hope that *The Lost Cinema of Mexico* can provide productive approaches that will help scholars and enthusiasts rediscover and recover the films that fill in these gaps.

## Notes

1. For more information on Golden Age films, see Charles Ramírez Berg, *The Classical Mexican Cinema: The Poetics of the Exceptional Golden Age Films* (Austin: University of Texas Press, 2015), Zuzana M. Pick, *Constructing the Image of the Mexican Revolution: Cinema and the Archive* (Austin: University of Texas Press, 2010), Dolores Tierney, *Emilio Fernández: Pictures in the Margins* (New York: Manchester University Press, 2007), Julia Tuñón, *Mujeres de*

*luz y sombra en el cine mexicano: La construcción de una imagen (1939–1952)* (Mexico City: Colegio de México and IMCINE, 1998), and Robert McKee Irwin and Maricruz Castro Ricalde's edited volume *Global Mexican Cinema: Its Golden Age* (London: Palgrave Macmillan and BFI, 2013). For additional information on the recent "renaissance" of Mexican cinema, see Ignacio M. Sánchez Prado, *Screening Neoliberalism* (Nashville: Vanderbilt University Press, 2014), Frederick Aldama, *Mex-Ciné: Mexican Filmmaking, Production, and Consumption in the Twenty-first Century* (Ann Arbor: University of Michigan Press, 2013), Misha MacLaird, *Aesthetics and Politics in the Mexican Film Industry* (New York: Palgrave Macmillan, 2013), Paul Julian Smith, *Mexican Screen Fiction* (Cambridge: Polity, 2014), Miriam Haddu's *Contemporary Mexican Cinema, 1989–1999* (Lewiston: E. Mellen Press, 2007), and Jorge Ayala Blanco's *La grandeza del cine mexicano* (Mexico City: Océano, 2004).

2. Seraina Rohrer, *La India María: Mexploitation and the Films of María Elena Velasco* (Austin: University of Texas Press, 2017), 3; Sergio de la Mora, "'Tus pinches leyes yo me las paso por los huevos.' Isela Vega and Mexican Dirty Movies," in *Latsploitation, Exploitation Cinemas, and Latin America,* eds. Victoria Ruétalo and Dolores Tierney (New York: Routledge, 2009), 247.

3. Published nearly thirty years ago, Charles Ramírez Berg's foundational study lays the groundwork for the field of Mexican film studies in the US today, establishing the centrality of the (at times limiting) paradigm of *mexicanidad*. *Cinema of Solitude: A Critical Study of Mexican Film, 1967–1983* (Austin: University of Texas Press, 1992).

4. Christian Wehr, ed., *Clásicos del cine mexicano: 31 películas emblemáticas desde la Época de Oro hasta el presente* (Madrid: Iberoamericana, 2016), 9.

5. Heather Levi, *The World of Lucha Libre: Secrets, Revelations, and Mexican National Identity* (Durham: Duke University Press, 2008), 186. Notably, there is a body of non-disparaging scholarship on El Santo that includes Álvaro A. Fernández, *Santo el enmascarado de plata: Mito y realidad de un héroe mexicano moderno* (Guadalajara: El Colegio de Michoacán/Universidad de Guadalajara, 2012), Kerry T. Hegarty, "From Superhero to National Hero: The Populist Myth of El Santo," *Studies in Latin American Popular Culture*, no. 31 (2013): 3–27, David Dalton, *Mestizo Modernity: Race, Technology, and the Body in Postrevolutionary Mexico* (Gainesville: University Press of Florida, 2018), 140–76, and Dolores Tierney, "*El vampiro y el sexo/The Vampire and Sex* (René Cardona, 1969): El Santo, sexploitation films and politics in Mexico 1968," *Porn Studies* (2019): 1–17.

6. A series of lamenting conversations between Mexican filmmakers and intellectuals (some of who were part of Nuevo Cine in the 1960s) were published in the industrial journal *Dicine,* including: "Problemas del cine mexicano: una mesa redonda" [Mexican Cinema's Problems: A Roundtable] (May–June 1984), which continued as "Una mesa redonda II" in the July–August 1984 issue, a three-part "El cine mexicano y sus crisis" [Mexican Cinema and Its Crises] (1987) featuring perspectives from members of the Colectivo Alejandro Galindo, and Nelson Carro's "Cine mexicano de los ochenta: ante el cadaver de un difunto" [1980s Mexican Cinema: Facing a Dead Man's Corpse] (1990).

7. José Antonio Monterrosas and Francisco Valenzuela, "Las películas del Santo no se pueden tomar en serio: director de la Cineteca," *Revés Online,* October 30, 2017, http://revesonline.com/2017/10/30/las-peliculas-del-santo-no-se-pueden-tomar-en-serio-director-de-la-cineteca/.

8. Seraina Rohrer notes that India María films were made for a pittance and yet consistently brought in significantly more revenue than their overhead.

9. Cineteca Nacional, "Información," https://www.cinetecanacional.net/controlador.php?opcion=contexto.

10. Vicente Gutiérrez, "El Santo no es digno para la Cineteca Nacional," *El Economista*, November 1, 2017, https://www.eleconomista.com.mx/arteseideas/El-Santo-no-es-digno-para-la-Cineteca-Nacional-20171101-0143.html.

11. "En esta esquina 'El Santo.' Y en la otra 'Pelayo,'" *El Universal*, November 6, 2017, https://www.eluniversal.com.mx/cultura/en-esta-esquina-el-santo-y-en-la-otra-pelayo?fb_comment_id=1111883032248282_1112140158889236.

12. "Que siempre sí, la Cineteca abre posibilidad de homenaje al Santo," *Medio Tiempo*, November 2, 2017, https://www.mediotiempo.com/lucha-libre/independientes/que-siempre-si-la-cineteca-abre-posibilidad-de-homenaje-al-santo. See also "Comunicado: El Santo contra la Cineteca Nacional," Cineteca Nacional, November 1, 2017, https://www.cinetecanacional.net/controlador.php?opcion=noticias&id=850.

13. "Triunfa El Santo en la Filmoteca," *Reforma*, Opinión, January 3, 2018, https://www.reforma.com/aplicacioneslibre/editoriales/editorial.aspx?id=126672&md5=6eee97609b65550a4dc182b810eb212d&ta=0dfdbac11765226904c16cb9ad1b2efe.

14. For more on Permanencia Voluntaria and Viviana García-Besné, see Colin Gunckel, "The Permanencia Voluntaria Archive and the Historical Study of Mexican Cinema," *Studies in Spanish and Latin American Cinemas* 16, no. 3 (Sept. 2019): 383–401.

15. Francisco Valenzuela and José Antonio Monterrosas, "Basta de menospreciar al cine popular: García-Besné," *Revés Online*, October 30, 2017, https://revesonline.com/2017/10/30/basta-de-menospreciar-al-cine-popular-garcia-besne/.

16. Gustavo R. Gallardo, "*Santo contra hombres infernales* Had an Outdoor Screening at the 15th FICM," October 27, 2017, https://moreliafilmfest.com/en/santo-contra-hombre-infernales-se-proyecto-al-aire-libre-en-el-15o-ficm/. The following year, a restoration of *Santo contra Cerebro del Mal* (filmed simultaneously with *Santo vs. Los hombres infernales*) premiered at the sixty-eighth Berlin International Film Festival. Chloë Roddick, "World Premiere of the New Restoration of *Santo contra Cerebro del Mal* at the 68th Berlinale," February 21, 2018, https://moreliafilmfest.com/en/version-restaurada-de-santo-contra-cerebro-del-mal-estrena-en-la-68a-berlinale/. Both films have an extraordinary history: they were shot in Cuba during the revolution and smuggled back to Mexico in a coffin just prior to Castro's victory.

17. Valenzuela and Monterrosas, "Basta de menospreciar," n.p.

18. Monterrosas and Valenzuela, "Las películas del Santo," n.p.

19. Aurelio de los Reyes García-Rojas, "Presentación," *Miradas al cine mexicano*, coord. Aurelio de los Reyes (Mexico City: IMCINE, 2016), 10.

20. For example, Eduardo de la Vega Alfaro's "The Decline of the Golden Age and the Making of the Crisis," in *Mexico's Cinema: A Century of Film and Filmmakers*, eds. Joanne Hershfield and David R. Maciel (New York: SR Books, 1999), 165–91. This is also easily observed through the chapter titles of Carl Mora's textbook-like *Mexican Cinema*: Chapter 4 "Golden Age, Crisis, and Retrenchment: 1947–1959," Chapter 5 "Decline, Renovation, and the Return of Commercialism 1960–1980," and Chapter 6 "To Rebuild a Ruined Cinema in a Ruined Country: 1981–1989"; Mora's Chapter 6 title cites a speech from IMCINE director Alberto Isaac in 1983.

21. Andrew Paxman notes that his approach "takes the death of the Golden Age as a given," "Who Killed the Mexican Film Industry? The Decline of the Golden Age, 1946–1960," *E.I.A.L.* 29, no. 1 (2018): 9–10.

22. de la Vega Alfaro, "The Decline of the Golden Age," 165.
23. Mora, *Mexican Cinema,* 78.
24. Paxman, "Who Killed," 15.
25. Mora, *Mexican Cinema,* 101–2.
26. Mora, *Mexican Cinema,* 101; Paxman, "Who Killed," 23.
27. Paxman, "Who Killed," 23.
28. Mora, *Mexican Cinema,* 116.
29. Mora, *Mexican Cinema,* 106.
30. Mora, *Mexican Cinema,* 107.
31. Emilio García Riera, *Historia del Cine Mexicano* (Mexico City: Secretaría de Educación Pública, 1985), 222.
32. Mora, *Mexican Cinema,* 75.
33. Mora, *Mexican Cinema,* 75.
34. de la Mora, "Tus pinches leyes," 247–8.
35. Mora, *Mexican Cinema,* 102.
36. This belief continued into our era of interest. Seraina Rohrer notes that "Mexploitation films rarely faced problems with the censorship board, simply because they were considered devoid of social or political commentary." Like La India María films, the vast majority of cinema treated in this volume were "categorized as harmless or purely to entertain," and censors missed the political content because they "foregrounded the profit-making aspect," *La India María,* 53.
37. Eduardo de la Vega Alfaro explores the conditions behind the censorship and eventual approval of four films, *Espaldas mojadas* (Alejandro Galindo, 1953), *El impostor* (Emilio Fernández, 1956), *El brazo fuerte* (Giovanni Korporaal, 1958), and *Rosa blanca* (Roberto Gavaldón, 1961), all of which were seen as critical of or undermining the Mexican state, *Cine, política y censura en la era del Milagro Mexicano* (Guadalajara: Universidad de Guadalajara, 2017), 17.
38. Ramírez Berg, *Cinema of Solitude,* 6.
39. García Riera, *Historia del Cine Mexicano,* 215.
40. Andrew Paxman, "Cooling to Cinema and Warming to Television: State Mass Media Policy, 1940–1964," in *Dictablanda: Politics, Work, and Culture in Mexico, 1938–1968,* eds. Paul Gillingham and Benjamin T. Smith (Durham: Duke University Press, 2014), 310; Paxman, "Who Killed," 25.
41. Mora, *Mexican Cinema,* 102.
42. Rohrer, *La India María,* 39.
43. For an excellent account of the transformation in funding with statistics of film production broken down by private, state, and independent, see Alejandro Pelayo, *La generación de la crisis: El cine independiente mexicano de los ochenta* (Mexico City: IMCINE & Conaculta, 2012), 59–78.
44. Ignacio M. Sánchez Prado, "The Golden Age Otherwise: Mexican Cinema and the Mediations of Capitalist Modernity in the 1940s and 1950s," in *Cosmopolitan Film Cultures in Latin America, 1896–1960,* eds. Rielle Edmonds Navitski and Nicolas Poppe (Bloomington: Indiana University Press, 2017), 241.
45. Sánchez Prado, "The Golden Age Otherwise," 242.
46. Dolores Tierney, *New Transnationalisms in Contemporary Latin American Cinemas* (Edinburgh: Edinburgh University Press, 2018).

47. This is clear with the framing of Leonardo García Tsao's "One Generation—Four Filmmakers: Cazals, Hermosillo, Leduc, and Ripstein," in *Mexican Cinema*, ed. Paulo Antonio Paranaguá (London: BFI, 1995), 209–23. Recent scholarship on auteurs from the era in question includes Manuel Gutiérrez Silva and Luis Duno Gottberg, eds., *The Films of Arturo Ripstein: The Sinister Gaze of the World* (New York: Palgrave Macmillan, 2019); Joe Hogan, "Paul Leduc: The Politics of Mexican Cinema in the 1970s," *Cinesthesia* 5, no. 1 (2015); and Kerry Hegarty, "Female Specters: The Gothic Horror Films of Carlos Enrique Taboada," *Flow Journal* 24, February 2014, www.flowjournal.org/2014/02/female-specters-carlos-enrique-taboada/.

48. Ramírez Berg, *The Classical Mexican Cinema*, 8.

49. Ramírez Berg, *The Classical Mexican Cinema*, 10.

50. "'Ganadoras del Ariel,' películas galardonadas, ahora en DVD," *Aristegui Noticias*, October 27, 2014, https://aristeguinoticias.com/2710/kiosko/ganadoras-del-ariel-peliculas-galardonadas-ahora-en-dvd/.

51. García Riera, *Historia del cine mexicano*, 157; IMCINE, "Premio Ariel," http://www.imcine.gob.mx/cine-mexicano/ariel/.

52. There seems to be a significant gap in critical scholarship about the history of the Ariel Awards. The only available information is from the arbiters of the prize itself: http://www.imcine.gob.mx/cine-mexicano/ariel/.

53. *El rebozo de Soledad* (Roberto Gavaldón, 1952), *Los Fernández de Peralvillo* (Alejandro Galindo, 1954) and *Desiertos mares* (José Luis García Agraz, 1994) were also released but fall outside of our timeframe, "'Ganadoras del Ariel.'"

54. Octavio Alfaro, "La Academia Mexicana lanza la segunda colección de las cintas ganadoras del Ariel en DVD," *Sensacine México*, February 19, 2018, https://www.sensacine.com.mx/noticias/noticia-18560804/.

55. López Rivera won the STPC's third experimental cinema contest with *Crónica de una familia* in 1985. Pelayo, *La generación*, 135.

56. Rohrer, *La India María*, 4.

57. Mora, *Mexican Cinema*, 104.

58. For the classic scholarship on New Latin American Cinema, see Michael Chanan, "Introduction," *Twenty-five Years of The New Latin American Cinema* (London: BFI, 1983), 2–8 and Ana M. López, "An 'Other' History: The New Latin American Cinema," *Resisting Images: Essays on Cinema and History*, eds. Robert Sklar and Charles Musser, (Philadelphia: Temple University Press, 1990), 308–30.

59. Octavio Getino and Fernando E. Solanas, "Hacia un tercer cine," *Hojas de cine: Testimonios y documentos del Nuevo Cine Latinoamericano*, vol. I (SEP and UAM, 1988), 29–62; Glauber Rocha, "Uma estética da FOME," *Revista Civilização Brasileiro* 3 (1965): 165–70; Julio García Espinosa, "For an Imperfect Cinema," trans. Julianne Burton, *Jump Cut* no. 20 (1979): 24–26, https://www.ejumpcut.org/archive/onlinessays/JC20folder/ImperfectCinema.html.

60. Second cinema, "la primera alternativa del primer cine," consists of auteur cinema and 1960s Argentine "nuevo cine" from directors like Leopoldo Torre Nilsson, Simón Feldman, Rodolfo Kuhn, David José Kohon, and Fernando Birri. Getino and Solanas, "Hacia un tercer cine," 40–41.

61. Paul Gillingham and Benjamin T. Smith, eds., *Dictablanda: Politics, Work, and Culture in Mexico, 1938–1968* (Durham: Duke University Press, 2014).

62. For more on the authorization process and prohibited content, see de la Vega Alfaro, *Cine, politica*, 17–20.

63. Marvin D'Lugo, Ana M. López, and Laura Podalsky, "Introduction: Troubling Histories," in *The Routledge Companion to Latin American Cinema*, eds. Marvin D'Lugo, Ana López, and Laura Podalsky (New York: Routledge, 2018), 9.

64. D'Lugo, López, and Podalsky, "Introduction," 10.

65. Aldama, *Mex-Ciné*; MacLaird, *Aesthetics and Politics*; Smith, *Mexican Screen Fiction*; Sánchez Prado, *Screening Neoliberalism*.

66. A *sexenio* is the six-year presidential term in Mexico that effectively organizes and reorganizes all bureaucratic dependencies with each new president. Given the close relationship between culture and the state, the *sexenio* thereby creates a high degree of precarity, especially for arts and humanities institutions, given the wide fluctuations in funding, policies, and appointed leadership every six years.

67. Cuauhtémoc Carmona Álvarez, coord., *El Estado y la imagen en movimiento: Reflexiones sobre las políticas públicas y el cine mexicano* (Mexico City: IMCINE & Conaculta, 2012); Ignacio Sánchez Prado, "Alegorías sin pueblo. El cine echeverrista y la crisis del contrato social de la cultura mexicana," *Chasqui* 44, no. 2 (2015): 50–67; Álvaro A. Fernández and Ángel Román Gutiérrez, eds., *A la sombra de los caudillos: El presidencialismo en el cine mexicano* (Mexico City: Universidad de Zacatecas & Cineteca Nacional, 2020).

68. Álvaro Vázquez Mantecón, *El cine súper 8 en México: 1970-1989* (Mexico City: Filmoteca UNAM, 2012); Jesús Alberto Cabañas Osorio, "El cine de ficheras: Un orden simbólico en espera de análisis," *Revista Iberoamericana de comunicación*, no. 25 (2013): 87–113; Violeta Lemus Martínez, "Erotismo, sexualidad e iconografía en el cine mexicano de *Ficheras* de los años 1970," *América* 46 (2015): 161–68; Silvana Flores, "El cine de rumberas y ficheras: Dos caras alternativas de una misma moneda," *Fonseca, Journal of Communication*, no. 20 (2020): 163–80; Carolyn Fornoff, "Musical Interludes in 1960s Mexican Melodrama: Crafting a Sonic Space of Exclusion," *Romance Notes* 58, no. 3 (2018): 507–18.

69. Olivia Cosentino, "Televisa Born and Raised: Lucerito's Stardom in 1980s Mexican Media," *The Velvet Light Trap*, no. 78 (Fall 2016): 38–52 and Olivia Cosentino, "Starring Mexico: Female Stardom, Age and Mass Media Trajectories in the 20th Century" in *The Routledge Companion to Gender, Sex and Latin American Culture*, ed. Frederick Luis Aldama (New York: Routledge, 2018), 196–205.

70. Norma Iglesias, *Entre yerba, polvo y plomo: Lo fronterizo visto por el cine mexicano*, vol. 1 (Tijuana: El Colegio de la Frontera Norte, 1991).

71. Norma Iglesias, "Reconstructing the Border: Mexican Border Cinema and Its Relationship to Its Audience," in *Mexico's Cinema: A Century of Film and Filmmakers* (New York: SR Books, 1999), 233–48.

72. María S. Arbeláez, "Low-Budget Films for Fronterizos and Mexican Migrants in the United States," *Journal of the Southwest* 43, no. 4 (Winter 2001): 637–57; Adán Ávalos, "The Naco in Mexican Film: *La banda del carro rojo*, Border Cinema, and Migrant Audiences," in *Latsploitation, Exploitation Cinemas, and Latin America*, eds. Victoria Ruétalo and Dolores Tierney (New York: Routledge, 2009), 185–97 and "¡Que Naco! Mexican *Popular* Cinema, *La Banda del Carro Rojo* and the Audience," in *Valuing Films: Shifting Perceptions of Worth*, ed. Laura Hubner (New York: Palgrave Macmillan, 2011), 106–20.

73. Laura Isabel Serna, "Chapter 6: *Al Cine*: Mexican Migrants Go to the Movies," *Making Cinelandia: American Films and Mexican Film Culture Before the Golden Age* (Durham: Duke University Press, 2014), 180–214.

74. For example, Desirée J. García explores how Fernando de Fuentes' film *Allá en el Ran-

*cho Grande* (1936) encouraged communities of Mexican migrant workers living in the United States to "strengthen their ties to each other and their homeland," "The Soul of a People: Mexican Spectatorship and the Transnational *Comedia Ranchera*," *Journal of American Ethnic History* 30, no. 1 (2010): 74. Even though de Fuentes' movie is clearly an example of a—if not, the—Golden Age *comedia ranchera*, García's argument nevertheless holds equally true for the films that came later: Mexican consumers, both at home and abroad, located themselves within a sea of changing cultural coordinates through moviegoing. Our argument here is that the films most frequently derided by scholars and historians are precisely the ones that are most beloved and consumed by the average Mexican viewer and therefore should be taken seriously.

75. Jaime Pensado, *Rebel Mexico: Student Unrest and Authoritarian Political Culture during the Long Sixties* (Stanford: Stanford University Press, 2013), 4.

76. Mora writes, "The basic problem was that as films became costlier and had to be produced on an assembly-line basis, there was an ever-greater reliance on "formulas"—*comedias rancheras*; films based on dance fads—cha-cha, Charleston, rock and roll; comedies; lacrimogenic melodramas' horror vehicles à la Hollywood; American-style Westerns; and "superhero" adventures in which masked cowboys or wrestlers took on a variety of evildoers and monsters," *Mexican Cinema*, 103.

77. See Elissa Rashkin, *Women Filmmakers in Mexico: The Country of Which We Dream* (Austin: University of Texas Press, 2001), 59–88.

78. Ilana Dann Luna begins this task in the "long 1990s" with *Adapting Gender: Mexican Feminisms from Literature to Film* (Albany: State University of New York Press, 2018).

79. Claudia Arroyo Quiroz, Álvaro Vázquez Mantecón, and David M. J. Wood, "Forgotten Cinemas: The Institutional Uses of Documentary in Twentieth-Century Mexico (1930–80)," *Studies in Spanish and Latin American Cinemas* 17, no. 2 (2020): 161–72.

## Bibliography

Aldama, Frederick Luis. *Mex-Ciné: Mexican Filmmaking, Production, and Consumption in the Twenty-first Century*. Ann Arbor: University of Michigan Press, 2013.

Alfaro, Octavio. "La Academia Mexicana lanza la segunda colección de las cintas ganadoras del Ariel en DVD." *Sensacine México*, February 19, 2018. https://www.sensacine.com.mx/noticias/noticia-18560804/.

Arbeláez, María S. "Low-Budget Films for Fronterizos and Mexican Migrants in the United States." *Journal of the Southwest* 43, no. 4 (Winter 2001): 637–57.

Ávalos, Adán. "The *Naco* in Mexican Film: *La banda del carro rojo*, Border Cinema, and Migrant Audiences." In *Latsploitation, Exploitation Cinemas, and Latin America*, edited by Victoria Ruétalo and Dolores Tierney, 185–97. New York: Routledge, 2009.

———. "¡Que Naco! Mexican *Popular* Cinema, *La Banda del Carro Rojo* and the Audience." In *Valuing Films: Shifting Perceptions of Worth*, edited by Laura Hubner, 106–20. New York: Palgrave Macmillan, 2011.

Arroyo Quiroz, Claudia, Álvaro Vázquez Mantecón, and David M. J. Wood. "Forgotten cinemas: The Institutional Uses of Documentary in Twentieth-Century Mexico (1930–80)," *Studies in Spanish and Latin American Cinemas* 17, no. 2 (2020): 161–72.

Ayala Blanco, Jorge. *La grandeza del cine mexicano*. Mexico City: Océano, 2004.

Cabañas Osorio, Jesús Alberto. "El cine de ficheras: Un orden simbólico en espera de análisis." *Revista Iberoamericana de comunicación*, no. 25 (2013): 87–113.

Carmona Álvarez, Cuauhtémoc, coord. *El Estado y la imagen en movimiento: Reflexiones sobre las políticas públicas y el cine mexicano*. Mexico City: IMCINE & Conaculta, 2012.

Carro, Nelson. "Cine mexicano de los ochenta: ante el cadaver de un difunto," *Dicine*, no. 33 (1990): 2–5.

Chanan, Michael. "Introduction." In *Twenty-five Years of the New Latin American Cinema*, edited by Michael Chanan, 2–8. London: BFI, 1983.

Cineteca Nacional. "Información." https://www.cinetecanacional.net/controlador.php?opcion=contexto.

Colectivo Alejandro Galindo. "El cine mexicano y sus crisis, primera parte." *Dicine*, no. 19 (May–June 1987): 12–13.

———. "El cine mexicano y sus crisis, segunda parte." *Dicine*, no. 20 (July–August 1987): 12–15.

———. "El cine mexicano y sus crisis, tercera parte." *Dicine*, no. 21 (Sept.–Oct. 1987): 16–18.

"Comunicado: El Santo contra la Cineteca Nacional." Cineteca Nacional, November 1, 2017. https://www.cinetecanacional.net/controlador.php?opcion=noticias&id=850.

Cosentino, Olivia. "Starring Mexico: Female Stardom, Age and Mass Media Trajectories in the 20th Century." In *The Routledge Companion to Gender, Sex and Latin American Culture*, edited by Frederick Luis Aldama, 196–205. New York: Routledge, 2018.

———. "Televisa Born and Raised: Lucerito's Stardom in 1980s Mexican Media." *The Velvet Light Trap*, no. 38 (Fall 2016): 38–52.

Cotter, Robert Michael "Bobb." *The Mexican Masked Wrestler and Monster Filmography*. Jefferson: McFarland and Company, 2008.

Dalton, David. *Mestizo Modernity: Race, Technology, and the Body in Postrevolutionary Mexico*. Gainesville: University Press of Florida, 2018.

de la Mora, Sergio. "'Tus pinches leyes yo me las paso por los huevos.' Isela Vega and Mexican Dirty Movies." In *Latsploitation, Exploitation Cinemas, and Latin America*, edited by Victoria Ruétalo and Dolores Tierney, 245–57. New York: Routledge, 2009.

De la Vega Alfaro, Eduardo. *Cine, política y censura en la era del Milagro Mexicano*. Guadalajara: Universidad de Guadalajara, 2017.

———. "The Decline of the Golden Age and the Making of the Crisis." In *Mexico's Cinema: A Century of Film and Filmmakers*, edited by Joanne Hershfield and David R. Maciel, 165–91. New York: SR Books, 1999.

De los Reyes García-Rojas, Aurelio. "Presentación." In *Miradas al cine mexicano*, coordinated by Aurelio de los Reyes, 9–11. Mexico City: IMCINE, 2016.

D'Lugo, Marvin, Ana M. López, and Laura Podalsky. "Introduction: Troubling Histories." In *The Routledge Companion to Latin American Cinema*, edited by Marvin D'Lugo, Ana M. López and Laura Podalsky, 1–14. New York: Routledge, 2018.

"En está esquina 'El Santo.' Y en la otra 'Pelayo.'" *El Universal*, November 6, 2017. https://www.eluniversal.com.mx/cultura/en-esta-esquina-el-santo-y-en-la-otra-pelayo?fb_comment_id=1111883032248282_1112140158889236.

Fernández, Álvaro A. *Santo el enmascarado de plata: Mito y realidad de un héroe mexicano moderno*. Guadalajara: El Colegio de Michoacán/Universidad de Guadalajara, 2012.

Fernández, Álvaro A., and Ángel Román Gutiérrez, eds. *A la sombra de los caudillos: El presidencialismo en el cine mexicano*. Mexico City: Universidad de Zacatecas & Cineteca Nacional, 2020.

Flores, Silvana. "El cine de rumberas y ficheras: Dos caras alternativas de una misma moneda." *Fonseca, Journal of Communication*, no. 20 (2020): 163–80.

Fornoff, Carolyn. "Musical Interludes in 1960s Mexican Melodrama: Crafting a Sonic Space of Exclusion." *Romance Notes* 58, no. 3 (2018): 507–18.

Gallardo, Gustavo R. "*Santo contra hombres infernales* Had an Outdoor Screening at the 15th FICM." October 27, 2017. https://moreliafilmfest.com/en/santo-contra-hombre-infernales-se-proyecto-al-aire-libre-en-el-150-ficm/.

"'Ganadoras del Ariel,' películas galardonadas, ahora en DVD." *Aristegui Noticias*, October 27, 2014. https://aristeguinoticias.com/2710/kiosko/ganadoras-del-ariel-peliculas-galardonadas-ahora-en-dvd/.

García, Desirée J. "The Soul of a People: Mexican Spectatorship and the Transnational *Comedia Ranchera*." *Journal of American Ethnic History* 30, no. 1 (Fall 2010): 72–98.

García Espinosa, Julio. "For an Imperfect Cinema." Translated by Julianne Burton. *Jump Cut* no. 20 (1979): 24–26. https://www.ejumpcut.org/archive/onlinessays/JC20folder/ImperfectCinema.html.

García Riera, Emilio. *Historia del Cine Mexicano*. Mexico City: Secretaría de Educación Pública, 1985.

García Tsao, Leonardo. "One Generation—Four Filmmakers: Cazals, Hermosillo, Leduc, and Ripstein." In *Mexican Cinema*, edited by Paulo Antonio Paranaguá, 209–23. London: BFI, 1995.

Getino, Octavio, and Fernando E. Solanas. "Hacia un tercer cine." In *Hojas de cine: Testimonios y documentos del Nuevo Cine Latinoamericano*, vol. 1, 29–62. SEP and UAM, 1988.

Gillingham, Paul, and Benjamin T. Smith, eds. *Dictablanda: Politics, Work, and Culture in Mexico, 1938–1968*. Durham: Duke University Press, 2014.

Greene, Doyle. *The Mexican Cinema of Darkness: A Critical Study of Six Landmark Horror and Exploitation Films, 1969–1988*. Jefferson: McFarland and Company, 2007.

———. *Mexploitation Cinema: A Critical History of Mexican Vampire, Wrestler, Ape-Man and Similar Films, 1957–1977*. Jefferson: McFarland & Company, 2005.

Gunckel, Colin. "The Permanencia Voluntaria Archive and the Historical Study of Mexican Cinema." *Studies in Spanish & Latin American Cinemas* 16, no. 3 (2019): 383–401.

Gutiérrez Silva, Manuel, and Luis Duno Gottberg, eds. *The Films of Arturo Ripstein: The Sinister Gaze of the World*. New York: Palgrave Macmillan, 2019.

Gutiérrez, Vicente. "El Santo no es digno para la Cineteca Nacional." *El Economista*, November 1, 2017. https://www.eleconomista.com.mx/arteseideas/El-Santo-no-es-digno-para-la-Cineteca-Nacional-20171101-0143.html.

Haddu, Miriam. *Contemporary Mexican Cinema, 1989–1999*. Lewiston: E. Mellen Press, 2007.

Hegarty, Kerry. "Female Specters: The Gothic Horror Films of Carlos Enrique Taboada." *Flow Journal*, February 25, 2014. www.flowjournal.org/2014/02/female-specters-carlos-enrique-taboada/.

Hegarty, Kerry T. "From Superhero to National Hero: The Populist Myth of El Santo." *Studies in Latin American Popular Culture*, no. 31 (2013): 3–27.

Hogan, Joe. "Paul Leduc: The Politics of Mexican Cinema in the 1970s." *Cinesthesia* 5, no. 1 (2015).

Iglesias, Norma. *Entre yerba, polvo y plomo: Lo fronterizo visto por el cine mexicano*, vol. 1. Tijuana: El Colegio de la Frontera Norte, 1991.

———. "Reconstructing the Border: Mexican Border Cinema and Its Relationship to Its Audience." In *Mexico's Cinema: A Century of Film and Filmmakers*, edited by Joanne Hershfield and David R. Maciel, 233–48. New York: SR Books, 1999.

IMCINE. "Premio Ariel." http://www.imcine.gob.mx/cine-mexicano/ariel/.

Lemus Martínez, Violeta. "Erotismo, sexualidad e iconografía en el cine mexicano de Ficheras de los años 1970." *América* 46 (2015): 161–8.

Levi, Heather. *The World of Lucha Libre: Secrets, Revelations, and Mexican National Identity*. Durham: Duke University Press, 2008.

López, Ana M. "An 'Other' History: The New Latin American Cinema." In *Resisting Images: Essays on Cinema and History*, edited by Robert Sklar and Charles Musser, 308–30. Philadelphia: Temple University Press, 1990.

López Aranda, Susana. "Problemas del cine mexicano: una mesa redonda." *Dicine*, no. 6 (May–June 1984): 3–4.

———. "Problemas del cine mexicano: Una mesa redonda II." *Dicine*, no. 7 (July–August 1984): 3–5.

Luna, Ilana Dann. *Adapting Gender: Mexican Feminisms from Literature to Film*. Albany: State University of New York Press, 2018.

MacLaird, Misha. *Aesthetics and Politics in the Mexican Film Industry*. New York: Palgrave Macmillan, 2013.

McKee Irwin, Robert, and Maricruz Castro Ricalde, eds. *Global Mexican Cinema: Its Golden Age*. London: Palgrave Macmillan and BFI, 2013.

Monterrosas, José Antonia, and Francisco Valenzuela. "Las películas del Santo no se pueden tomar en serio: director de la Cineteca." *Revés Online*, October 30, 2017. http://revesonline.com/2017/10/30/las-peliculas-del-santo-no-se-pueden-tomar-en-serio-director-de-la-cineteca/.

Mora, Carl. *Mexican Cinema: Reflections of a Society, 1896–2004*. Jefferson, NC: McFarland & Company, 2005.

Paxman, Andrew. "Cooling to Cinema and Warming to Television: State Mass Media Policy, 1940–1964." In *Dictablanda: Politics, Work, and Culture in Mexico, 1938–1968*, edited by Paul Gillingham and Benjamin T. Smith, 299–320. Durham: Duke University Press, 2014.

———. "Who Killed the Mexican Film Industry? The Decline of the Golden Age, 1946–1960." *E.I.A.L.* 29, no. 1 (2018): 9–33.

Pelayo, Alejandro. *La generación de la crisis: El cine independiente mexicano de los ochenta*. Mexico City: IMCINE & Conaculta, 2012.

Pensado, Jaime. *Rebel Mexico: Student Unrest and Authoritarian Political Culture during the Long Sixties*. Stanford: Stanford University Press, 2013.

Pick, Zuzana M. *Constructing the Image of the Mexican Revolution: Cinema and the Archive*. Austin: University of Texas Press, 2010.

"Que siempre sí, la Cineteca abre posibilidad de homenaje al Santo." *Medio Tiempo*, November 2, 2017. https://www.mediotiempo.com/lucha-libre/independientes/que-siempre-si-la-cineteca-abre-posibilidad-de-homenaje-al-santo.

Ramírez Berg, Charles. *Cinema of Solitude: A Critical Study of Mexican Film, 1967–1983*. Austin: University of Texas Press, 1991.

———. *The Classical Mexican Cinema: The Poetics of the Exceptional Golden Age Films*. Austin: University of Texas Press, 2015.

Rashkin, Elissa. *Women Filmmakers in Mexico: The Country of Which We Dream*. Austin: University of Texas Press, 2001.
Rocha, Glauber. "Uma estética da FOME." *Revista Civilização Brasileiro* 3 (1965): 165–70.
Roddick, Chloë. "World Premiere of the New Restoration of *Santo contra Cerebro del Mal* at the 68th Berlinale." February 21, 2018. https://moreliafilmfest.com/en/version-restaurada-de-santo-contra-cerebro-del-mal-estrena-en-la-68a-berlinale/.
Rohrer, Seraina. *La India María: Mexploitation and the Films of María Elena Velasco*. Austin: University of Texas Press, 2017.
Sánchez Prado, Ignacio M. "Alegorías sin pueblo. El cine echeverrista y la crisis del contrato social de la cultura mexicana." *Chasqui* 44, no. 2 (2015): 50–67.
———. "The Golden Age Otherwise: Mexican Cinema and the Mediations of Capitalist Modernity in the 1940s and 1950s." In *Cosmopolitan Film Cultures in Latin America, 1896–1960*, edited by Rielle Edmonds Navitski and Nicolas Poppe, 241–66. Bloomington: Indiana UP, 2017.
———. *Screening Neoliberalism: Transforming Mexican Cinema, 1988–2012*. Nashville: Vanderbilt University Press, 2014.
Serna, Laura Isabel. *Making Cinelandia: American Films and Mexican Film Culture Before the Golden Age*. Durham: Duke University Press, 2014.
Smith, Paul Julian. *Mexican Screen Fiction*. Cambridge: Polity, 2014.
Tierney, Dolores. *Emilio Fernández: Pictures in the Margins*. New York: Manchester University Press, 2007.
———. *New Transnationalisms in Contemporary Latin American Cinemas*. Edinburgh: Edinburgh University Press, 2018.
———. "*El vampiro y el sexo/The Vampire and Sex* (René Cardona, 1969): El Santo, Sexploitation Films and Politics in Mexico 1968." *Porn Studies* (2019): 1–17.
"Triunfa El Santo en la Filmoteca." *Reforma*, Opinión, January 3, 2018. https://www.reforma.com/aplicacioneslibre/editoriales/editorial.aspx?id=126672&md5=6eee97609b65550a4dc182b810eb212d&ta=0dfdbac11765226904c16cb9ad1b2efe.
Tuñón, Julia. *Mujeres de luz y sombra en el cine mexicano: La construcción de una imagen (1939–1952)*. Mexico City: Colegio de México & IMCINE, 1998.
Valenzuela, Francisco, and José Antonio Monterrosas. "Basta de menospreciar al cine popular: García-Besné." *Revés Online*, October 30, 2017. https://revesonline.com/2017/10/30/basta-de-menospreciar-al-cine-popular-garcia-besne/.
Vázquez Mantecón, Álvaro. *El cine súper 8 en México: 1970–1989*. Mexico City: Filmoteca UNAM, 2012.
Wehr, Christian, ed. *Clásicos del cine mexicano: 31 películas emblemáticas desde la Época de Oro hasta el presente*. Madrid: Iberoamericana, 2016.

# 1

# I KNOW IT'S ONLY ROCK AND ROLL, BUT I LIKE IT

Popular Music and the Advent of the *Churro*

BRIAN PRICE

Early rock movies are some of the most maligned and misunderstood in Mexican film history. Despite their popularity throughout the late 1950s and 1960s, to say nothing of their relative profitability, these films are considered a blemish on the smooth surface of national film production. While other commercial B-genres like wrestling movies and sex comedies draw occasional nods from the academy, movies about rock and roll and youth culture get dismissed as trivial consumer garbage targeting adolescent masses or overlooked, as if they never existed.[1] Film historian Jorge Ayala Blanco dedicates a number of pages to describing them, among other things, as insignificant, passive, anodyne, and bad caricature.[2] Emilio García Riera suggests that one rock film—Benito Alazraki's *A ritmo de twist* (1962), which I will discuss later—was so badly made, so bereft of artistry, and so banal in its writing that the director withdrew in shame from making films for about a decade.[3] Similarly, none of the major studies on Mexico's film history published in the US academy even deigns to cast a condescending glance at them. Film critic David William Foster makes no mention of 1960s rock movies in *Mexico City in Contemporary Film* even though the inclusion of the capital cityscape constitutes one of the pioneering characteristics of rock cinema. Foster's case is particularly appropriate since his book focuses on the way that the capital city is constructed and narrativized through film, but I could have just as easily cited Susan Dever's oversight of melodramas like *Amor a ritmo de go go* (Miguel M. Delgado, 1966) in her otherwise excellent *Celluloid Nationalism and Other Melodramas* or Andrea Noble's omission of rock films and other popular commercial genres when discussing the post-revolutionary formation of a national cinema audience in *Mexican National Cinema*. To wit, the only time that Charles Ramírez Berg mentions a rock film in *Cinema of Solitude* is when he laments about the hackneyed double standard of female identity in *Cinco de chocolate y uno de fresa* (Carlos Velo, 1968).[4] Only Eric Zolov, in his landmark study on the emergence of counterculture in Mexico, gives rock films any serious thought when he correctly observes that, throughout the midcentury, the film industry recognized that the rising generation of youth was at least as influenced by foreign music and movies as it was by homegrown icons, and met the demands of young viewers by building upon "a long-standing genre of musical drama and comedies" and hoping "to emulate the marketing success of rock 'n' roll-based dramas originating in the United States."[5] Beyond this, only a handful of isolated essays about rock film are emerging in Mexico, and most of them appear in online journals or blogs.

This tension between critical snobbism and public jouissance reveals more about institutional bias than it does about the quality of the films. Film institutes and critics prefer to focus their attention on art-house cinema or movies clearly identified with a national project. If we were to follow the lead of these critics, it would be easy to give into naysaying and dismiss rock films as unworthy of critical attention. However, these movies are important because they attest in many ways to changes in Mexican society and filmmaking. Just as Foster makes a compelling argument in favor of accounting for the representation of urban landscapes in contemporary Mexican film on the basis that life is necessarily linked to geographic space, there is also a soundscape that accompanies existence. Popular music constitutes an important if sometimes overlooked idiom within film language that is central to creating an affective response among viewers.[6] In their rush to write these films out of history, scholars miss three important points. First, early rock films are as much a product of the national folkloric tradition as they are of the Hollywood gristmill. They gave visual and aural space to an emerging and evolving cosmopolitan ethos that broke with the provincial post-revolutionary nationalism of early sound film. Second, these movies were moneymaking machines that provided the capital necessary for loftier art-house-style cinema. As popular commercial films, they cultivated a new audience of viewers by appealing to young people, placing their interests, styles, and culture front and center. Third, national rock films domesticated foreign cultural influences and promoted homegrown musical talent. In essence, these movies became the primary vehicle for showcasing national artists, thereby creating a multiplatform star system that was essentially autonomous from the US system.

This chapter offers an overview of the emergence of early rock movies, specifically those made between 1957 and the end of the 1960s, which I will define here as movies where rock music plays an important role in the diegesis of the film and not simply as soundtrack or backdrop. The first section considers how rock and roll came to Mexico and the changes that it signified for the national film industry. As rock music grew in popularity with middle- and upper-class audiences, films depicting new dance trends, fashion, and music displaced traditional folkloric musicals and offered Mexican youth an alternative to the rigid nationalist imagination. The second section considers how rock films became promotional vehicles for emerging, homegrown musical talent. There I will argue that, throughout the 1960s, domestic film studios produced large numbers of low-budget boilerplate rock films—or *churros*—in order to draw in large crowds of younger spectators.[7] Notwithstanding the slapstick gags, banal wordplay, and stock caricatures present in nearly every one of these films, 1960s rock *churros* played an important role in promoting local musical talent and instructing adolescent audiences in the latest foreign dance trends. By the same token, they also became vehicles for criticizing and undermining the subversive countercultural gesture.

## Transitional Films of 1957

Rock and roll made landfall in Mexico in the mid-1950s around the same time that the cha-cha and mambo were introduced from the Caribbean and quickly became an aspirational symbol of status and modernity. Early songs were composed by adult musicians, performed by large jazz orchestras, heard primarily in cabarets and nightclubs, and marketed as a new dance style to middle-class audiences with disposable income for purchasing records.⁸ As Michael Lydon reminds us, the music industry is synonymous with business and rock music "was never an art form that just happened to make money, nor a commercial undertaking that sometimes became art."⁹ It was always already a consumer commodity with all of the attendant social status that accompanies high-end goods. As such, rock and roll became a status symbol for a growing middle class that had benefitted from decades of sustained economic increases. By the 1950s, transnational record companies like RCA Victor and Columbia Records were figuring out how to exploit the Latin American market and, due to its geographic proximity, relative economic well-being, and preexisting cultural infrastructure, Mexico became the focus of efforts to sell US music abroad. Sensing challenges from transnational corporations and the impending loss of market dominance, local record labels like Orfeón began claiming their own share of the airwaves by contracting local talent to cover popular US tunes.¹⁰ Most of these early recordings, commonly referred to as *refritos,* amounted to little more than workaday translations. Musicians recorded the instrumental backing tracks note for note, in most cases, but delivered the lyrical content in Spanish and often very literally. Neil Sedaka's "Calendar Girl" was immediately picked up and covered by Los Rebeldes del Rock as "Calendario de amor" while Little Richard's "Lucille" was transformed into "Lucila" by Los Yakis, with lead singer Benny Ibarra using Little Richard's gospel-influenced groans as a vehicle for Hispanicizing the name. *Refritos,* while not original masterpieces of national music, gave many Mexican citizens their first taste of rock and roll and functioned as a kind of sentimental education for an entire generation of young musicians and listeners.

While rock and roll was steadily working its way onto the airwaves, filmmakers recognized the potential benefits of cashing in on an emerging adolescent youth culture and closely followed the US production model. As a number of scholars have pointed out, Mexican filmmakers enjoyed a close relationship with Hollywood.¹¹ Throughout World War II, Mexican melodramas played in theaters across the US and Mexican actors starred in a number of important Hollywood productions. This proximity meant that Mexican filmmakers enjoyed access to US studios, production processes, press kits, and a large supply of raw film stock. This gave Mexico a decided advantage over other Latin American industries which struggled to find the material means for creating local productions. Moreover, Mexico's geographic proximity made distribution of Hollywood movies feasible. This access gave them up-to-date information about what was working in the US market, and film producers were able to catch the wave of early rock films, wasting no time in crafting their own films almost simultaneously with their US counterparts. Market trends in both countries appear to have also run similar paths. The waning popularity of Golden Age nationalist cinema paralleled what was happening in the post-war US market. Thomas Doherty suggests that "the decline of Classical Hollywood cinema and the rise of the privileged American teenager" created the conditions for the emergence of low-budget cinematic fare aimed at exploiting the interests of adolescent viewers.[12]

Hollywood recognized that the rising generation of adolescents craved films about their own experiences, concerns, and culture. Film executives began crafting stories that would reflect those interests, giving rise to what Doherty has called the "teenpic." He argues that films about rock and roll should be categorized as "exploitation" films because these movies "are *triply* exploitative, simultaneously exploiting sensational happenings (for story value), their notoriety (for publicity value), and their teenage participants (for box-office value)."[13] Filmmakers at Azteca and Churubusco—the two most prominent producers of rock films through the 1950s and early 1960s—followed suit. They specifically targeted a demographic that had been largely overlooked by the purveyors of cultural products. With the exception of films like Luis Buñuel's *Los olvidados* [*The Young and the Damned*] (1950), where adolescents were portrayed as victims of a negligent social apparatus, young people had only limited experience being on-screen protagonists. More often than not, they were relegated to secondary roles and were used to elicit emotional responses from viewers. But those roles always depended on and were subservient to adult leads. Adolescent experiences, concerns, and culture were largely ignored.

Many of the first movies to incorporate rock and roll were juvenile delinquency films that expressed anxiety over the new moralities of the large post-war adolescent population. Modern rock and roll was expressly tied to the moral degeneracy in films like Richard Brooks's *Blackboard Jungle* (1955), which marked the first time that rock and roll appeared on the big screen. The movie begins with a prologue extolling the virtues of the US educational system and expressing concern about the rising threat of juvenile delinquency. Even though the prologue assures audiences that the "scenes and incidents depicted here are fictional," the filmmakers believe that "public awareness is the first step toward a remedy for any problem" and, in this way, the film presents itself as a public service announcement. This text is accompanied by a jazzy take on military-style drumming, suggesting that the film is the first line of defense in the war against delinquency. The message scrolls to the top of the screen and fades as the drum section seamlessly counts in Bill Haley's "Rock Around the Clock." An extended version of the song plays through the opening credits and into the first scene as Glenn Ford approaches the high school where he'll be teaching, cutting his way through a bunch of young hooligans dancing in the courtyard. All of this, of course, indicates that the music of young people somehow correlates to the violence and rebelliousness that will make up the majority of the film's content.

As soon as *Blackboard Jungle* hit Mexico City theaters, it was almost immediately imitated, or maybe more correctly "covered," by Mexican filmmakers. Within a year, Fernando Cortés directed *Viva la juventud* (1956) and José Díaz Morales put out *Juventud desenfrenada* (1956). Both movies showed at the large Art Deco–style Teatro Orfeón, and both enjoyed rather long runs: *Viva la juventud* screened for eight weeks and *Juventud desenfrenada* showed for six. Like their US predecessor, these two movies were morality tales and, on those rare occasions when rock music is heard, it cues reflections on social problems. *Juventud desenfrenada* is a perfect example of a filmic *refrito*. In every way, it copies the introduction of *Blackboard Jungle*.[14] The movie opens with a nighttime shot of a dance school as a trumpet spits out a slinky minor blues melody. The camera pans downward to the rearview mirror of a car where a young woman applies makeup as an off-screen narrator ominously explains that "un rostro nuevo ha aparecido en todas las ciudades del mundo: la adolescencia delincuente" [a new face has appeared in all the cities of the world: juvenile delinquency]. It then cuts to a long, dark alleyway where a man runs while firing a pistol at the police who pursue him. "Donde esperamos encontrar a hombres y mujeres madurados en el vicio" [Where we might expect to find men and women acquainted with vice], the voice informs us, "surgen ahora jóvenes apenas salidos de la niñez, asaltantes de bancos, robacoches, maleantes que llegan al robo y al crimen envilecidos por las drogas" [young people barely out of childhood become bank robbers, carjackers, ne'er-do-wells who turn to thievery and crime under the influence of drugs]. The voice then explains that the story we are about to watch has been taken from the pages of police reports and committed to film in order to dissuade young people from falling into evil pathways. The narrator's final words coincide with the title card superimposed upon a snare drum solo and Gloria Ríos's rendition of "Rock Around the Clock." The beat-for-beat similarities between these two introductions allow us to connect the ideological project of US delinquency films like *Blackboard Jungle* with their Mexican refried versions. Music in these films is not portrayed as the root cause of delinquency but rather as a symptom of broader social problems. Delinquency films express serious concerns about the corrupting foreign influences that are represented by music and demonstrate the degree to which filmmakers and local government were concerned about the deleterious effects of music and foreign cultural intervention on Mexican youth.[15]

Rock and roll made its definitive appearance on Mexican screens in 1957 when four movies premiered within months of each other: *Los chiflados del rock 'n roll* (José Díaz Morales), *La locura del rock 'n roll* (Fernando Méndez), *Al compás del rock and roll* (José Díaz Morales), and *Locos peligrosos* (Fernando Cortés).[16] I refer to these films as "transitional rock films" for two reasons: first, they mark the first conscientious but partial move away from the cowboy musicals of the Golden Age and, second, because, read collectively, they illustrate the ambivalence in Mexican society toward the incipient rock gesture. As might be expected from the preceding year's offering of delinquency films, not everyone was on board with the new musical trend. However, change was coming, and the transition from the *comedia ranchera* to modern rock and roll films implied several narrative and thematic changes that were unevenly distributed and adopted, depending on the film. The most obvious was the move away from provincial landscapes. The hills, plains, and ranches that had characterized much of early sound film were replaced by cityscapes, streetlights, and cabarets. Most of these films clearly situate themselves within a modern city that is quickly catching up to its northern neighbor in terms of wealth and cultural practice. These early rock films were also among the first to emphasize the immediacy of contemporary society, a gesture which supersedes the backward glancing nostalgia of the folkloric musical. The change of scenery and temporality also demanded changes in casting. Wealthy ranchers, singing cowboys, and beautiful maidens gave way to record producers and sound engineers, bandleaders and dancers, and, more importantly, high school and university students. Unlike their provincial counterparts, these urban youth question and mock authority figures like policemen, teachers, executives, and store owners. Maybe the most striking development in these casting decisions was the emergence of modern female characters who broke the mold of the submissive Mexican woman. For the most part women in early Mexican film occupy secondary roles to their male costars, generally fulfilling the role of the love object around which the tensions of the story develop. We have to look no further than *Allá en el Rancho Grande* (Fernando de Fuentes, 1936) or *Los tres García* (Ismael Rodríguez, 1947) to verify this. Only on rare occasions, such as *Santa* (Antonio Moreno, 1932) and *Río Escondido* (Emilio Fernández, 1948), do female leads take a more active role in determining the outcome of the story. The emergence of strong female leads in rock films alluded to the transformation of gender roles in Mexican society, a development that, as we will see, was not generally considered a welcomed change.

The first transitional film to hit the theaters was Spanish exile José Díaz Morales's *Los chiflados del rock 'n roll*. Díaz Morales arrived in Mexico from Spain at the end of 1936 and, over the course of a thirty-year career, directed ninety-one films, usually three a year but sometimes as many as five. Most of his films in the 1940s were religiously themed melodramas where women were portrayed as problematic threats to male virtue, a trend in his filmmaking that continued well into the 1950s. The moralizing melodrama machine that Díaz Morales created was perfectly suited to capitalizing on new cultural trends. After producing the delinquency film *Juventud desenfrenada*, Díaz Morales shifted his gaze toward the profitability of rock and roll and moved quickly. In January, he started shooting *Los chiflados del rock 'n roll* at Estudios Churubusco, and filming lasted about two weeks. The film premiered on February 27, 1957, at Teatro Orfeón, a few blocks from the Alameda Central in downtown Mexico City and ran for three weeks. Billed as one of the first authentic rock films, *Los chiflados* tells the story of three musicians who attempt to woo the rough-edged niece of a wealthy *norteño* rancher in the hopes of obtaining her dowry to fund a nightclub in Mexico City. Yet, *Los chiflados* is a rock film in name only, which became apparent a few weeks before it was released. When a report began circulating out of Tijuana that Elvis Presley had remarked that he would rather kiss three Black women than one Mexican, the promotional campaign used to market *Los chiflados* to Mexican audiences was immediately altered to denigrate Presley and his music. Posters were modified to depict him as effeminate and pernicious and worthy of being shot by a firing squad of sombrero-wearing revolutionaries while the three lead characters of the film were portrayed as wholesome and the movie as enriching family entertainment.[17] Of course, the brouhaha had little to do with the thematic content of the film and more with publicity. It exploited, to use Doherty's term, a salient current event to sell tickets. But, when watching the film, it is apparent that the lack of rock performances was not a postproduction decision. Rock and roll was never planned to play an integral part of the story.

The first clue was the decision to assemble a cast of older, well-established performers to draw in a reliable ticket-buying crowd. The ensemble cast included aging icons of the traditional folkloric repertoire: Agustín Lara, Pedro Vargas, and Luis Aguilar. Lara had turned sixty a few months before filming started and Vargas was fifty-one. That left the thirty-nine-year-old Aguilar to take the romantic lead opposite Rosita Arenas, twenty-four, who made frequent appearances in rock films over the next couple of years. Maybe more important than age, however, were their respective musical backgrounds. By this time, Lara was one of Mexico's most cherished balladeers, having composed sentimental favorites like "Farolito" and "Arráncame la vida." Vargas trained as an opera singer, recorded tangos in Argentina, and solidified his reputation as a well-known *ranchera* singer and actor during the Golden Age of Mexican cinema. Aguilar built up his credentials as a *comedia ranchera* leading man, starring in more than 150 films over the course of his career. Understandably, then, the songs they perform throughout the film are ballads and *rancheras*. Zolov suggests that the reference to rock and roll in the title underscores the prevailing notion of rock as a passing fad.[18] And while that may be true—Díaz Morales was unquestionably attempting to cash in on the newest dance sensation sweeping the nation—it still doesn't account for why the film is composed primarily of these traditional songs when the title suggests that it is a rock film. Aside from two brief numbers by Mario Patrón's orchestra and an incongruous German newsreel called "Rock N Roll Fieber" about a dance competition that gets cut into the film without even taking the time to edit out the opening credit sequence, there is not much modern music. Instead, *Los chiflados* heavily favors the traditional national repertoire. Lara performs three of his own songs ("Flor de lis," "Se me hizo fácil," and

"Rosa de Francia") while comic actor Lalo "El Piporro" González offers up a scene-stealing rendition of his own humorous *ranchera* song "El cascarazo," easily the most entertaining musical number of the whole film. Additionally, a series of traditional *rancheras* like José Alfredo Jiménez's "Serenata huasteca" and Cuco Sánchez's "Qué manera de perder" and "Fallaste corazón" round out the musical offering. The emphasis, then, is clearly centered on folkloric music that older audiences, ostensibly the targets of the promotional campaign touting the movie as wholesome family entertainment, would want to listen to. It is, in essence, a *comedia ranchera* set in the present.

As soon as he wrapped *Los chiflados del rock and roll*, Díaz Morales got to work on his next film, *Al compás del rock 'n roll*, which appeared on screen in May. In the meantime, however, Fernando Méndez's *La locura del rock 'n roll* offered an important counterpoint to Díaz Morales's modern *comedia ranchera* both in tone and style. Like *Los chiflados*, Méndez's move was shown in the downtown area, this time at the Cine Palacio Chino, a large theater that opened its door in 1940 and boasted seating for four thousand on two levels. It premiered on March 29, 1957, and showed there for four weeks. But unlike its predecessor, *La locura* captured the youthful aspect of rock counterculture, portrayed the financial aspirations of the rising generation, and even offered glimpses into growing demands for equal rights for women in a modernizing society.

The first major difference from *Los chiflados* was its shift in focus away from rural landscapes and older leading men. *La locura del rock 'n roll* is clearly situated in an urban environment dominated by adolescents and the symbols of their rising affluence within Mexican society. The film opens with a narrative exposition about the importance of two local centers of higher education, the humanities-oriented Universidad Nacional Autónoma de México (UNAM) and the vocational Instituto Politécnico Nacional (IPN). The narrator explains that the students of both institutions form one large close-knit family where youthful bouts of competition take place on the sports field. This message of fraternal togetherness—and its corollary to the metaphor of the post-revolutionary family—is ironically undermined by images of the students fighting both on and off the field. The sequence includes footage from student gatherings, sporting events, and campus landscapes, and indicates that upward mobility is achieved by taking advantage of the educational opportunities available through the economic well-being of the nation. While this somewhat clunky opening feels more like a promotional video for local universities, it creates a sense of social and cultural difference for university students, where humanities students are pitted against vocational students.[19] This is part and parcel of the film's overall logic. Conflict is what drives the narrative forward. However, while the opening narration would have us think that the immediate tension lies between two collegiate institutions, it is, on the contrary, between the sexes.[20]

The real story revolves around tensions between members of a coed university orchestra that is codirected by Juan (Juan García Esquivel) and Teresa (Lilia Prado). As the expositional narration finishes, Juan and Teresa stand in front of a poster announcing a battle of the bands between Los Rítmicos from UNAM and Los Armónicos from IPN. They discuss their excitement about finally being able to perform and express their shared dream of becoming famous. The emphasis of the dialogue centers on their mutual success. This seemingly egalitarian position is undermined, however, when the couple argues about what to call the band, since tradition states that orchestras take the name of the bandleader. Teresa imagines a marquee announcing La Orquesta de Teresa García. Juan fires back that his name should take prominence, presumably because he is the male bandleader. They eventually agree to share the limelight, but tempers flare up again when a wealthy friend offers to hire the orchestra to play in his cabaret. The catch is that he only wants the women to play, asserting that the joint needs something new. The orchestra splits along gender lines and a sort of cold war between the lovers ensues. Pressure grows as the women draw large crowds to the restaurant while their male counterparts remain unemployed. The film then appears to advocate in favor of sexual emancipation: women are the profitable breadwinners and their boyfriends must rely upon them for support and entertainment. Yet, the film rejects these emancipatory feminist politics over the course of the movie.

The most conservative moment in the film's gender politics comes near the end when female band members voluntarily cede their autonomy to male leadership. When introducing the final number at the intercollegiate battle of the bands, Teresa credits the arrangement of their number to Juan, who sits brooding at the back of the gymnasium. At the mention of his name, the camera cuts to a close-up that registers Juan's surprise at receiving mention for his contribution. As the applause dies down, Teresa says that no one is better qualified than he to direct the orchestra, which she underscores by granting him ownership and calling it his. She makes her public submission even more explicit when she tells him in a pleading tone that his place is at the head of the group, that everyone in the band wants him to lead, and that she especially wants him there. With breathy undertones, she asks him to come and direct them. A long tracking shot follows his every move as Juan cuts a path through the applauding male audience. When he finally arrives on stage, the band members begin caterwauling "The Bridal Chorus," as if to suggest that Teresa's final submission to Juan has finally prepared the grounds for their inevitable marriage. Teresa's decision to allow the pouting Juan to take the reins for the big performance can be read in two ways. The initial impulse might be irritation at what clearly appears to be straightjacketing her agency, sacrificing her own position as bandleader and assuming the role of band member. But, it might also be argued that her gesture is the most conclusive act of agency in the whole film because, in fact, there does not appear to be any social pressure on her to resign her post. Rather, she hands over the proverbial (and literal) baton as an act of reconciliation and a gesture of love. The seemingly ambiguous finale then allows for both interpretations. Far from perfect in this regard, *La locura del rock 'n roll* establishes a pattern for musical film in the 1960s that openly advocates the sexual and political agency of female characters while subtly undermining that agency.

If *Los chiflados* and *La locura* illustrate the ambivalent, transitional nature of these 1957 films both in their wary embrace of rock music and their somewhat regressive gender politics, Fernando Cortés's *Locos peligrosos* marks a decidedly conservative reaction to the influx of rock and roll. It premiered on August 8, 1957, at the Teatro Chapultepec, where it showed for three weeks. Better than any other film from the period, *Locos peligrosos* dramatizes the incipient conflict between established musical-moral values and the insurgency of modern music. Federico (Germán Valdés aka Tin-Tan) and Pedro (Luis Aguilar) are two musicians who work at a music school under the direction of a classical maestro, Don Julio (Julio Villareal). Deciding that classical music is out of step with modern musical trends, the two friends begin playing rock and roll, obtain a recording contract, produce a number of hit singles, and achieve international notoriety.[21] In the process, however, Federico indefinitely postpones marriage to his longtime girlfriend Minerva, who also happens to be Don Julio's daughter, alleging the need to save more money. Trouble begins when both of the young musicians decide to pursue the affections of their producer, culminating with a raucous musical showdown during Carnival in Havana. The film concludes with both men renouncing rock and roll and returning to the music school where they are received with open arms both by their former teacher and his daughter. Thus, the movie bears all the marks of a delinquency film, while at the same time all of the draw for audiences hoping to hear some modern music. Throughout *Locos peligrosos*, "modern music" is perceived as a pathway to improving socioeconomic status. During a televised variety show, a jazz orchestra led by the kinetic Puppy Lane, played by Ramón Valdés, performs a swinging number while Pedro attempts to woo the program's producer María Mercedes (Ariadna Welter).[22] She rejects his advances and informs him that, as a classical musician, he is a nobody, and that she is not interested in dating someone with no future. Pedro then joins his maestro on stage for a sedate performance of Franz Lizst's *Liebestraum* while the camera records the boredom felt by the members of the rock and roll group. Midway through the piece, Pedro remembers the producer's rejection and spices up the performance by improvising a jazzy solo that leads to a jump-and-jive version of Lizst's melody, much to the dismay of his conductor and the approval of the audience and his love interest. After Federico and Pedro improvise flirtatious lyrics over the melody, María begins to warm up to her would-be suitor. Later Federico, who had always been reticent to play rock and roll because his future father-in-law Don Julio adamantly rejects any deviation from the musical canon, asks his girlfriend Minerva (Yolanda Varela) to support his new musical direction because he has already received a number of recording contracts that will allow them to marry. In this manner, rock and roll is not simply an expression of youthful vitality and rebellion but also a means to financial independence.[23] This success comes at a moderate price as the duo must perform under the Anglicized names of Fred and Peter and record original tunes as well as translated covers of US chart toppers like "Sixteen Tons."

    The decision to abandon canonical music takes the two performers down the path of immorality. The more successful Federico becomes, the more he postpones his wedding to Minerva and chases after María Mercedes, eventually following her to Cuba during Carnival in an attempt to win her affections. When a tabloid photo shows the two boarding an airplane for the Caribbean,

Minerva breaks down and cries while her father declares her to be another helpless "víctima del rock and roll" [victim of rock and roll]. Later Pedro and Federico discover that they have both come to the island for the same reason and attempt to undermine each other's chances with María. In this manner, *Locos peligrosos* evinces the same moralistic concern about juvenile delinquency that appeared in earlier films. Even though Valdés, forty-one at the time of shooting, and Aguilar, thirty-nine, were far from adolescents at this point in their careers, both play capricious, immature characters in desperate need of paternal guidance from the older schoolmaster and domestication at the hands of their sweethearts. But whereas *Juventud desenfrenada* and other delinquency films blamed disintegration of family order on the abuse of alcohol and narcotics, *Locos peligrosos* identifies the culprit as modern music. In this regard the title explicitly indicates societal perceptions of rock and roll's potentially deleterious effects; it is construed both as madness in its rejection of good behavior as well as dangerous to the individual and the bedrock institution of marriage.

In this regard, the trip to Cuba during Carnival—with all of its bacchanalian excess, transitory liminality, and periodic framework for transgression—allows for the expression and expulsion of foolishness prior to a return to normalcy. Though the two friends might have been lured into the dangerous world of rock and roll for a brief period, they nevertheless reconcile themselves to polite society, family values, and the musical canon. The film concludes with a complete resolution: Don Julio is directing Minerva as she practices a classical piece when, from the other room, they hear Federico and Pedro accompanying her on the cello and piano. The harmonizing of their instruments communicates the proverbial return of the prodigals. Don Julio removes the black band that he had draped around the statue of Beethoven, and two photographs of Mozart and Chopin that had previously fallen to the ground during a rock and roll number magically jump back on the wall. But what is even more telling about the film's support of traditional musical culture emerges when the trio is joined by the local organ grinder, a folkloric throwback to pre-revolutionary culture, whose organ cranks out the same tune in perfect pitch and harmony.[24] The end of the film restores order, balance, and tradition.

Taken as a whole, the transitional films of 1957 point to radical and rapid changes in Mexican society. Young people wanted movies about themselves, and filmmakers, though not completely ready to embrace the rock gesture, were sufficiently interested in exploring the financial possibilities of a genre that met those demands. At the same time, however, they found themselves hedging their bets. They warned against the dangers of juvenile delinquency while projecting examples of it on screen. They flirted with female emancipation only to kneecap it with tropes of submission. They hinted that modern music might in fact be a worthy economic and professional pursuit while countering that financial success comes at the cost of moral ruin. They also opened the door for the mass-produced commercial movies that provided modern music and stories about adolescent experience for adolescents. But they did so by plugging these new elements into the existing structure of the *comedia ranchera.*

## The Rock *Churro*

One way to read the transitional rock films is as a kind of market test, where industry executives attempted to figure out which model would be the most popular and profitable. What they discovered was a goldmine in the positive, upbeat, celebratory *La locura del rock 'n roll* version of the genre, and they immediately set out to produce large numbers of low-budget boilerplate rock films in order to draw in large crowds of younger spectators. These films are frequently and pejoratively referred to as *churros,* evoking the cheap fried pastries commonly found in restaurants and street carts. Jesús Salvador Treviño, writing in 1979, observes that these "were films geared to the lowest common denominator of popular taste and lacked the ambition of serious filmmaking that had marked the films of Mexico's 'golden era' in the 1940s. The churros were cheaply made, mostly by *productores privados*: private, profit-minded independent producers with few or no artistic pretensions."[25] The term *churro* acquires the same dismissive, elitist tone expressed by the critics quoted at the outset of this essay and is almost universally employed as a way of dismissing popular filmmaking. And yet, like its pastry counterpart, the filmic *churro* satisfies a craving for light, enjoyable cinematic fare and creates its own market niche. From the industry point of view, and above and beyond any artistic aspirations, rock *churros* were moneymaking machines, and no one understood that better than Sam Katzman. Katzman was, first and foremost, a businessman who maintained no high notions about the purity of art. He was the most notorious, not to mention successful, producer of pulpy genre films in Hollywood and had a keen nose for sniffing out the next big trend and then milking it for all its worth. In 1962 Katzman related that the total cost to make *Twist around the Clock* (Oscar Rudolph, 1961) was $250,000 and that, in less than six months, the film had grossed more than $6,000,000. From a business perspective the choice was obvious: "of course I'm gonna make more *Twist* movies!"[26] Mexican filmmakers were quick to adopt Katzman's pragmatic approach. The key for Mexican studios was to produce a lot of rock films and to produce them quickly.

As yet there is no consensus on exactly how many rock films were produced during the 1960s, largely because critics have not settled on a concrete definition for what constitutes a rock film. Some choose movies where music plays a significant role in defining the contours of the narrative while others are happy to count any project where rock music is played. Chronicler Federico Rubli sets a low bar of about 44 films, apparently selecting only representative movies. Novelist Federico Arana identifies about 65 films in *Guaraches de ante azul* (1985), one of the most well-documented chronicles of national rock counterculture. Gustavo Zamora, by contrast, counts 222 movies by scouring bibliographic sources, looking over cast listings, and counting any film starring pop and rock icons, including *luchador* films starring El Santo, Luis Buñuel's *Simón del desierto* (1965), and at least one Cantinflas movie, *Un Quijote sin mancha* (Miguel M. Delgado, 1969), demonstrates Zamora's encyclopedic impulse. In this last film, an older Cantinflas dresses up as a hippie and infiltrates a dance party. Club-wielding police officers storm the building and carry the dancers down to the local station where they will spend the night. While the young people seem completely content playing their guitars and hanging out in the cell, Cantinflas gets annoyed and tells them to knock off the racket. He then lectures the young people about their moral responsibilities and civic duties, chastising them for their bohemian ways. So, while there is technically some rock music in *Un Quijote sin mancha*, in its denunciation of rock music and culture it is definitely not a rock film. In short, if there is a rock song present in the soundtrack, or if a musician makes a cameo appearance, Zamora counts it. In the figure below, I have compiled the findings of all three sets and compared them with García Riera's annual production numbers in *Historia documental del cine mexicano*.

This data allows us to take a broad view and make a couple of generaliza-

Table 1.1. Comparative data on Mexican rock film production, 1955–1969

| Year | Total Film Production[a] | Rubli[b] | % | Arana[c] | % | Zamora[d] | % |
|---|---|---|---|---|---|---|---|
| 1955 | 91 | - | - | - | - | 2 | 2% |
| 1956 | 101 | - | - | 6 | 6% | 8 | 8% |
| 1957 | 104 | - | - | 8 | 8% | 18 | 17% |
| 1958 | 135 | - | - | 5 | 4% | 12 | 9% |
| 1959 | 116 | 1 | 1% | 1 | 1% | 7 | 6% |
| 1960 | 114 | 2 | 2% | 4 | 4% | 14 | 12% |
| 1961 | 74 | 2 | 3% | 3 | 4% | 8 | 11% |
| 1962 | 81 | 8 | 10% | 10 | 12% | 18 | 22% |
| 1963 | 86 | 4 | 5% | 7 | 8% | 16 | 19% |
| 1964 | 113 | 6 | 5% | 12 | 11% | 25 | 22% |
| 1965 | 97 | 12 | 12% | 13 | 13% | 24 | 25% |
| 1966 | 98 | 7 | 7% | 12 | 12% | 41 | 42% |
| 1967 | 93 | 1 | 1% | 2 | 2% | 24 | 26% |
| 1968 | 103 | 1 | 1% | 1 | 1% | 41 | 40% |
| 1969 | 88 | - | - | - | - | 8 | 9% |

*Notes:* a. Emilio García Riera, *Historia documental del cine mexicano* (Guadalajara and Mexico City: Universidad de Guadalajara, Gobierno de Jalisco, Conaculta, Instituto Mexicano de Cinematografía, 1994).
b. Federico Rubli, *Estremécete y rueda* (México: Chapa Ediciones, 2007).
c. Federico Arana, *Guaraches de ante azul* (Madrid: Espoz y Mina, 2002).
d. Jorge Zamora, *El rock de los 60 en el cine mexicano*. Last modified February 5, 2013. http://filmografiadelrockmexicano.wordpress.com.

tions. First, following the transitional films of 1957, production of rock *churros* ramped up slowly through the latter part of the 1950s, generally accounting for less than 10 percent of overall films, and built up steam through the first half of the 1960s as rock and roll proved its durability and profitability as a youth dance fad and increasingly saturated the airwaves. Second, about halfway through the 1960s, studios dramatically increased production, with rock music appearing in at least 25 percent of all movies throughout the decade and almost 50 percent of all movies made in 1964 and 1965. This increased interest coincides with a number of important developments in the pop music world. Elvis Presley had become one of the most important film icons in the US, starring in twenty-seven feature-length films between 1960 and 1969, averaging about three lead roles per year. At the same time, the beach party subgenre took theaters by storm, making Frankie Avalon and Annette Funicello household names among teenagers in the US. In Mexico, a similar star system emerged around César Costa, Enrique Guzmán, and Angélica María. Beatlemania followed hard on the heels of the Liverpool quartet's first US tour in 1964 and was spurred on by their appearances on television variety shows like *The Ed Sullivan Show* and films like *A Hard Day's Night* (Richard Lester, 1964) and *Help!* (Richard Lester, 1965). Third, by the end of the 1960s, rock filmmaking went into a steep decline. However, unlike the *comedia ranchera*, which waned because it could not speak to the modernizing aspirations of a nation perched upon the precipice of first-world status, rock movies died out due to institutional backlash against counterculture following the 1968 student protests and the massacre at the Plaza de las Tres Culturas. By the early 1970s, after the Halconazo and the Avándaro rock festival, film studios nixed nearly every rock-related project, and countercultural filmmakers were forced underground.[27] These cancellations were likely influenced by the Echeverría administration, which showed open hostility toward counterculture and controlled a large portion of film production budgets.[28] Rock films would not begin to appear in theaters again until the mid- to late-1980s.

In the remaining pages, I focus on two 1960s rock *churros*: Benito Alazraki's *A ritmo de twist* (1962) and Miguel M. Delgado's *Amor a ritmo de go go* (1966). To be sure, there are many more that need serious discussion. However, I find these two films to be compelling examples for two main reasons. First, they both demonstrate the ways that film studios capitalized on the popularity of rock music to promote national musicians and to sell their films; second, the contrast between their styles and intent demonstrates the unresolved tensions that were present in the transitional films we saw earlier.

Benito Alazraki's *A ritmo de twist* (1962) is, to my mind, the exemplary 1960s rock *churro*. Filmed, edited, and released to theaters within a two-month period, the movie ran for four weeks at the Cine Mariscala near the Palacio de Bellas Artes. In the film, Matusalén (Manuel "El Loco" Valdés) is a slacker student with no aspirations to graduate whose uncle offers to pay for his studies in England if the younger man can keep the family dressmaking business afloat while the uncle goes on a trip.[29] Recognizing the untapped financial resources of his classmates, he puts together a campaign that markets the dresses with rock music. When a rival swimsuit maker attempts to undercut his business through some dirty tricks, Matusalén challenges him to a competition to see who makes the best dresses. The rest of the movie is a series of musical scenes stitched together with brief narrative fragments, a flimsy story of unrequited love, a passel of campy jokes, and a smattering of silly slapstick scenes. The flick is light entertainment; it certainly does not aspire to highbrow filmmaking. Even so, it is still worth noting for the things that it does well.

*A ritmo de twist*, like many rock *churros* from the period, created an alternate star system that launched the careers of many teen idols and future heavy hitters in the Mexican music scene. Younger audiences could now more easily identify with the actors on screen as opposed to longing for older leading men and women. Mario Patrón, who provided soundtracks for almost all of the transitional films and starred in a couple of them, would later become a central figure in the Mexican jazz scene and composer of popular ballads. Teen idol César Costa, lead singer and guitar player for Los Black Jeans, starred in about twelve *churros* throughout the 1960s including *Dile que la quiero* (1963), continued recording up through the 1980s, and then enjoyed an on-screen comeback as a sitcom actor in the 1990s. Maybe even more surprising was the fact that Costa's backup singer in the band was none other than Plácido Domingo. And then there is Enrique Guzmán, the lead singer of Los Teen Tops, arguably the most important male teen heartthrob of the time. *A ritmo de twist* features on-screen musical performances from the five most important pioneer bands in Mexico: Los Rebeldes del Rock, Los Hooligans, Los Crazy Boys, Los Teen Tops, and Los Beatniks. Eight musical numbers totaling almost forty minutes are crammed into this seventy-five-minute film. Most of the bands get one performance that takes place in a party setting where young people have congregated to dance. In this sense, *A ritmo de twist* is not far removed from dance programs like *American Bandstand*, which ran on US television from 1952 to 1989 and gave exposure to popular bands every week.[30] By giving these bands screen time and a chance to perform their music in a scene where young people were clearly dancing and enjoying themselves, *A ritmo de twist* and other films in the genre played an important role in forging profitable careers for all of these musicians.[31]

Churros did not just promote the bands but also Spanish-language covers of foreign tunes as well as homegrown, original compositions. All but one of the songs in *A ritmo de twist* is a cover of a US hit. Los Rebeldes offer up a straightforward Spanish version of Neil Sedaka's "Calendar Girl" as do Los Hooligans with their rendition of Dodie Stevens's "Pink Shoelaces." Alberto Vásquez gets more creative when he channels Elvis Presley while singing Paul Anka's "Tonight, My Love, Tonight." Two of the songs are admirably imaginative translations, namely Los Crazy Boys's "La pulga," which covers Hank Ballard's "The Twist" and Los Teen Tops's take on the Larry Williams's hit "Boney Maroney," which they render as "Popotitos." Even the tune "Tampico Twist," performed by Los Beatniks and later reprised during the final dance number, is a cover of a popular tune composed by Johnny Grande, Frank Beecher, and Johnny Kay, all members of Bill Haley's backing band, the Comets. The only original tune in the film is María Eugenia Rubio's "Cándida," which she had previously performed in *Jóvenes y rebeldes* (Julián Soler, 1961). Just as the *comedia ranchera* had helped establish and popularize the classic folk songs like "Allá en el Rancho Grande," *A ritmo de twist* consecrated and canonized all the major bands of Mexico's early rock period. Almost all of these tunes became the classical songs of Mexico's early rock canon and their commercial success is intimately linked to the popularity of this *churro*.

Rock *churros* also functioned as instructional videos for kids eager to dance like their US counterparts. The didactic impulse of *A ritmo de twist* cannot be overstated. As Paul Reinsch observes, early rock movies offered "teen performances of recorded music and demonstrations of how to dance to this new music."[32] *A ritmo de twist* opens with a three-minute-long scene in which Los Rebeldes del Rock perform a refried version of "Calendar Girl." Fulfilling its promotional mission, the camera takes in the band with lead singer Johnny Laboriel, one of the few Black musicians in Mexico to ever make it to the screen, crooning away, and then cuts quickly to the band's logo on the bass drum so that the audience knows who's playing, and then to an elevated panoramic shot of young people dancing. From here the sequencing of this and nearly every musical number afterward falls into a predictable pattern of four to five images: a medium shot of the band, a panoramic view of the party, a close-up on one dancing couple with an obligatory downward tilt to take in the movement of feet and hips, another panorama of the crowd, and then back to the band. This cycle repeats itself with minor variations throughout the entirety of the song. There is a similar sequence near the end of the film when Liza Rossel, after performing a truly outstanding thirty-second drum solo, spends nearly three minutes dancing the twist on stage to recorded music. The camera tracks her every move from nearly every imaginable angle, allowing the viewers to consume both the dance step and Rossel as a fetishized sexual commodity.

While *churros* like *A ritmo de twist* commercialized and celebrated the emerging youth culture, not all did so. Some *churros* maintained a decidedly conservative line, choosing to cash in on modern dance trends while simultaneously alerting viewers to the potential dangers of rock music. Zolov describes the approach as a policy of containment designed to counteract the influence of foreign music, style, and ideologies. Looking specifically at music, he points to the ways the *refritos* stave off the potential damage of US and British music by domesticating its language through translation. "By introducing the musical rhythms of foreign performers, but with 'homegrown' lyrics and a clean-cut image more palatable to the concerns of adults," he argues, record companies "discovered a formula for naturalizing a cultural phenomenon previously regarded as controversial and even subversive."[33] The same thing happened with film. In this regard, films like Miguel M. Delgado's *Amor a ritmo de go go* (1966) can be read as an extension of the ideological project of *Locos peligrosos*. The movie has another threadbare plot stitched together by repetitive musical performances and chauvinistic attitudes toward bikini-clad dancers and female drivers. Don Guillermo, a wealthy older man played by Raúl Astor, who is infatuated with a young go-go dancer named Lupe, portrayed by Rosa María Vásquez, attempts to buy her affections with a new convertible. While resisting his advances, she agrees to exchange dance lessons for the car so she doesn't have to take the bus to work anymore. The would-be suitor hires a handsome instructor named Raúl, played by crooner Javier Solís, to teach her how to drive. Raúl eventually falls in love with his student and attempts to dissuade her from dancing in clubs and accepting these kinds of offers. The vehicle itself becomes a symbol of the "upwardly mobile aspirations and frivolous consumption" of the modernizing country in that it is both a luxury item available to only the financially well off and the object which facilitates views of modern roadways and the city.[34]

Musical numbers are, like those in many early rock films, primarily floor shows filmed in upscale nightclubs where musicians and dancers perform for a seated audience. But there is a significant change in the composition of the audience members. In *Amor a ritmo de go go,* the spectators are mostly young people and most wear everyday street clothes. There are no tuxedos or any of the other outward trappings of wealth that were common in earlier transition films like *La locura*. This, of course, points toward the democratization of rock music as the 1960s progressed and the economic benefits of the Mexican Miracle continued to improve financial conditions for urban middle classes. The line between middle- and upper-class dissolves somewhat as the driving instructor Raúl finds himself sitting at the table next to a well-dressed older man. The club has become more heterogeneous regarding both the age and social status of its clients. Notably the scenes underscore the visual component of these performances. The center of the action are the scantily clad female dancers who have no singing role. Music is provided by Los Hooligans and Los Rocking Devils, and one song is performed by Blanca Estrada, a female lead singer for the second band.[35] However she and the band are located to the side of the stage, out of sight and almost out of mind. The main attraction, as demonstrated by both the camera time dedicated to dancing and the reactions of patrons, are the female dancers. Their only function is to provide gyrating bodies for the male gaze.

And there is an implicit moral judgment levied against those who engage in the production and consumption of rock music. Like *Locos peligrosos*, *Amor a ritmo de go go* places financial gain at odds with moral integrity. Lupe dances to earn a living, but in doing so, she transforms herself into a commodity for the club's male clientele. It is noteworthy that her skimpy onstage costume is not a symbol of joyous sexual liberation but a calculated commodification of her body. This is, in fact, the underlying logic of Don Guillermo's proposed gift: the car is a form of currency to be exchanged for romantic favors. However, Lupe negotiates the terms of their agreement, asserting control over her own body by suggesting that she will only teach him how to dance. The more she becomes romantically involved with Raúl, however, the more this commercialized exchange of bodies and goods becomes problematic. Raúl does not approve of Lupe's dancing and criticizes her for performing for the lurid gaze of the clients and using her charms to obtain the vehicle. He hopes to make her a respectable woman by inviting her out on a date for drinks and dancing *a la antigua*. When the jukebox begins playing the tropical bolero "Espera"—one of the actor Javier Solís's biggest hits—the couple takes to the floor, embraces, and dances slowly while Raúl croons the lyrics. Here the intimacy of Latin music, with its slow, swaying rhythm and close bodily contact between partners, contrasts favorably with the isolated jerking of go-go. The camera gives us a nearly uninterrupted two-shot of the couple gazing into each other's eyes, dangerously close to kissing, and the soft low lighting creates the necessary ambiance. This setting marks a sharp distinction from the garish colors and oversaturated lighting taken in by a wide-angle camera during go-go scenes. This in fact is key to understanding this conservative *churro*'s take on music, dancing, and love. Modern rock and roll, the film suggests, leads to isolation, voyeurism, and even sexual exploitation while the traditional tropical repertoire enables sensuality, love, and intimate personal engagement.

Throughout this chapter I have argued that early rock movies emerged from and against the grain of post-revolutionary folkloric musicals. They did so as the *comedia ranchera* lost its foothold with young audiences that craved modern, cosmopolitan sights and sounds. This was particularly true of urban middle-class youth who increasingly identified with the global popular counterculture that spread throughout the 1960s. As Laura Podalsky so precisely argues, these were young people who sought out filmic stories about their own culture within a rapidly changing world where characters who looked and sounded like them "navigate[d] successfully between the 'old world' and the 'new,' between their parents and themselves, between the traditional and the modern; and who . . . provide[d] a spatio-temporal bridge bringing audiences up-to-date and into the world beyond national borders."[36] And while even a cursory glance at the existing body of scholarly literature about Mexican film reveals a stunning disregard for anything resembling rock and roll, these movies are an important part of the film industry's attempt to transition away from the post-revolutionary film models. Not only were they instrumental in modernizing Mexican cinema, they were wildly popular. They drew large crowds and created audiences, taught adolescents new dance steps, and exposed viewers to modern sights and sounds that connected with the broader youth culture of the day. Music historian Elijah Wald observes a similar disdain among music critics when he notes that, even though history is generally written by the winners, the case of popular music—and for our purposes, music film—is somewhat different. "The victors tend to be out dancing," he writes:

while the historians sit at their desks, assiduously chronicling music they cannot hear on mainstream radio. And it is not just the historians: The people who choose to write about popular music, even while it is happening, tend to be far from average consumers and partygoers and often despise the tastes and behavior of their more cheerful and numerous peers.[37]

When all is said and done, rock *churros* will never live up to the expectations of serious film critics and historians who pooh-pooh them for being frivolous, lightminded, and fun. But they do not have to. When all is said and done, these films were just about rock and roll, and people liked them.

## Notes

1. Wrestling films have been productively studied in David Wilt, "El Santo: The Case of a Mexican Multimedia Hero," *Film and Comic Books*, eds. Ian Gordon, Mark Jancovich, and Matthew P. McAllister (Jackson: University Press of Mississippi, 2007); Kerry Hegarty, "From Superhero to National Hero: The Populist Myth of El Santo," *Studies in Latin American Popular Culture* 31 (2013): 3–27; and David S. Dalton, "Intenciones enmascaradas en la pantalla plateada. El Santo y el mimetismo imperial," *Alambique* 4.1 (2016): article 5. For insightful analyses on *fichera* films, see Sergio de la Mora, *Cinemachismo: Masculinities and Sexuality in Mexican Film* (Austin: University of Texas Press, 2006) and Vek Lewis, *Crossing Sex and Gender in Latin America* (New York: Palgrave Macmillan, 2010).

2. Jorge Ayala Blanco, *La búsqueda del cine mexicano (1968–1972)* (Mexico City: Editorial Posada, 1986), 223–24.

3. Emilio García Riera, *Historia documental del cine mexicano* (Guadalajara and Mexico City: Universidad de Guadalajara, Gobierno de Jalisco, Conaculta, Instituto Mexicano de Cinematografía, 1994), 167. Despite this judgment, Alazraki remained a constant presence in the Mexican film industry. He directed at least forty films between 1953 and 1995 and served in a number of administrative positions including a three-year stint as the director for the Corporación Nacional Cinematográfica (Conacine).

4. Susan Dever, *Celluloid Nationalism and Other Melodramas: From Post-Revolutionary Mexico to fin de siglo Mexamérica* (Albany: State University of New York Press, 2003); Andrea Noble, *Mexican National Cinema* (London & New York: Routledge, 2005); Charles Ramírez Berg, *Cinema of Solitude: A Critical Study of Mexican Film, 1967–1983* (Austin: University of Texas Press, 1992).

5. Eric Zolov, *Refried Elvis: The Rise of Mexican Counterculture* (Berkeley: University of California Press, 1999), 30.

6. David William Foster, *Mexico City in Contemporary Mexican Cinema* (Austin: University of Texas Press, 2002). Foster argues that "there is a real Mexico City, but that real Mexico City has no meaning in and of itself. It has meaning only to the extent that its materiality is inserted into a semiotic process for the substantiation of meaning. . . . The challenge, then,

becomes the demonstration of how individuals create the city through their lives and how their lives are circumscribed in significant and often violent ways by the city" (x–xi).

7. In her outstanding book *La India María: Mexploitation and the Films of María Elena Velasco* (Austin, University of Texas Press, 2017), Seraina Rohrer argues that, "Like the term *cine popular*, *churro* is not exclusively used to describe low-budget Mexican films with low production values, but all uses of this word are derogatory and bear culturally determined and overtly negative associations, implying that the films have little, if any, cultural value," 29. While I agree that the term has been used almost exclusively as a pejorative, because the project of this book and this essay is to recuperate and recover films that have been pushed aside by high-minded bias, I will use *churro* here in keeping with common parlance.

8. Zolov, *Refried Elvis*, 1–16.

9. Michael Lydon, "Rock for Sale," in *Side-Saddle on the Golden Calf*, ed. George H. Lewis (Pacific Palisades: Goodyear, 1972), 314.

10. José Agustín reports that, in addition to the record companies, rock and roll entered the country through cross-border exchanges of albums, magazines, instruments, and films. *La casa del sol naciente: De rock y otras rolas* (Mexico City: Nueva Imagen, 2006), 108.

11. See Noble, *Mexican National Cinema*; Carl J. Mora, *Mexican Cinema: Reflections of a Society, 1896–2004* (Jefferson, NC: McFarland & Company, 2005); Misha MacLaird, *Aesthetics and Politics in the Mexican Film Industry* (New York: Palgrave Macmillan, 2013); and Ignacio M. Sánchez Prado, *Screening Neoliberalism: Transforming Mexican Cinema, 1988–2012* (Nashville: Vanderbilt University Press, 2014).

12. Thomas Doherty, *Teenagers and Teenpics: The Juvenilization of American Movies in the 1950s* (Philadelphia: Temple University Press, 2002), 12.

13. Doherty, *Teenagers and Teenpics*, 7.

14. This is not to say that these moralistic openings were entirely alien to Mexican filmmaking. Luis Buñuel's *Los olvidados* (1950) opens with the same kind of voiceover introduction.

15. Concerns about bad behavior were nothing new for Mexican society. As Katherine Elaine Bliss and Ann S. Blum point out, as early as the 1920s citizens complained about the moral degradation that accompanied modernization. They write, "The associations among youth, entertainment, public spaces, and sexual behavior were hardly new in 1920s and 1930s Mexico City; for example, public officials had long lamented the participation of young women—and, to some extent, of young men—in sexual commerce in the city's parks and public walkways. However, parental and official concerns over adolescent sexual behavior reached new heights in this period of rapid cultural and demographic transformation of the capital," "Dangerous Driving: Adolescence, Sex, and the Gendered Experience of Public Space in Early-Twentieth-Century Mexico City" in *Gender, Sexuality, and Power in Latin America since Independence*, eds. William E. French and Katherine Elaine Bliss (Lanham: Rowman & Littlefield, 2006). Ebook.

16. The variability of spellings in these titles attests to how new the musical genre was. Films bounced back and forth between "rock and roll" and "rock 'n roll." To date, historians employ both terms. I generally prefer "rock and roll" but will use the spelling that appears on the title card for each individual film.

17. For a more thorough discussion of this, see Zolov, *Refried Elvis*, 41–46.

18. Zolov, *Refried Elvis*, 43.

19. For a great discussion of the rivalries between UNAM and IPN in the late 1950s, see Jaime M. Pensado, *Rebel Mexico: Student Unrest and Authoritarian Political Culture during the Long Sixties* (Stanford: Stanford University Press, 2013), 61–66.

20. Chances are that Díaz Morales was paying close attention to Méndez's film because his next production, *Al compás del rock and roll,* appeared in theaters two months later and bears more than a striking resemblance to *La locura del rock 'n roll.* When a traditional orchestra loses its radio contract following an on-air fight, the male musicians are forced to take a job washing dishes at a local restaurant while their girlfriends start a rock and roll band. The ensuing battle of the sexes emasculates the men. The movie runs so close to the storyline of *La locura,* in fact, that very little else can or should be said about it.

21. Germán Valdés earned his fame portraying the picaresque character Tin Tan and deserves serious consideration as one of Mexico's first proto–rock and roll stars for his first feature-length film, *El hijo desobediente* (Humberto Gómez Landero, 1945).

22. Ramón Valdés, younger brother of Germán Valdés, would later go on to garner immense popularity for his role as Don Ramón on the television series *El chavo del ocho.*

23. The financial viability of a profession in popular music is also the central concern of *El hijo desobediente,* in which Valdés's character, Tin Tan, triumphs in his dream of becoming a performer in Mexico City despite the early objections of his *norteño* ranching father.

24. Anyone who has spent any time walking around downtown Mexico City knows that this is the purest nationalist fantasy because there are no perfectly tuned organs anywhere.

25. Jesús Salvador Treviño, "The New Mexican Cinema," *Film Quarterly* 32, no. 3 (Spring 1979): 26.

26. Internet Movie Database, "Sam Katzman," *Internet Movie Database,* http://www.imdb.com/name/nm0441947/.

27. There are a few rock-themed films that were completed, including Álvaro Salazar's *Bikinis y rock* (1972), which essentially recycled the premise of *A ritmo de twist* and highlighted bands like El Ritual, Peace and Love, and Bandido; and Jaime Humberto Hermosillo's *La verdadera vocación de Magdalena* (1973), starring Angélica María and the members of the band La Revolución de Emiliano Zapata. But, aside from these outliers, rock film was forced underground as directors like Sergio García Michel turned to independent Super 8 filmmaking to capture concerts and countercultural stories.

28. See Iván Eusebio Aguirre Darancou's chapter about Super 8 filmmaking in this book.

29. The force of rock films is strong in the Valdés family. Manuel "El Loco" Valdés is the younger brother of Germán Valdés and Ramón Valdés, stars who I have already discussed. To my knowledge there has not been any discussion of this family's prominence in early rock films yet.

30. Indeed, in a similar vein, Laura Podalsky proposes that the accumulation of musical scenes in Argentine rock cinema "parece seguir la gramática de *los shows musicales* de la televisión argentina del momento," in "El rock, el cine, la televisión y las culturas juveniles en los 1960s en la Argentina," *Actas del V Congreso Internacional de AsAECA* (Buenos Aires: Universidad de Quilmes, 2016), 1488.

31. Well, technically not for Plácido Domingo, who, though he sang with Los Black Jeans, never appeared on screen as a rock and roller.

32. Paul N. Reinsch, "Music over Words and Sound over Image: 'Rock Around the Clock' and The Centrality of Music in Post-Classical Film Narration," *Music and the Moving Image* 6, no. 3 (Fall 2013), 12.

33. Zolov, *Refried Elvis,* 72.

34. Zolov, *Refried Elvis,* 76.

35. And lyrics to the song, "Si soy graciosa" by Los Rocking Devils, underscore some of

these themes: "Bailo y canto, canto y bailo los ritmos modernos de calidad. Pero lo que anhelo brindar consuelo y hacerle reír a la humanidad. Si soy graciosa, seré famosa" [I dance and I sing, I sing and I dance quality modern rhythms. But I want to bring consolation and laughter to mankind. If I am graceful, I will be famous].

36. Laura Podalsky, "Cosmopolitanism, Modernity and Youth in the 1960s: The Transnational Wanderings of Teen Idols from Argentina, Mexico and Spain," *Transnational Screens* 11, no. 2 (2020): 137.

37. Elijah Wald, *How the Beatles Destroyed Rock and Roll: An Alternative History of American Popular Music* (Oxford and New York: Oxford University Press, 2009), 97.

## Bibliography

Arana, Federico. *Guaraches de ante azul*. Madrid: Espoz y Mina, 2002.
Ayala Blanco, Jorge. *La búsqueda del cine mexicano (1968–1972)*. Mexico City: Editorial Posada, 1986.
Conway, Christopher. *Heroes of the Borderlands: The Western in Mexican Film, Comics, and Music*. Albuquerque: University of New Mexico Press, 2019.
Dalton, David. "Intenciones enmascaradas en la pantalla plateada. El Santo y el mimetismo imperial," *Alambique* 4.1 (2016): article 5.
de la Mora, Sergio. *Cinemachismo: Masculinities and Sexuality in Mexican Film*. Austin: University of Texas Press, 2006.
Dever, Susan. *Celluloid Nationalism and Other Melodramas: From Post-Revolutionary Mexico to fin de siglo Mexamérica* (Albany: State University of New York Press, 2003).
Doherty, Thomas. *Teenagers and Teenpics: The Juvenilization of American Movies in the 1950s*. Philadelphia: Temple University Press, 2002.
Foster, David William. *Mexico City in Contemporary Mexican Cinema*. Austin: University of Texas Press, 2002.
García Riera, Emilio. *Historia documental del cine mexicano*. Guadalajara and Mexico City: Universidad de Guadalajara, Gobierno de Jalisco, Conaculta, Instituto Mexicano de Cinematografía, 1994.
Hegarty, Kerry. "From Superhero to National Hero: The Populist Myth of El Santo." *Studies in Latin American Popular Culture* 31 (2013): 3–27.
Internet Movie Database, "Sam Katzman," *Internet Movie Database*, http://www.imdb.com/name/nm0441947/.
Lewis, Vek. *Crossing Sex and Gender in Latin America*. New York: Palgrave Macmillan, 2010.
Lydon, Michael. "Rock for Sale." In *Side-Saddle on the Golden Calf*, edited by George H. Lewis, 313–21. Pacific Palisades: Goodyear, 1972.
MacLaird, Misha. *Aesthetics and Politics in the Mexican Film Industry*. New York: Palgrave Macmillan, 2013.
Mora, Carl J. *Mexican Cinema: Reflections of a Society, 1896–2004*. Jefferson, NC: McFarland & Company, 2005.
Noble, Andrea. *Mexican National Cinema*. London & New York: Routledge, 2005.
Pensado, Jaime. *Rebel Mexico: Student Unrest and Authoritarian Political Culture during the Long Sixties*. Stanford, CA: Stanford University Press, 2013.
Podalsky, Laura. "El rock, el cine, la televisión y las culturas juveniles en los 1960s en la Argen-

tina." *Actas del V Congreso Internacional de AsAECA*, 1482–91. Buenos Aires: Universidad de Quilmes, 2016.

———. "Cosmopolitanism, Modernity and Youth in the 1960s: The Transnational Wanderings of Teen Idols from Argentina, Mexico and Spain." *Transnational Screens* 11:2 (2020): 136–54.

Ramírez Berg, Charles. *Cinema of Solitude: A Critical Study of Mexican Film, 1967–1983*. Austin: University of Texas Press, 1992.

Reinsch, Paul N. "Music over Words and Sound over Image: 'Rock Around the Clock' and the Centrality of Music in Post-Classical Film Narration." *Music and the Moving Image* 6, no. 3 (Fall 2013): 3–22.

Rohrer, Seraina. *La India María: Mexploitation and the Films of María Elena Velasco*. Austin: University of Texas Press, 2017.

Rubli, Federico. *Estremécete y rueda*. Mexico City: Chapa Ediciones, 2007.

Sánchez Prado, Ignacio M. *Screening Neoliberalism: Transforming Mexican Cinema, 1988–2012*. Nashville: Vanderbilt University Press, 2014.

Treviño, Jesús Salvador. "The New Mexican Cinema." *Film Quarterly* 32, no. 3 (Spring 1979): 26–37.

Tenorio Trillo, Mauricio. *Historia y celebración: México y sus centenarios*. Mexico City: Tusquets, 2009.

Wald, Elijah. *How the Beatles Destroyed Rock and Roll: An Alternative History of American Popular Music*. Oxford & New York: Oxford University Press, 2009.

Wilt, David. "El Santo: The Case of a Mexican Multimedia Hero." *Film and Comic Books*, edited by Ian Gordon, Mark Jancovich, and Matthew P. McAllister, 199–220. Jackson: University Press of Mississippi, 2007.

Zamora, Jorge. *El rock de los 60 en el cine mexicano*. Last modified February 5, 2013. http://filmografiadelrockmexicano.wordpress.com

Zolov, Eric. *Refried Elvis: The Rise of Mexican Counterculture*. Berkeley: University of California Press, 1999.

# 2

# ON VIRGINS, MALINCHES, AND *CHICAS MODERNAS*

The Star Power of Lorena Velázquez in *Lucha Libre* Cinema

DAVID S. DALTON

Few stars of Mexican cinema have left a more lasting mark on the national film industry than Lorena Velázquez. The actress leveraged her success in the controversial Miss Mexico 1956 pageant—in which she took first runner-up—for a long career on the silver screen.[1] Her forays in the national film industry began in 1956 with the production of *¡Viva la juventud!* (Fernando Cortés), but she consolidated her star power during the Mexploitation epoch, which lasted from the early 1960s through the late 1980s. Her first role in this new era came in *La nave de los monstruos* (Rogelio A. González, 1960), where she played one of two Venusian sisters who employ their irresistible sexuality in an attempt to conquer Earth. Her first *lucha libre* film was *Santo vs. los zombies* (Benito Alazraki, 1962), where she played a damsel-in-distress. Over the next year she would appear in two very different, yet equally iconic, *lucha libre* roles: Zorina, Queen of the Vampire Women in *Santo contra las mujeres vampiro* (Alfonso Corona Blake, 1962) and Gloria Venus, a fictional *luchadora*, in *Las luchadoras contra el médico asesino* (René Cardona, 1963). This chapter analyzes how Velázquez's performances interfaced with evolving attitudes surrounding the role of women in 1960s Mexican society. Her parts tended to engage the traditional duality between the Virgin of Guadalupe and La Malinche, and she performed both ends of the spectrum with confidence. The fact that she could play such distinctive roles so well suggests that we view her performances through the lens of the *chica moderna*. Indeed, throughout her performances and her own private life, Velázquez took advantage of changing attitudes surrounding gender to harness a degree of star power that few people, regardless of gender, could rival.

Velázquez's success was especially remarkable given that the early part of her career coincided with the emergence of the so-called Mexploitation era, when the national film industry had to negotiate new funding and distribution realities that led to inexpensive, often lower-quality productions.[2] Studies published within Mexico have yet to adopt the word Mexploitation.[3] Nevertheless, Seraina Rohrer notes that this term serves as a useful umbrella for a wide array of films ranging from *lucha libre* cinema to the sexy *fichera* and violent border films—or any combination of these—that found great commercial success from the 1960s through the 1980s.[4] The perceived lack of prestige in the Mexploitation era has certainly contributed to the fact that, despite numerous studies on the Golden Age star system, very little has been written about the following generation.[5] Rohrer conjectures that this may reflect the fact that Mexploitation stars earned less than their Hollywood and (presumably) Golden Age counterparts, but she also belongs to a current of criticism that proclaims that Mexploitation "produce[d] its own stars."[6] Of course, most scholarship continues to prioritize the movement's male actors like El Santo, los Hermanos Almada, and others.[7] That said, we should recognize that Velázquez launched an eight-decade career by performing gender in a way that attracted moviegoers as she navigated the Mexploitation landscape.

She accepted the roles available to her, and her films tended to dialogue with—and frequently, to uncritically reproduce—both the Virgin trope, which emphasized adherence to strict sexual norms and motherhood, and the la Malinche trope, which embodied treason and sexual promiscuity.[8] Though la Malinche was originally a figure that intersected female and indigenous subjectivity, Sandra M. Cypess notes that, by midcentury, authors and cultural producers began to employ "La Malinche as a subtext to comment on male-female relations [regardless of race] in Mexico."[9] As with any binary, this one attracted criticism both for its simplicity and its serious implications for Mexican women at large. This held especially true regarding the national cinema, where, according to Jean Franco, directors "often seem[ed] to position the woman spectator as accessory to her own subordination."[10] Little, if any, empirical data exists to provide clues as to how Mexican women internalized the discourses of midcentury cinema, but even a cursory viewing of the films makes it clear that the movies reinforced patriarchal ideologies. Nevertheless, Velázquez's performances participated in cultural movements that aimed to break down this binary by opening a dialogue on female performativity.

Viewed in this light, the actress's performances in *lucha libre* cinema are especially tantalizing due to their paradoxically conservative yet liberatory potential with regard to the opportunities offered to women at that time. As Judith Butler argues:

> performativity cannot be understood outside of a process of iterability, a regularized and constrained repetition of norms . . . This iterability implies the "performance" is not a singular "act" or event, but a ritualized production, a ritual reiterated under and through constraint, under and through the force of prohibition and taboo . . . but not . . . determining it fully in advance.[11]

The binary of Virgin/Malinche may sit at the background of Velázquez's *lucha libre* films, but her performances also trouble or refine this binary. One could argue, along with Itala Schmelz, that Velázquez's performances elicited the specter "not only of male sexual fantasies, but of a patriarchal society's fears regarding the progress of women's liberation and their participation in politics."[12] The actress's characters—both "good" and "bad"—interfaced with notions of the *chica moderna*, whom Joanne Hershfield defines as a (modern) woman who is "'up-to-date' in her appearance, her dress, and her attitudes."[13] Anne Rubenstein notes that *chicas modernas* had to "[remain] chaste until marriage and faithful afterward," but she also asserts that they enjoyed greater autonomy than had previous generations.[14] Interestingly, Hershfield tracks the *chica moderna* through the mid-1930s, thus ending her discussion decades prior to the beginning of Velázquez's career. This is because most Mexican media began to imagine modern women as threatening and deviant following the election of Manuel Ávila Camacho (1940–1946).[15] Indeed, Rubenstein notes that one of the few spaces that continued to allow for positive representations of *chicas modernas* was the comic book industry.[16] It should thus come as no surprise that *luchador* (and especially *luchadora*) cinema—

themselves products of comic book culture—would produce entertaining, positive representations of the *chica moderna*. Across her roles, Velázquez interpreted very different versions of femininity; in so doing, she provided a valuable roadmap that considered many different ways that women could thrive in the quickly modernizing nation.

The actress's cultivation of a star image is especially noteworthy given Rohrer's observation that "Mexploitation stars were directly linked to a certain character type."[17] As such, actors generally garnered fame only after iconic performances, and as a result, they remained typecast throughout their careers. Velázquez certainly became the "chica-Santo por excelencia" [Santo girl *par excellence*] after appearing alongside the *luchador* in five separate films.[18] That said, she achieved star status by playing surprisingly distinctive roles that placed her as both damsel-in-distress and villain.[19] She added yet another role type to her résumé when she played Gloria/Loreta Venus, a *luchadora* and superhero. Regarding this part, she later confided the following:

> "¡Que nadie se entere de que hice una película de luchadoras!," me dije, pero me llevé una sorpresa agradable porque fue un éxito y ¿sabes? Todo el mundo se enteró, igual con las de El Santo. Otras películas con argumentos dizque más serios y profundos no tuvieron el éxito popular que tenían estas películas.[20]
>
> ["Please don't let anyone find out that I made a film about *luchadoras*," I said to myself, but I was pleasantly surprised because it was successful, you know? Everyone found out about it, just like they did with El Santo's films. Other movies with supposedly deeper or more serious plots didn't have the popular success that these [*luchador/a*] ones had.]

Velázquez thus came to embrace her *lucha libre* roles as audiences celebrated her brand. She consciously based her on-screen persona on María Félix by building a transgressive image that centered on questions of performativity in modern Mexico.[21] Clearly, the uniting thread across her performances was the notion of *chica moderna*; she cultivated and performed this ideal in different ways both in her films and in her personal life. I begin this chapter with a discussion of the films where she appeared alongside El Santo; in these movies, Velázquez's *chica moderna* characters interfaced with the Virgin/Malinche dichotomy in different ways: her "good" characters articulated Guadalupan traits that a *chica moderna* should supposedly strive to achieve;

her *femme fatale* characters embodied the threats that modern women supposedly posed in a changing society. I finish the essay with a discussion of her *luchadora* films, where she interpreted a professional *luchadora* and helped to construct new articulations of Mexican femininity. While the films discussed below tended to communicate simplistic notions of female performativity, Velázquez leveraged her ability to play these roles as a means to forward her career as an independent, modern woman.

### The *Chica Moderna* in a Supporting Role: Velázquez as Villain and Damsel-in-Distress

Velázquez interprets a fairly stereotypical version of *chica moderna* in *Santo vs. los zombies*. El Santo had appeared in other films previous to this one, but *Santo vs. los zombies* catapulted him to cinematic stardom.[22] What is more, the film coincided with his transition from *rudo* [heel or villain] to *técnico* [hero] in the wrestling ring.[23] Because El Santo remained a relatively unknown quantity in the national film industry, producers depended on other cast members—particularly Velázquez—to draw audiences. Velázquez's interpretation of Gloria Sandoval depends on the construction of the *chica moderna*, particularly that Mexploitation iteration that accedes to patriarchal authority figures—generally fathers or fiancés—for guidance.[24] An against-the-grain reading of the film suggests that Gloria enlists male assistance because she desperately seeks to restore patriarchal order in her life after her father goes missing. Director Benito Alazraki emphasizes Gloria's sanctity during an early scene where the young woman meets with her boyfriend and his friends (all of whom happen to be her father's students) to tell them that her father has disappeared. Her performativity plays to Mexican, and indeed Western, notions of femininity that hold women to be frail and defenseless. Her shawl vaguely alludes to the image of the Virgin, while her voice is soft and high-pitched. While she is the one who speaks, she remains marginalized in the frame; the camera pans to the left as she speaks, thus placing her male interlocutors in the center of the shot while relegating Gloria to the corner.

The mise-en-scène suggests that the female protagonist has no business embarking alone on adventures. In one scene, she enters the woods in heels and a skirt—a wardrobe choice that highlights the modern fashion sense (but not common sense) of a true *chica moderna*—while a group of zombies stalks her.²⁵ Her garb makes her unable to escape her lumbering antagonists, and the creatures take her to a cave where her uncle has transformed her father into a cybernetic-cadaver slave who is helping him carry out diabolical acts of kidnapping, murder, and robbery.²⁶ Gloria only survives because El Santo arrives and kills her foes. When she asks the wrestler why her uncle would do this, the wrestler replies that the man did this "por ambición, por riquezas y por poder" [due to unrighteous ambition and a lust for riches and power]. This film certainly posits El Santo as a hypermasculine hero who must save "good" Mexicans from corporeal colonization, but it also reinforces the film's gender politics, particularly the notion that men must both protect and impart wisdom to women, especially if they are young *chicas modernas*.²⁷ As the film ends, El Santo leaves Gloria with her boyfriend, a man who will once again provide her the patriarchal structure that she apparently needs; their pending marriage suggests that, similar to the Virgin, Gloria Sandoval will dedicate the rest of her days to motherhood and other traditional female roles.

Velázquez's performance of gender changes significantly in her role as Zorina in *Santo contra las mujeres vampiro*. One of the most successful Mexploitation productions ever made, this movie continues to enjoy cult status not only in Mexico but also in the United States and Europe.²⁸ The producers seemed more concerned with satisfying the heterosexual male gaze than with providing meaningful avenues for the articulation of female identity. Indeed, Marco Antonio Santiago asserts that the film's success had more to do with Velázquez's beauty than El Santo's presence.²⁹ Director Alfonso Corona Blake both strips Zorina of her agency and accentuates her seductive potential by relegating her to the role of Satan's preferred concubine. She sits on a throne in her Mexico City crypt and orders other vampires—both male and female—to do her bidding. Unlike many Mexploitation horror films, which built on science fiction to posit a city destroyed by technology, this film suggests a gothic, Eastern European aesthetic as the true danger.³⁰ One of the strangest things about this particular film is that, despite a title—and even cover art—that prepares its audience for a showdown between El Santo and Zorina, neither one of these characters plays a particularly large role in the actual film. The majority of the movie follows Tundra (Ofelia Montesco), a vampire priestess who must reawaken Zorina and present her with her heiress, Diana Orlof (María Duval), who will soon be the new queen of the vampires. The other principal character is Professor Orlof, Diana's father, and the man who ultimately contracts El Santo to save his daughter.

The titular villains are vampire women, but it is worth noting that El Santo only ever physically fights with the male-vampire slaves of Zorina and Tundra. Played by Fernando Osés, Guillermo Hernández, and Nathanael León—all of whom were real-life *luchadores*—these characters could engage in specially choreographed spectacles where Velázquez's Zorina could not.[31] Indeed, aside from Tundra and, on one short occasion, Zorina, none of the vampire women ever leave their crypt; rather, they passively await Diana's wedding. This observation emphasizes the fact that, rather than pose a physical threat to Mexico, the vampire women's rejection of traditional female roles, coupled with their provocative sexuality, represents a spiritual threat.[32] According to Gabriel Eljaiek-Rodríguez, "se genera, entonces, una oposición entre las figuras femeninas de Tundra [y Zorina], la perversa vampira-bruja que busca esclavizar a los hombres, y Diana, una chica moderna que aprecia la monogamia, el matrimonio y los valores tradicionales" [an opposition is generated between the feminine figures of Tundra (and Zorina), the perverse vampire-witch who seeks to enslave men, and Diana, a *chica moderna* who appreciates monogamy, marriage, and traditional values].[33] The vampire women come to embody contemporaneous societal fears regarding the evolving role of women—particularly those who are modern and sexually liberated—as they stalk Diana and try to contaminate her.

The vampire women challenge the conservative views on sexuality that permeated 1960s Mexico in many ways. Their dress associates them quite literally with the trope of the "vamp," which Ana M. López defines as "the flipside of saintly mothers."[34] Perhaps more subversively, the director also hints at possible homoerotic ties between the devil's wives.[35] Naief Yehya notes that the specter of lesbianism haunts much of Mexploitation cinema, where (particularly female) "sexuality is often depicted as a threat."[36] The lesbian potential to this film rings particularly clear when viewed through the lens of Eve Sedgwick's discussion of the erotic triangle.[37] Unlike most erotic triangles from Western literature, where two men vie for a woman, this film depicts numerous women who share a single man. Similar to the erotic triangles of her study, however, the most interesting relationship in the harem is that which exists among the devil's wives. The vampire women remain detached from Lucifer throughout the film, and Zorina's anxiousness to replace herself as the devil's preferred bride could reflect her desire to emancipate herself from her husband so she can spend her time with her true muses: the vampire women. Viewed in this light, El Santo exorcizes the most transgressive tendencies that the vampire women exhibit when he sets fire to their crypt and burns them to death. In so doing, he metaphorically saves Diana and ensures that she can marry her fiancé and continue to live as a "good," heterosexual *chica moderna* with a commitment to motherhood and a patriarchal family.

José Díaz Morales's *Atacan las brujas* (1968) explores this theme further. The movie feels like a remake of *Santo contra las mujeres vampiro* because it employs many of the stylistic elements that differentiated that film from other Santo movies. Once again, *Atacan las brujas* revolves around a harem of women, wives of Beelzebub. Witches rather than vampires, these characters aim to make the dual (human) sacrifice(s) of the virgin Ofelia (María Eugenia San Martín) and a servant of Goodness (El Santo). In an attempt to capture—and build on—the magic that had made *Santo contra las mujeres vampiro* so successful, José Díaz Morales greatly expanded the roles of both El Santo and Velázquez in this film. Indeed, the opening credits place the names of the two stars alongside each other as equals, a move that was quite uncommon in Santo movies, where even superstars like Blue Demon were only listed after El Santo. This fact almost certainly reflects Velázquez's professional savvy. In a 2009 interview, she said that her sister, the well-known actress Tere Velázquez, who was involved in Shakespearian drama, had teased her for accepting a role in *Atacan las brujas*. As Velázquez explained, by this point in her career, working with El Santo "me empezó a dar un poco de cosa, y decidí cobrarle más a El Santo, ¡y me lo pagó! Porque quería que trabajara con él; así que dije: 'que digan misa pero yo estoy cantada'" [started to make me a bit uncomfortable, and I decided to charge El Santo more. And he paid me! Because he wanted me to work with him; so I said "haters gonna hate, but I couldn't be happier"].[38] As this quotation shows, El Santo and the producers recognized her appeal and rewarded her accordingly. Even as the role she played validated the binary of Virgin/Malinche through her portrayal of a *femme fatale*, Velázquez was clearly building a successful career and advocating for herself as a young, successful *chica moderna*. While her role as the head witch may have lacked the critical acclaim of other productions, the actress knew she could use it to build her brand and further her popularity and professional growth. The fruits of her labor ring clear as we consider the fact that she leveraged her star power to secure greater compensation. The *luchador* could easily have hired someone else to play the queen of the witches, but he recognized that Velázquez's collaboration would benefit the film and, by extension, his own bottom line. The film thus functioned as a vessel through which both El Santo and Velázquez could project, and further construct, their own star power.

The key role of sexuality in both actors' star image shines through in an early scene from *Atacan las brujas,* where Velázquez's character, Mayra, conspires to corrupt El Santo through temptations that would make him an unworthy superhero. Interestingly, Mayra chooses not to seduce the wrestler herself, instead asking her underling, Medusa (Edaena Ruiz), to do it. In this scene, El Santo travels to the old mansion of the witches to investigate, and Medusa suddenly appears out of thin air. The wrestler follows her into the home and watches as she attempts to seduce him in lingerie. Greene argues that this scene showcases the desire of directors to engage mature themes.[39] That said, the counter-macho aesthetic remains at the fore when a non-diegetic voiceover of Santo's thoughts says, "tengo que mantenerme alerta y salir de aquí. Estoy siendo objeto de una seducción infernal" [I must remain vigilant and escape from here. I am currently the object of an infernal seduction]. Medusa lays down on a bed and invites him to come to her; El Santo lifts her head as if to acquiesce, and then he drops her in disgust. In doing so, the wrestler upholds what Rubenstein refers to as his "counter-macho" values: far from seeking sexual gratification, the wrestler upholds conservative sexual norms and expects the same from others.[40] Javier Pereda and Patricia Murrieta-Flores note that "during this time [the 1960s], sexual morality was seen as one of the most essential elements of male heroes in popular culture," a fact that emphasizes the importance of (Catholic) faith in the heroic profile.[41] El Santo certainly recognized that his star power depended on his ability to uphold conservative norms of sexuality, a fact made clear with his attempts to block the distribution of his scandalous film *El vampiro y el sexo* (René Cardona, 1969).[42]

If overt sexuality threatened the star image of El Santo, then it could have destroyed the career of—or significantly limited the roles available to—a *chica moderna* like Velázquez. Indeed, this fact may shed light on why Velázquez did not play the seductress in the aforementioned scene. Such a performance would have affected the celebrity image that she had so carefully cultivated both on and off the screen for more than a decade. As such, it appears that the decision to cast Edaena Ruiz here reflected the two actresses' asymmetrical star power. Ruiz appeared in only a handful of films during a short career that lasted from 1965 to 1968, and she rarely had named roles. Unlike Velázquez, who enjoyed relative freedom in picking and choosing her parts, Ruiz had to accept the roles that other actresses had turned down. Where Velázquez consciously worked to avoid typecasting, Ruiz may have been open to leveraging her sexuality for gaining parts in films because this would have opened professional opportunities she would otherwise lack.[43] What is especially interesting is that, in recent years, Velázquez has leaned into more sexualized roles. In the romantic comedy *Amor de mis amores* (Manolo Caro, 2013), for example, she plays the elderly mother of one of the leads, and she engages in frequent sex—often for comedic effect—with her twenty-something-year-old lover. Her willingness to play this role in 2013 suggests that her avoidance of overtly sexual parts during the 1960s was a conscious decision aimed at protecting her star image. She could play a desirable and attractive *femme fatale*, but she had to make sure to protect her professional image as a respectable *chica moderna*.

Viewed in this light, the power dynamic between Mayra and Medusa reflects a similar one that existed between the actresses who played them. We see this power differential especially clearly when Mayra learns of Medusa's failure to corrupt the masked superhero and berates her. This section of the film fleshes out Mayra's hegemony in the harem. Mayra's total control over the sexuality of the other witches alludes to a queer, though not necessarily lesbian, relationship between the wives of the devil. Given the historical referent of 1960s Mexico, it would certainly not seem out of the ordinary that the wives of the devil could engage in lesbian activity given its problematic status in post-revolutionary society.[44] That said, any representation of such a relationship could not be explicit. *Atacan las brujas* represents a moment where Velázquez felt confident enough to push the envelope: she could direct the queen of the witches to order a botched seduction, but she still preferred to avoid appearing in overly suggestive or explicit shots herself.[45] The film left no question in adult viewers' minds about how sexuality interfaced with villainy and heroism even as it remained ostensibly appropriate for young children. In asserting Velázquez's characters' uncontested dominance among the harem of wives of the devil, both *Atacan las brujas* and *Santo contra las mujeres vampiro* posit Velázquez's character as a Malinche figure whose power reflects her preferential seat alongside the devil.

Velázquez's iconic performances of both Zorina and Mayra exemplified her ability as a successful *chica moderna* to build her star persona. That said, the roles themselves associated her characters with transgression and la Malinche. This fact rings especially clear as we recognize how Zorina and Mayra are ultimately expendable appendages to their master. As Octavio Paz has so problematically argued in *El laberinto de la soledad* (1950), la Malinche exists in the Mexican imaginary as a feminine figure who opened herself up to Cortés, a man who took advantage of her abilities when he needed her but abandoned her immediately after she ceased to be useful.[46] Mayra and Zorina thus embody *la chingada*, women who dedicate themselves to a lover who will never remain loyal to them. Corona Blake emphasizes Zorina's ties to la Malinche by having her search for a replacement for herself in the devil's harem while Díaz Morales explores the indigenous element of La Malinche's identity through his emphasis on human sacrifice. Even as *Atacan las brujas* builds on popular Christian imageries of the devil, then, it also equates pre-Columbian cosmologies and deities with Satanism. Certainly, the actresses in this film are much more closely aligned with the *mestizo* state than with indigenous society.[47] Nevertheless, they perform a type of "barbarism" that popular and official discourses ascribed to pre-Columbian societies. In the end, the original sin of both the witches and the vampire women is that they have aligned themselves with the devil; had they sided with the proper patriarch—Christ, in this case—then they would pose no threat to themselves nor to Mexico. In this way, these films upheld the Virgin/Malinche dichotomy. That said, her *luchadora* films troubled this binary by positing urban, professional *chicas modernas* as the protagonists. These characters did not embody the treachery that one would associate with la Malinche, but they also tended to reject Guadalupan ideals of motherhood and submissiveness.

## *Luchadoras* and Family: *Chicas Modernas* in Velázquez's *Luchadora* Films

No discussion of Velázquez's performance of female identity in *lucha libre* cinema is complete without a discussion of her role as Loreta/Gloria Venus in a trilogy of *luchadora* films that aimed to exploit the market that El Santo had opened by casting female *luchadoras* rather than male masked wrestlers. Nelson Carro alludes to these films' significance when he argues that they belonged to a movement when, in the early 1960s, "todos los géneros cansados y a punto de agotarse fueron revitalizados por la presencia del *sexo débil* en los papeles protagónicos" [all the genres, exhausted and about to fade away, were revitalized by the presence of the *weaker sex* in protagonist roles].[48] This is not to say that heroic women had not appeared in Mexican cinema previously; one need look no further than the *soldadera* cinema. Nevertheless, where *soldadera* films tended to depict women who "subordinate [their] needs to those of [their] mate[s] for the love of *pater* and *patria*," *luchadora* films starred urban women in their late twenties who—like Velázquez and many other actresses who interpreted them—had chosen a career over traditional marriage and motherhood.[49] These films thus chipped away at the binary of Virgin/Malinche. Schmelz asserts that "solamente pueden existir dos tipos de mujeres [en el cine de *luchadores*], santas y putas" [there can only be two types of women (in *luchador* cinema): saints and whores].[50] *Luchadora* cinema challenges this claim by imagining *chicas modernas* who exist beyond this binary.

There were obvious limits to the rethinking of the Malinche/Virgin trope. Directors were careful not to let their characters commit social taboos that would associate them with immorality and la Malinche. Nevertheless, these films were key to expanding the representation of women in society. Ilana Dann Luna argues that "for women to be recentered in narrative fiction—literature or film—it stands to reason that a degree of subversion was and still is required and that this subversion must take place over time, and repeatedly, to push back against the weight of 'universal' (sexist) culture."[51] As such, these films' greatest legacy is that they opened a new space from which to center their stories on women. Indeed, while Ana Lau Jaiven does not mention this cinema directly, it clearly participated in those movements that laid the framework for "the new wave of feminism" in Mexico, where women came to question and subvert their continued marginalization.[52] We see this clearly in *Las luchadoras contra el médico asesino* (1963), where the wrestling women challenge any notion of women as damsels-in-distress because they prove far more adept than their boyfriends at stopping the mad scientist.[53] At the same time, the following films, *Las luchadoras contra la momia* (René

Cardona, 1964) and *Las lobas del ring* (René Cardona, 1965), bring these independent wrestling women back into the Guadalupan fold as Velázquez's character comes to embrace the values of family and (possibly) motherhood along with her career.

Unlike her male peers, who moved to cinema after successful careers in professional wrestling, Velázquez—who never wrestled professionally—made her way into the cinematic ring through a combination of sex appeal and popularity as an actress.[54] Given that women's wrestling had existed since 1935, the decision to cast actresses rather than professional *luchadoras* did not reflect a lack of women for the part but a desire to appease the heterosexual male gaze.[55] Indeed, director René Cardona often switched Velázquez out with professional-wrestling doubles during fight scenes that required technical finesse. The actress later said that she had no desire to learn to wrestle for the role since she had been cast primarily for her looks.[56] She also tells that she did not want a double for *Las lobas del ring* "because the woman they hired to do my scenes was really fat. I asked her not to eat so much, but she never once stopped eating."[57] This comment sheds greater light on Velázquez's priorities in establishing and maintaining her star power. She carefully constructed a persona on the silver screen; even when cast as a *luchadora*, she knew that her principal role was not to fight but to grace the screen with her normative beauty, which depended on her slim figure, light skin, and generally European features. In most cases, casting a double did not conflict with her goals; however, she expressed concern when a double could undermine her carefully cultivated persona and image.

Of course, the political project of the producers of *luchadora* cinema went beyond simply providing a means for Velázquez to build her star power. They aimed to normalize and popularize women's wrestling in order to promote its reinstatement and growth in the capital, where it had been prohibited since 1956; the ban remained in place until 1986.[58] This ban—purportedly due to the sport's supposed immorality—applied only to Mexico City. Women could wrestle in other cities like Monterrey, but they could not compete in the country's largest market. Perhaps for this very reason, the *luchadora* films downplayed the notion of greatness in the ring and accentuated the erotic spectacle that the athletes created with their graceful femininity. As Greene notes, these movies tended to linger on the *luchadoras'* presence in the locker room—and the tantalizing potential that they may shower—more than on their fighting.⁵⁹ This fact rings through most clearly in the decision to name Velázquez's character Gloria Venus in *Las luchadoras contra el médico asesino*. This name explicitly refers to her character as a glorified Venus, a not-too-subtle reference to her erotic appeal as a sex goddess. That said, *luchadora* cinema took steps to make itself more like its *luchador* counterpart in subsequent productions. For example, when Velázquez reprised her role in *Las luchadoras contra la momia* and, later, in *Las lobas del ring*, they changed her character's name—with no explanation—to Loreta Venus.⁶⁰ This made the protagonist's name sound more like that of the actress who interpreted her, a fact that furthered the *lucha libre* aesthetic of people playing fictionalized versions of themselves. Of course, the fact that she maintained the second name of Venus reminds us that her sex appeal remained key to her brand. What is more, her adoption of the name Loreta coincided with storylines where she had to acquiesce to the knowledge and strength of her male counterparts.

The problematic interplay between autonomy and subservience is especially clear in *Las luchadoras contra la momia*, perhaps the most well-known *luchadora* film and the second of the three that starred Velázquez. In an early scene, Loreta and her North American teammate, Golden Ruby (Elizabeth Campbell), enter the changing room after a particularly difficult fight. They are surprised when a professor approaches them in search of Armando, Loreta's boyfriend. Dressed in their wrestling leotards, the *luchadoras* allow their boyfriends into the locker room, and the professor explains that a mystical Asian cult called El Dragón Negro wants an ancient codex that he and his colleagues recently found.⁶¹ Immediately after he divulges this fact, an ostensibly Asian assassin, not-so-subtly named Mao (a yellowface performance by the *luchador*, actor, and scriptwriter Jesús "Murciélago" Velázquez), pokes his head through an air vent and shoots the professor dead with a poison dart.⁶² The *luchadoras* and their boyfriends decide to find Armando's uncle, Dr. Luis Trelles (Víctor Velázquez), the last surviving anthropologist with knowledge of the codex. Despite being the titular characters, Loreta Venus and Golden Ruby only ever play a supporting role to Dr. Trelles and their boyfriends, none of whom will appear in the duo's following film, *Las lobas del ring*.⁶³ A principal theme is the wrestling women's relative helplessness in a patriarchal society. Loreta and Golden Ruby can never fight off male opponents when they confront members of

El Dragón Negro (they can generally knock three or four to the ground, but when reinforcements come, they are aptly contained).

The *luchadoras* ultimately succeed in spite of themselves. At no point do they directly defeat their adversaries—be they Asian cults or resurrected Aztec mummies. In an early scene, they (along with Armando) confront the members of El Dragón Negro. Armando explains that he possesses one codex needed for identifying the mummy, while the cult has another. The cult leader suggests a special fight pitting Loreta and Golden Ruby against two supposedly Chinese *luchadoras*, interpreted by the Mexican *luchadoras* Irma González and Chabela Romero, who are experts in jiu jitsu, which is a Japanese (rather than Chinese) art.[64] The winner will claim the loser's codex. Even the *luchadoras*' victory in the ring comes as a tactical loss; the group takes the codices to Dr. Trelles's home so that the archeologist can decipher them. Unbeknownst to them, El Dragón Negro has placed a camera in their apartment that allows the cult leaders to spy on them as they decipher the writings.[65] The film emphasizes Trelles's patriarchal role by having him impart the knowledge that he has obtained from the codices to the *luchadoras* and to their boyfriends. It is at this moment that Trelles reveals that a great treasure lies hidden deep within the bowels of a pre-Columbian pyramid.

Cardona depends on his viewers' familiarity with the 1960s Mexican star system to further emphasize Trelles's patriarchal legitimacy within the film. The professor is played by Víctor Velázquez, Lorena Velázquez's real-life stepfather. Indeed, she adopted his last name—she was born as María de la Concepción Lorena Villar—when she began her career, perhaps in an effort to align herself with the well-respected actor and benefit from his connections as she began her career in the mid-1950s. By the 1960s, however, she seems to have been the one assisting her stepfather in finding work. He had an uncredited role as a coroner in *Santo contra las mujeres vampiro;* his stepdaughter's connections may have even played a role in the decision to cast him as an inspector in *Santo en el museo de cera* (Alfonso Corona Blake, 1963) the following year. While one can speculate about the extent to which Lorena Velázquez's popularity contributed to her stepfather's roles in the Santo movies, it is beyond question that he secured the role of Professor Trelles as a result of his familial relationship with his stepdaughter. Even as he plays the patriarchal figure in the film, the fact that Víctor Velázquez received this role at all reflects his stepdaughter's professional success, some of which trickled down to him. At the same time, however, audiences would have understood that, as her stepfather, he had the patriarchal role in their relationship.

Trelles's authority rings clear in the second half of the film. After the characters accidentally (and somewhat stupidly) awaken a mummy by stealing a necklace from a former human sacrifice, the creature awakens and travels by night to reclaim his jewels. Following the scene in the pyramid, the camera cuts to the professor's home, where the two *luchadoras* sleep next to each other in a bed while their boyfriends sleep on couches. These shots emphasize the fact that, while Dr. Trelles allows everyone to spend the night, he forbids them from engaging in sexual activity in his home. The *luchadoras* may be independent women who do not exhibit the motherly attributes of the Virgin (their commitment to their careers inhibits that), but they still abstain from premarital sex because such behavior would cast them as irredeemably lost Malinche figures. At the same time, this scene challenges the assertion of Greene that "there is virtually no interaction between Loreta and Golden Ruby outside the ring that does not involve or revolve around the men in their lives."[66] By showing these women together without their respective men, the film privileges the homosocial relationship between the *luchadoras*—who are the film's true draw—over the male characters. Indeed, the shot invites its viewers to fantasize of possible amorous ties between the female leads without explicitly depicting a relationship that would have been taboo at that time.

The following sequence once again subordinates these *luchadoras* to the male characters who resolve the problems facing them. In an especially outlandish coincidence, gangsters from El Dragón Negro congregate outside of Dr. Trelles's home and prepare to ambush the occupants precisely when the mummy arrives. The resulting skirmish leaves every member of the cult dead; the mummy has to return to his pyramid without reclaiming the lost necklace because the sun rises. If Greene is correct that El Dragón Negro is the film's true antagonist, then we should note that, once again, a male character dispatches them.[67] Even the scene that pits Loreta and Golden Ruby against the mummy emphasizes their subordinate position to men. The mummy incapacitates Golden Ruby, and, in unconvincing choreography, Loreta engages him in futile hand-to-hand combat. Only after the men place a sack over the mummy's head does the group take control. They return the stolen jewels to their rightful place and the pyramid crumbles to the ground when the mummy clumsily knocks over a pillar. The film ends as the party drives away from the pyramid. The *luchadoras* are the titular characters, but they have mostly played a subordinate role to their male counterparts.

Our discussion of *Las luchadoras contra la momia* provides an important perspective for discussing *Las lobas del ring*. The movie begins with several *lucha libre* executives who decide to have a contest between all of the *luchadoras* of the country. The monetary prize of one million pesos causes the *rudas*, led by the evil Sonia La Borrada (Sonia Infante), to form a conspiracy to incapacitate their competition. Sonia orders the kidnappings and killings of several *luchadoras*, both *técnicas* and *rudas*, throughout the movie. Loreta and Golden Ruby lead a group of *técnicas* who agree to split their winnings among themselves. This storyline allows Cardona to play into a somewhat simplistic vision of good versus evil that ends up associating the *técnicas* with the Virgin and the *rudas* with la Malinche. This rebranding of the *luchadoras* almost certainly reflects the commercial interests of professional wrestling associations that wanted to promote female wrestling to audiences in Mexico City and throughout the country.[68] Cardona even casts men who do not enjoy watching women's *lucha libre* as uncouth and uncultured. One grotesquely overweight male fan, for example, draws the ridicule of his peers when he constantly shouts "¡Quiero ver sangre!" [I want to see blood!] in a discredited attempt to mock female matches as less exciting than male ones. That said, even as the characters defend female *lucha libre*, they do so not by asserting the technical skills of women wrestlers but by claiming that female fights and choreographies please the male gaze.

The film does not portray women as true equals to men. When the *luchadoras* learn about the one-million-peso prize, they immediately go to the gym of Jesús "Murciélago" Velázquez—a real-world *luchador* who wrote the screenplay to this film in which he played a fictional version of himself—and ask him to teach them how to fight better. Cárdenas Pérez argues that this section emphasizes the work that *luchadoras* had to put into their craft.[69] Nevertheless, it is strange that these professional women suddenly feel the need to turn to male experts despite the fact that they are already professionals. More than perhaps any other *luchadora* film, this one plays with notions of female performativity. The film's very title, as well as its tagline ("Intimate problems and the wickedness of friends are resolved in the ring") wink toward the film's problematic treatment of gender throughout. Many of the *luchadoras* embody different stereotypes (or inversions) of Mexican femininity and gender relations. One *luchadora*, for example, is a poet who constantly beats her husband for comedic effect (and when he finally hits her back at the end of the film, Cardona portrays it as a restoration of order). Sonia plays the role of conniving vamp particularly well; Golden Ruby plays to the stereotype of the tall North American bombshell with an endearing accent. Cardona emphasizes her exotic beauty when he places her alongside an especially short love interest. As they dance, her boyfriend complains that no one takes him seriously because he is short. Golden Ruby mischievously replies, "hago crecer a los chaparros" [I make little men grow]. The man's face lightens with bewildered ecstasy as she lifts him above her head. Later, she chases away people that make fun of him. The inclusion of this scene, of course, reflects the desire for some adult humor in this family-friendly film, but it also emphasizes a comedic reversal of midcentury constructs of gender and sexuality.

Once again, however, the most interesting articulation of gender comes from Loreta. The director goes out of his way to refashion her as a Guadalupan figure. She is certainly a *chica moderna* who remains single, middle-class, and independent, but in this film we learn that she has entered the "unbecoming" world of female wrestling in order to take care of her mother following the death of her father.[70] What is more, she tells Miguel, her fiancé, that once he graduates from medical school she will be able to retire and allow him to take care of her.[71] This segment of the film recasts Loreta's character and motivation; rather than reflecting a desire to make her voice heard in a patriarchal order that would prefer to silence her, her independence reflects, more precisely, the fact that the circumstances of her life have made it impossible for her to depend on a male provider. Her relationship with Miguel reminds the viewers that Loreta views wrestling as a short-term occupation that she can and will renounce once she is married. The carefully written circumstances surrounding Loreta's decision to wrestle professionally emphasize the conditions under which the film's writers believed they could justify a middle-class woman's decision to work without sacrificing her maternal instinct. The film operates within a construct of gender where the refusal to enter into the twin institutions of marriage and motherhood would make a woman particularly irredeemable. As such, it cements Loreta's commitment to her family through the final chapter of the film. Several criminals break into Loreta's home and kidnap both her mother and Golden Ruby immediately prior to the championship fight between Sonia and Loreta. As usual, Golden Ruby throws several of her male attackers to the ground, but they soon overwhelm her and tie her to a chair. When the criminals tell Loreta that they will kill her mother if she defeats Sonia, Loreta and her opponent discuss a plan to throw the match in a way that will not raise suspicion. Cárdenas Pérez argues that the kidnapping of Loreta's mother serves as the logical result of the *luchadora*'s desire for a successful career.[72] While he is correct that her mother would not have been kidnapped if Loreta had not become a *luchadora*, her willingness to throw the match shows that she ultimately values family over professional success.

The circumstances that allow for Loreta's ultimate victory emphasize the character's overall dependence on benevolent males. Golden Ruby unties the ropes that bind her to her chair, but instead of fighting her way out of the warehouse with Loreta's mother (which one would ostensibly expect from a movie about *luchadoras*), she goes to a phone and calls Jesús "Murciélago" Velázquez's gym—rather than the police—and begs the *luchadores* to save her. While narratively disappointing, this ending makes sense given that the real-life Jesús "Murciélago" Velázquez wrote the script. Beyond using the film to advocate for women's wrestling, he also used it to promote his own brand. The *luchador* and his friends arrive to the warehouse while Loreta and Sonia fight in the ring, and they immediately arrange for Golden Ruby and Loreta's mother to attend the fight. Loreta quickly defeats her opponent after she sees her mother and Golden Ruby in the audience, thus claiming the winnings for herself and the other *técnicas*. As the circumstances of her victory show, this *luchadora* film is less about women's emancipation than it is about subordinating them to the "proper" male authority. Loreta will soon end her fighting career and get married; what is more, this film has validated a binary of good women whose attributes align them with the Virgin and bad women whose penchant for betrayal aligns them with la Malinche. While it champions women's *lucha libre*, it does so through a misogynistic discourse that, rather than celebrating the *luchadoras*' technical abilities, ultimately sexualizes them. This is not to say that wrestling does not hold emancipatory value for individual women; indeed, those who participate in this activity are able to achieve a degree of independence they otherwise may not have. Rather, *Las lobas del ring* emphasizes the fact that these women have to navigate a patriarchal system if they wish for greater autonomy.

As this chapter has shown, Lorena Velázquez's *lucha libre* repertoire—not to mention her star persona—engages the notion of *chica moderna* in numerous ways. Her characters certainly negotiated the Virgin/Malinche binary, but in many cases they did so in ways that embodied elements of both of these archetypes. We see this in her *luchadora* films, where, similar to many modern, professional women, Gloria/Loreta Venus ignores the maternal drives of the Virgin and eschews a traditional lifestyle of heterosexual marriage and motherhood, opting instead to pursue a professional career. In the films that placed her alongside El Santo, she tended to play more explicitly Guadalupan or Malinche figures; nevertheless, the notion of *chica moderna* sat at the heart of her performances in these films as well. In films like *Santo vs. los zombies* she embodied the values of abnegation and family that the state continued to promote among women, while in films like *Santo contra las mujeres vampiro* and *Atacan las brujas* she more precisely encapsulated the fears that resonated throughout the country of *chicas modernas* who would upend traditional constructs of gender in the nation. In the end, the actress articulated her gendered performance in a way that reverberated with audiences and garnered her great fame. While occasionally problematic, her performances extended her a great deal of agency, allowing her to construct one of the most long-lasting and successful acting careers of anyone in the history of Mexican cinema.

## Notes

1. Velázquez claims she lost due to a corrupt process that favored Irma Arévalo, who was the daughter of President Ruiz Cortines's personal physician, cited in Rogelio Agrasánchez, *Bellezas del cine mexicano/Beauties of Mexican Cinema* (Harlingen, Texas: Agrasánchez Film Archive, 2001), 192. In any case, she would later win the pageant in 1960, though her acting career ultimately kept her from representing the country. See Juan Manuel Vázquez, "¡Hasta un novio perdí por culpa de *El Santo!*" and Itala Schmelz, *El futuro más acá* (Mexico City: Universidad Autónoma de México, 2006), 119.

2. Carl J. Mora, *Mexican Cinema: Reflections of a Society*, 3rd edition (Jefferson: McFarland & Co., 2005), 105.

3. Victoria Ruétalo and Dolores Tierney. "Introduction: Reinventing the Frame: Exploitation and Latin America" in *Latsploitation, Exploitation Cinemas, and Latin America* (New York: Routledge, 2009), 4.

4. Seraina Rohrer, *La India María: Mexploitation and the Films of María Elena Velasco* (Austin: University of Texas Press, 2017), 32–48.

5. John Mraz, *Looking for Mexico: Modern Visual Culture and National Identity* (Durham: Duke University Press, 2009), 118–51.

6. Rohrer, *La India María*, 49; Sergio de la Mora "'Tus pinches leyes yo me las paso por los huevos.' Isela Vega and Mexican Dirty Movies," in *Latsploitation, Exploitation Cinemas, and Latin America*, eds. Victoria Ruétalo and Dolores Tierney (New York: Routledge, 2009), 247–8; Álvaro A. Fernández Reyes, *Santo: El Enmascarado de Plata: Mito y realidad de un héroe mexicano moderno.* (Zamora: D.R. El Colegio de Michoacán, 2012), 64–66.

7. For discussion on El Santo, see Rafael Aviña, "Santo el enmascarado de plata," *Cinémas d'Amérique latine* 19 (2011): 26; David Dalton, *Mestizo Modernity: Race, Technology, and the Body in Postrevolutionary Mexico* (Gainesville: University of Florida Press, 2018), 150; Evan Lieberman, "Mask and Masculinity: Culture, Modernity, and Gender Identity in the Mexican Lucha Libre Films of El Santo," *Studies in Hispanic Cinemas* 6, no. 1 (2009): 13; Anne Rubenstein, "El Santo's Strange Career," in *The Mexico Reader: History, Culture, Politics*, eds. Gilbert M. Joseph and Timothy J. Henderson (Durham: Duke University Press, 2002), 576–8. For a discussion on the Brothers Almada, see Ryan Rashotte, *Narco Cinema: Sex, Drugs, and Banda Music in Mexico B-Filmography* (New York: Palgrave MacMillan, 2015), 43–101. Rohrer's work on María Elena Velasco represents an important exception to this general focus on male actors.

8. Octavio Paz, *El laberinto de la soledad. Postada. Vuelta a El laberinto de la soledad* (Mexico City: FCE, 2004), 94–5. See also Rosario Castellanos, "Otra vez Sor Juana," in *Obras II: Poesía, teatro y ensayo*, comp. Eduardo Mejía. (Mexico City: FCE, 1998), 468.

9. Sandra Cypess, *La Malinche in Mexican Literature: From History to Myth* (Austin: University of Texas Press, 1991), 129.

10. Jean Franco, *Plotting Women: Gender and Representation in Mexico* (New York: Columbia University Press, 1988), 159.

11. Judith Butler, *Bodies That Matter: On the Discursive Limits of "Sex"* (London: Routledge, 1993), 95.

12. Schmelz, *El future más acá*, 119. This argument holds especially true given Miguel Ángel Fernández Delgado's observation that Mexploitation cinema was directed at urban audiences in Mexico City who were most directly affected by the country's evolving gender landscape, "An X-Ray of Mexican Science Fiction Films," in *El futuro más acá*, ed. Itala Schmelz (Mexico City: Universidad Autónoma de México, 2006), 139.

13. Joanne Hershfield, *Imagining la Chica Moderna: Women, Nation, and Visual Culture in Mexico, 1917–1936* (Durham: Duke University Press, 2008), 5.

14. Anne Rubenstein, *Bad Language, Naked Ladies, and Other Threats to the Nation: A Political History of Comic Books in Mexico* (Durham: Duke University Press, 1998), 46.

15. Rubenstein, *Bad Language*, 46.

16. Rubenstein, *Bad Language*, 46–50.

17. Rohrer, *La India María*, 49.

18. The term chica-Santo serves as a clear allusion to the famous Bond girls that came about in the 1960s. Indeed, the connection between *lucha libre* cinema and James Bond runs deeper than just attractive female characters. Films like *Operación 67* (René Cardona, 1967) showed El Santo as a Mexican spy on par with 007.

19. Indeed, the relationship between El Santo and Lorena Velázquez was such that she became one of very few—if any—costars who would ever see the *luchador* without his mask. Juan Manuel Vázquez, "¡Hasta un novio perdí por culpa de *El Santo!*"

20. Cited in Itala Schmelz, "Las edecanes del mal," *Luna Córnea* 27 (2004): 76.

21. Agrasánchez Jr., *Bellezas del cine mexicano*, 178.

22. Tiziana Bertaccini, *Ficción y realidad del héroe popular* (Mexico City: Universidad Iberoamericana, 2001), 102.

23. Kerry T. Hegarty, "From Superhero to National Hero: The Populist Myth of El Santo," *Studies in Latin American Popular Culture* 31 (2013): 14.

24. Doyle Greene, *Mexploitation Cinema: A Critical History of Mexican Vampire, Wrestler, Ape-Man and Similar Films, 1957–1977.* (Jefferson: McFarland & Company, 2005), 29.

25. For a discussion of the fashion choices of *chicas modernas*, see Hershfield, *Imagining*, 5.

26. Dalton, *Mestizo Modernity*, 155.

27. Dalton, *Mestizo Modernity*, 156–7.

28. Bertaccini, *Ficción y realidad*, 103; Antonio Lázaro-Rebol, "The Reception of Latin America Exploitation Cinemas in Spanish Subcultures," in *Latsploitation, Exploitation Cinemas, and Latin America*, eds. Victoria Ruétalo and Dolores Tierney (New York: Routledge, 2009), 43–45.

29. Marcos Antonio Santiago, "El pollo cinéfilo," *Boletín: Facultad de Matemáticas* 269 (March 2009): 7. http://tifon.fciencias.unam.mx/boletin/2009/Marzo/269.pdf.

30. Tania Negrete and Héctor Orozco, "From the Countryside to the Capital, and from the Capital to Space," in *El futuro más acá*, ed. Itala Schmelz (Mexico City: Universidad Autónoma de México, 2006), 201.

31. Greene, *Mexploitation Cinema*, 59.

32. Rocío Pérez-Gañán, "Perversas latinoamericanas en el cine de terror: evolución y configuración de una cotidianidad transformadora, conflictual y decolonizante," *Contemporánea* 7, no. 1 (2017): 176. See also Greene, *Mexploitation Cinema*, 57.

33. Gabriel Eljaiek-Rodríguez, *Selva de fantasmas: El gótico en la literatura y el cine latinoamericanos* (Bogotá: Pontificia Universidad Javeriana, 2017), 175.

34. Ana M. López, "Tears and Desire: Women and Melodrama in the 'Old' Mexican Cinema," in *The Latin American Cultural Studies Reader*, eds. Ana del Sarto, Abril Trigo, and Alicia Ríos (Durham: Duke University Press, 2004), 450.

35. Delfin Romero Tapia notes that numerous films from the 1960s and 1970s highlighted the lesbian potential of female vampires, *La representación del héroe*, 139–40.

36. Naief Yehya, "Cosmic Femmes, the Urban Apocalypse, and Other Singularities of Future Film Archaeology," in *El futuro más acá*, ed. Itala Schmelz (Mexico City: Universidad Autónoma de México, 2006), 213.

37. Eve Kosofsky Sedgwick, *Novel Gazing Queer Readings in Fiction* (Durham: Duke University Press, 1997), 21–22.

38. Vázquez, "¡Hasta un novio perdí por culpa de *El Santo!*," n.p.

39. Greene, *Mexploitation Cinema*, 166.

40. Rubenstein, "El Santo's Strange Career," 576–8.

41. Javier Pereda and Patricia Murrieta-Flores, "The Role of Lucha Libre in the Construction of Male Identity," *Networking Knowledge: Journal for the MeCCSA Postgraduate Network* 4, no. 1 (2011): 9; José Luis Barrios, "Female Aliens, or, How to Be a G-Rated *Fichera*," in *El futuro más acá*, ed. Itala Schmelz (Mexico City: Universidad Autónoma de México, 2006), 161–3. See Vinodh Venkatesh, *Capitán Latinoamérica: Superheroes in Cinema, Television, and Web Series* (Albany: State University of New York Press, 2020).

42. See Dolores Tierney, "*El vampiro y el sexo/The Vampire and Sex* (René Cardona, 1969): El Santo, Sexploitation Films and Politics in Mexico 1968," *Porn Studies* 6, no. 4 (2019): 411–27.

43. One Mexican actress who made a career out of appearing in dirty movies was Isela Vega. See Sergio de la Mora, "'Tus pinches leyes,'" 245–58.

44. Emily Hind, *Femmenism and the Mexican Woman Intellectual from Sor Juana to Poniatowska: Boob Lit* (New York: Palgrave MacMillan, 2010), 63–64.

45. Several critics have noted that producers tended to film family-friendly versions of their movies for domestic audiences while exporting versions with exotic nudity for international audiences. See Barrios, "Female Aliens," and Greene, *Mexploitation Cinema*, 85 and 105.

46. Paz, *El laberinto*, 94.

47. For a discussion of the binary between *mestizo* and indigenous, see Joshua Lund, *The Mestizo State: Reading Race in Modern Mexico* (Minneapolis: University of Minnesota Press, 2012), x–xvii; Pedro Ángel Palou, *El fracaso del mestizo* (Mexico City: Paidós, 2014), 14; Dalton, *Mestizo Modernity*, 1–14.

48. Nelson Carro, *El cine de luchadores* (Mexico City: Rosette, 1984), 42.

49. Arce, *Mexico's Nobodies*, 102. See also Oswaldo Estrada, *Troubled Memories: Iconic Mexican Women and the Traps of Representation* (Albany: State University of New York Press, 2018), 141–83.

50. Schmelz, "Las edecanes," 78.

51. Ilana Dann Luna, *Adapting Gender: Mexican Feminisms from Literature to Film* (Albany: State University of New York Press, 2018), 3.

52. Ana Lau Jaiven, *La nueva ola del feminismo en México. Conciencia y acción de lucha de las mujeres* (Mexico City: Planeta, 1987), 141–2.

53. Greene, *Mexploitation Cinema*, 119–21.

54. Alfonso Morales, "Missiles and Marionettes," in *El futuro más acá*, ed. Itala Schmelz (Mexico City: Universidad Autónoma de México), 183; Fernández Delgado, "An X-Ray," 145.

55. Ricardo Cárdenas Pérez, "Representaciones y roles femeninos en el cine mexicano de luchadoras," *Balajú. Revista de Cultura y Comunicación* 4, no. 7 (2017): 40–44.

56. Agrasánchez Jr., *Bellezas del cine mexicano*, 190–2.

57. Agrasánchez Jr., *Bellezas del cine mexicano*, 192.

58. Cárdenas Pérez, "Representaciones y roles," 39. Several scholars have noted that male-dominated *lucha libre* movies also aimed to undermine censorship, particularly the sport's ban from television. See Dalton, *Mestizo Modernity*, 147–8; Greene, *Mexploitation Cinema*, 62; Heather Levi, *The World of Lucha Libre: Secrets, Revelations, and Mexican National Identity* (Durham: Duke University Press, 2008), 181–6.

59. Greene, *Mexploitation Cinema*, 109.

60. Greene, *Mexploitation Cinema*, 125–6.

61. The depiction of El Dragón Negro is quite racist; it conflates Japanese and Chinese cultures while at the same time signaling communism as a threat to Mexican modernity. See Greene, *Mexploitation Cinema*, 126, 134.

62. As far as I can determine, there was no familial relationship between Lorena Velázquez and Jesús "Murciélago" Velázquez.

63. Venkatesh notes a similar dynamic in *Las luchadoras contra el robot asesino* (René Cardona, 1968), where the *luchadoras* ultimately become "sidekicks" to the male detectives.

64. Cárdenas Pérez, "Representaciones y roles," 47. The inclusion of these Mexican *luchadoras* in this scene was a key element to *luchadora* cinema because it gave audiences a chance to

view a fight between *luchadoras*. This was especially important for Mexico City viewers since the city had banned women from wrestling.

65. David Wilt notes that the camera functions more like a movie camera than one placed by spies to bug the home, "*Las luchadoras contra la momia*," *The Elizabeth Campbell Filmography* (blog), last modified December 2006, http://terpconnect.umd.edu/~dwilt/luchamom.htm.

66. Greene, *Mexploitation Cinema*, 132.

67. Greene, *Mexploitation Cinema*, 20.

68. Levi notes a deep symbiotic relationship between the sport of lucha libre and lucha libre cinema, *The World of Lucha Libre*, 186–90.

69. Cárdenas Pérez, "Representaciones y roles," 45.

70. Cárdenas Pérez, "Representaciones y roles," 48.

71. There were certainly more *luchadoras* films that came out after this, but this was the last one starring Velázquez as Loreta (Ariadne Welter was recast in the role of Gloria Venus in *Las mujeres panteras*, 1967). The film thus should be read as the story of how Loreta finishes her wrestling career.

72. Cárdenas Pérez, "Representaciones y roles," 52.

## Bibliography

Agrasánchez, Rogelio, Jr. *Bellezas del cine mexicano / Beauties of Mexican Cinema*. Harlingen, Texas: Agrasánchez Film Archive, 2001.

Arce, B. Christine. *Mexico's Nobodies: The Cultural Legacy of the Soldadera and Afro-Mexican Women*. Albany: State University of New York Press, 2017.

Aviña, Rafael. "Santo el enmascarado de plata." *Cinémas d'Amérique latine* 19 (2011): 25–38.

Barrios, José Luis. "Female Aliens, or, How to Be a G-Rated *Fichera*." In *El futuro más acá*, edited by Itala Schmelz, 149–69. Mexico City: Universidad Autónoma de México, 2006.

Bertaccini, Tiziana. *Ficción y realidad del héroe popular*. Mexico City: Universidad Iberoamericana, 2001.

Butler, Judith. *Bodies That Matter: On the Discursive Limits of "Sex."* London: Routledge, 1993.

Cárdenas Pérez, Ricardo. "Representaciones y roles femeninos en el cine mexicano de luchadoras." *Balajú. Revista de Cultura y Comunicación* 4, no. 7 (2017): 37–59.

Carro, Nelson. *El cine de luchadores*. Mexico City: Rosette, 1984.

Castellanos, Rosario. "Otra vez Sor Juana." In *Obras II: Poesía, teatro y ensayo*, compiled by Eduardo Mejía, 467–70. Mexico City: FCE, 1998.

Castro Ricalde, Maricruz, and Robert McKee Irwin. *El cine mexicano "se impone": Mercados internacionales y penetración cultural en la época dorada*. Mexico City: UNAM, 2011.

Cypess, Sandra. *La Malinche in Mexican Literature: From History to Myth*. Austin: University of Texas Press, 1991.

Dalton, David. *Mestizo Modernity: Race, Technology, and the Body in Postrevolutionary Mexico*. Gainesville: University of Florida Press, 2018.

de la Mora, Sergio. "'Tus pinches leyes yo me las paso por los huevos': Isela Vega and Mexican Dirty Movies." In *Latsploitation, Exploitation Cinemas, and Latin America*, edited by Victoria Ruétalo and Dolores Tierney, 261–74. New York: Routledge, 2009.

Eljaiek-Rodríguez, Gabriel. *Selva de fantasmas: El gótico en la literatura y el cine latinoamericanos.* Bogotá: Pontificia Universidad Javeriana, 2017.

Estrada, Oswaldo. *Troubled Memories: Iconic Mexican Women and the Traps of Representation.* Albany: State University of New York Press, 2018.

Fernández Delgado, Miguel Ángel. "An X-Ray of Mexican Science Fiction Films." In *El futuro más acá,* edited by Itala Schmelz, 131–48. Mexico City: Universidad Autónoma de México, 2006.

Fernández Reyes, Álvaro A. *Santo: El Enmascarado de Plata: Mito y realidad de un héroe mexicano moderno.* Zamora: D.R. El Colegio de Michoacán, 2012.

Franco, Jean. *Plotting Women: Gender and Representation in Mexico.* New York: Columbia University Press, 1988.

Greene, Doyle. *Mexploitation Cinema: A Critical History of Mexican Vampire, Wrestler, Ape-Man and Similar Films, 1957–1977.* Jefferson: McFarland & Company, 2005.

Hegarty, Kerry T. "From Superhero to National Hero: The Populist Myth of El Santo." *Studies in Latin American Popular Culture* 31 (2013): 3–27.

Hershfield, Joanne. *Imagining la Chica Moderna: Women, Nation, and Visual Culture in Mexico, 1917–1936.* Durham: Duke University Press, 2008.

Hind, Emily. *Femmenism and the Mexican Woman Intellectual from Sor Juana to Poniatowska: Boob Lit.* New York: Palgrave MacMillan, 2010.

Jaiven, Ana Lau. *La nueva ola del feminismo en México.* Mexico City: Planeta, 1987.

Lázaro-Rebol, Antonio. "The Reception of Latin America Exploitation Cinemas in Spanish Subcultures." In *Latsploitation, Exploitation Cinemas, and Latin America,* edited by Victoria Ruétalo and Dolores Tierney, 38–54. New York: Routledge, 2009.

Levi, Heather. *The World of Lucha Libre: Secrets, Revelations, and Mexican National Identity.* Durham: Duke University Press, 2008. Kindle.

Lieberman, Evan. "Mask and Masculinity: Culture, Modernity, and Gender Identity in the Mexican Lucha Libre Films of El Santo." *Studies in Hispanic Cinemas* 6, no. 1 (2009): 3–17.

López, Ana M. "Tears and Desire: Women and Melodrama in the 'Old' Mexican Cinema." In *The Latin American Cultural Studies Reader,* edited by Ana del Sarto, Abril Trigo, and Alicia Ríos, 441–58. Durham: Duke University Press, 2004.

Luna, Ilana Dann. *Adapting Gender: Mexican Feminisms from Literature to Film.* Albany: State University of New York Press, 2018.

Lund, Joshua. *The Mestizo State: Reading Race in Modern Mexico.* Minneapolis: University of Minnesota Press, 2012.

Mora, Carl J. *Mexican Cinema: Reflections of a Society.* 3rd edition. Jefferson: McFarland & Co., 2005.

Morales, Alfonso. "Missiles and Marionettes." In *El futuro más acá,* edited by Itala Schmelz, 169–84. Mexico City: Universidad Autónoma de México, 2006.

Mraz, John. *Looking for Mexico: Modern Visual Culture and National Identity.* Durham: Duke University Press, 2009. Kindle.

Negrete, Tania, and Héctor Orozco. "From the Countryside to the Capital, and from the Capital to Space." In *El futuro más acá,* edited by Itala Schmelz, 185–200. Mexico City: Universidad Autónoma de México, 2006.

Palou, Pedro Ángel. *El fracaso del mestizo.* Mexico City: Paidós, 2014.

Paz, Octavio. *El laberinto de la soledad. Postada. Vuelta a El laberinto de la soledad.* Mexico City: FCE, 2004.

Pereda, Javier, and Patricia Murrieta-Flores. "The Role of Lucha Libre in the Construction of Male Identity." *Networking Knowledge: Journal for the MeCCSA Postgraduate Network* 4, no. 1 (2011): 1–19.

Pérez-Gañán, Rocío. "Perversas latinoamericanas en el cine de terror: evolución y configuración de una cotidianidad transformadora, conflictual y decolonizante." *Contemporánea* 7, no. 1 (2017): 167–91.

Rashotte, Ryan. *Narco Cinema: Sex, Drugs, and Banda Music in Mexico's B-Filmography*. New York: Palgrave MacMillan, 2015.

Rohrer, Seraina. *La India María: Mexploitation and the Films of María Elena Velasco*. Austin: University of Texas Press, 2017.

Rubenstein, Anne. *Bad Language, Naked Ladies, and Other Threats to the Nation: A Political History of Comic Books in Mexico*. Durham: Duke University Press, 1998.

———. "El Santo's Strange Career." In *The Mexico Reader: History, Culture, Politics*, edited by Gilbert M. Joseph and Timothy J. Henderson, 570–78. Durham: Duke University Press, 2002.

Ruétalo, Victoria, and Dolores Tierney. "Introduction: Reinventing the Frame: Exploitation and Latin America." In *Latsploitation, Exploitation Cinemas, and Latin America*, 1–12, New York: Routledge, 2009.

Santiago, Marcos Antonio. "El pollo cinéfilo." *Boletín: Facultad de Matemáticas* 269 (March 2009): 7. http://tifon.fciencias.unam.mx/boletin/2009/Marzo/269.pdf

Schmelz, Itala. *El futuro más acá*. Mexico City: Universidad Autónoma de México, 2006.

———. "Las edecanes del mal." *Luna Córnea* 27 (2004): 76–81.

Sedgwick, Eve Kosofsky. *Novel Gazing: Queer Readings in Fiction*. Durham: Duke University Press, 1997.

Syder, Andrew, and Dolores Tierney. "Importation/Mexploitation: Or, How a Crime-Fighting, Vampire-Slaying Mexican Wrestler Almost Found Himself in an Italian Sword-and-Sandals Epic." In *Horror International*, edited by Steven Jay Schneider and Tony Williams, 33–55. Detroit: Wayne State Press, 2005.

Tapia, Delfín Romero. *La representación del héroe: mujeres, luchadores y otros personajes en las películas del Santo*. Villahermosa: Universidad Juárez Autónoma de Tabasco, 2010.

Vázquez, Juan Manuel. "'¡Hasta un novio perdí por culpa de El Santo!': Lorena Velázquez." *Jornada* (Mexico City, Mexico), Feb. 14, 2009. https://www.jornada.com.mx/2009/02/14/index.php?section=espectaculos&article=a08n1esp.

Venkatesh, Vinodh. *Capitán Latinoamérica: Superheroes in Cinema, Television, and Web Series*. Albany: State University of New York Press, 2020.

Wilt, David. "Las luchadoras contra la momia." *The Elizabeth Campbell Filmography* (blog). Last modified December 2006. http://terpconnect.umd.edu/~dwilt/luchamom.htm.

Yehya, Naief. "Cosmic Femmes, the Urban Apocalypse, and Other Singularities of Future Film Archaeology." In *El futuro más acá*, edited by Itala Schmelz, 201–19. Mexico City: Universidad Autónoma de México, 2006.

# 3

## THE MEXICAN *SUPEROCHERO* MOMENT

Countercultural Nations and Utopian
Assemblages in Small Format

IVÁN EUSEBIO AGUIRRE DARANCOU

This chapter focuses on the cultural phenomenon of small-format film production that, in the context of the lost decades of Mexican cinema, began with the violent eruption of state violence in the Plaza de las Tres Culturas in Tlatelolco on the fateful date October 2, 1968. A tragic event that was to be repeated in 1971 with the Halconazo (Corpus Christi Massacre), Tlatelolco became the marking point for an incipient and short-lived, albeit extremely active, production circuit of filmmakers using the small format of Super 8mm film. Introduced to the country during the 1950s, Super 8 was a documentarian device, an upper- and middle-class commodity, and a marker of the modernization that Mexico was experiencing in those decades. In the aftermath of Tlatelolco, Mexican filmmakers began using it in a variety of ways to explore and exploit its political, cultural, social, and artistic potentialities. Particularly in the 1970s, the *superochero* cultural sphere established itself as a space where young filmmakers came together to share an extremely wide variety of cultural production.[1] Responding directly to the overbearing presence of both the authoritarian state of the Luis Echeverría administration (1970–1976), which used state institutions to capture and domesticate dissident voices and filmmakers, and the increasing strength of mass-media industries that began to be coupled with advertising agencies, *superocheros* sought to change the forms of political engagement, in line with the anti-colonial struggles of the Global South and in conversation with the Third Cinema theorizations emanating from South America. With aesthetic roots in the experimental gaze of *La fórmula secreta* (Rubén Gámez, 1965) and *El grito* (Leobardo López Arretche, 1968), their production encompassed well over two hundred films and included low-budget Westerns, erotic films, political communiqués, avant-garde experimentalism, political documentaries, rock documentaries, and rock operas.

Within this sphere, Sergio García Michel (1945–2010) was a central figure whose cultural work involved not only production but also chronicling the diverse history of the small format, establishing various film collectives, founding the important Foro Tlalpan cultural center, and teaching film production, both in small workshops (*talleres*) and in university classrooms. Situated in the *superochero* production corpus, García Michel's oeuvre allows us to understand the creative use of a particular format in the construction of an alternative aesthetics and cultural politics. The radical nature (in both form and content) of his films is made visible in the constant reiteration of anti-capitalist, anti-patriarchal, anti-nationalist, and utopic subjects, both on-screen in the representation and off-screen in the affective engagements that the original screenings demanded due to their technical limitations. I refer to these as "countercultural nations" not only because of the subversion and recirculation of nationalist visual and audial tropes but also due to the emphasis García Michel placed on building and maintaining alternative cultural spheres and networks, both national and international, where Super 8 could circulate.

In other words, by reusing the visual, literary, and audial tropes of the *mestizo* national(ist) project, and by circulating these repurposed images and sounds in alter-capitalist circuits, García Michel and the *superocheros* created alternative nations and national projects, much beyond being moments of bourgeois escapism; in this sense, they created countercultural nations. In the history of Golden Age cinema sponsored under the aegis of the *alemanista* state (1946–1952), and the independent cinema of the 1970s with ties to and support from the Echeverría administration via Rodolfo Echeverría as president of the Banco Nacional Cinematográfico, Super 8 appeared as a circuit that, in spite of the technological and cultural limitations imposed by the medium, could offer the possibility to imagine cinema as a space outside the overarching influence of both state and capitalist logics.[2] García Michel's interventions best exemplify what he described as the "fourth cinema" that Mexican Super 8 promised to be, resting specifically upon the representations of female sexuality in disruptive and politicized tones that generate what film critic Teresa Rizzo refers to as a molecular sexuality, explosive forces capable of destabilizing normative social and gender orders.[3] Through an aesthetics that diverges from the centralization of male experience within the representation of counterculture, García Michel's films become instances where the potential affective engagements incorporate spectators as cinematic subjects outside the heteronormative order of Mexican nationalism.

To better understand García Michel's unique interventions within the *superochero* movement and the greater film industry of the 1970s and 1980s, this chapter focuses on his three most famous and widely circulated films: *El fin* (1970), *Ah, verdá . . . ?* (1974) and *Un toke de roc* (1988). Each of these will be contextualized and counterpointed with other films that share some of the common themes. These include the representation of state violence and political escapism, topics that García Michel centralizes in his oeuvre and that reappear in *Mi casa de altos techos* (David Celestinos, 1970) and *Lux externa* (José Agustín, 1973/2003/2008); political praxis and collaborative filmmaking in the work of the Cooperativa de Cine Marginal, specifically in *Otro país* (1972); the representations of class oppression and conflict in films such as *Víctor Ibarra Cruz* (Eduardo Carrasco Zanini, 1971); and finally sexual liberation and eroticism in *Chuchulucos y arrumacos para burgueses* (Rafael Montero, 1974).[4] In the context of contests, festivals, and film cooperatives, these films stand out for their use of cinema as a tool of political action. Susana Draper, in recovering the various ways in which Mexican culture responded to the events of 1968, focuses on how Super 8 was seen as a format and potential political tool in that it implied a "manifest form of political intervention of the image. This does not have to do with filming about, but rather with making a change of and in the image as a place of transformation of aesthetic habits."[5] This transformation rests not only with the ability of the format to penetrate social spaces prohibited either due to censorship (prison cells, political meetings) or technical limitations (rock concerts, outdoor spaces) but also with the ways in which film was seen as a way to generate alternative subjectivities, sexualities, and political actions beyond representation itself.[6]

Jesse Lerner and Rita González have emphasized how Sergio García Michel—and the rest of the *superocheros* active in the production and distribution circuit—not only produced films but also constructed spaces where other filmmakers could showcase their work.[7] In these spaces, the mobilization that his films make of the iconography and soundscape of *mestizo* and state-sponsored nationalism mutate in processes of becoming. Following Rosi Braidotti, I argue that these films generate a utopian nationalism infused by countercultural aesthetics and politics where the end result is not simply the reification nor the rejection of a collection of social values, iconographies, and soundscapes that make up *mestizo* nationalism. Rather, in the words of Braidotti, these Super 8 representations of mutated becomings, changes, and transformations can be viewed as "alternative representations and social locations for the kind of hybrid mix we are in the process of becoming ... materialistic mappings of situated, embedded and embodied, positions."[8] Contextualized within other films focused on representing and critiquing the variety of countercultural manifestations in Mexico, García Michel's filmic interventions generate alternative sociabilities (on- and off-screen) grounded in the aesthetics of both global counterculture and Mexican nationalisms. These cinematic assemblages include the visual representations that García Michel directly controls while also engaging the viewers with the music of Mexican rock figures such as Botellita de Jerez, Rockdrigo González, Three Souls in My Mind, Cecilia Toussaint, and Jaime López, whose musical soundscapes are and become integral components of these mutated and countercultural utopian nationalisms.[9]

In a 1971 article titled "El cinito ha muerto, ¡Viva el cine!," journalist José de la Colina wrote how "while 35mm and 70mm are chained to an industry, a system, and big money, 8mm represents a place where filmmakers can operate freely, a territory in which one can film everything one wants, in the way one wants."[10] Echoing what film theorists such as Jonathan Gunter saw in the format at this crucial moment of anti-capitalist struggles across the Global South, Mexican filmmakers eagerly used the small format as a medium with which to decentralize cinematic production.[11] Beginning with the Primer Concurso Nacional de Cine Independiente [First National Competition of Independent Cinema] arranged by the Centro de Arte Independiente Las Musas in 1970, the *superocheros* spanned nine contests organized by various institutions, including the Secretaría de Cultura y Deportes of the Asociación Nacional de Actores and the Comité de Difusión Cultural de la Escuela de Economía de la UNAM, and produced over two hundred films to be screened and distributed in cities like Zacatecas, Puebla, Querétaro, Guadalajara, Tepic, Villahermosa, and others.

Within this extremely diverse production, in 1974 García Michel and other *superocheros* published a pamphlet-manifesto titled "Toward a Fourth Cinema," where they position themselves in a particular mode of countercultural production that sought to question the effectiveness of a political cinema. By focusing on the potential of Super 8 film as an "antidote to the alienating media, giving back to the individual their function as subject, making them a direct participant in the work of cinema," these producers creatively exploited the limitations of the format in its production (especially in terms of sound) and distribution (the inability to mass produce copies).[12] In line with the cinematic style of Third Cinema in other Latin American countries, García Michel understood the radical potentiality of Super 8—a potentiality echoed in the digital technologies of today—as one that activated cinema as an open medium, where the political message rested less on the representational level and more on the awakening of a mode of viewing.[13] In the manifesto, fourth cinema is "brief, concise and impacting; something like a *poster* or—with due allowance—it must have the force of an *advertisement*."[14] Given his training as an advertising agent during the last years of the 1960s—something he shares with novelist Fernando del Paso, whose representation of the student movement and youth culture and politics in *Palinuro de México* (1977) rings close to García Michel's playful yet politically committed cinematic gaze—this understanding of fourth cinema as one that "raises consciousness, but does not form it" shapes the way in which to comprehend the greater Super 8 production of Mexico in this decade.[15] As Lerner and González specify, the distance from Third Cinema lies not in the political content of the films themselves but in the form and commitment to a political subjectivity whose appearance in the 1960s and 1970s can also be reflexively observed in the literature of the Onda or the music of La Onda Chicana, specifically through the figure of youth, from naïve adolescents to rebellious young adults.[16]

The topics of the first two contests in 1970 and 1971 were respectively "Nuestro país" [Our Country] and "La problemática actual" [The Current Problem]. Responding to this, most of the films presented in these two years worked around the realities of state violence against students, the representation of non-normative social subjects, the use of film as a political tool and finally, self-critiques of youth and countercultural spheres. Following Christopher Dunn, an approach to Latin American countercultures must take into account how these (counter)cultural spheres emerge as a response to conservative moral structures, authoritarian governments, and revolutionary insurgency, as well as modernization and the rise of consumerism.[17] Although the films presented belong to this countercultural sphere and indubitably emerge from a politics and aesthetics informed by globalization, youth culture, rock and roll, and leftist politics, their particular approaches reveal nuances and tensions within the *superocheros* themselves.

Beginning with *Mi casa de altos techos* (David Celestinos, 1970), the *superocheros* focus their attention on the impact of authoritarian violence directed against students, and a critical assessment of this for revolutionary action. Celestinos's short film reflects on the role of the artist in politics by telling the story of two painters studying at the prestigious Academia de San Carlos, each of whom passes through a process of self-reflection informed by the Tlatelolco massacre of October 2, 1968, the realization of the poverty and class conflict present in the nation, and their negotiation with global counterculture. Opening with the two students entering the imposing doors of the Academia, the film emphasizes their respective differences as politically intersectional. The first student appears as a fair-skinned young man with long hair and beard who will remain throughout the film within the confines of the school grounds, leaving only to symbolically "escape" with a young woman to the refuge of the forest. The second student is portrayed with darker skin and clothing that visually marks him as a middle-class youth, perhaps a first-generation student like so many of those that participated in the political actions of the 1960s. After the opening sequence entering the Academia, the film becomes a story of a broken camaraderie whose existence revolved around the space of the school, metaphorically extended to a critical reflection of the nation itself. As the students walk through the school, a voiceover says, "Esta es mi casa. Mi diario sufrir y mi esperanza. En ella siempre hay un hueco para mí, un casillero, un banco, una tela desnuda y un amigo . . . no estoy solo, está mi hermano, mi camarada" [This is my house. My daily suffering and my hope. In it there is always a nook for me, a locker, a bench, a naked cloth, and a friend . . . I am not alone, my brother is there, my comrade]. The pair soon separates, however, and the bearded student remains inside while his comrade exits in order to experience the city. In a visual reference to *La fórmula secreta*, whose opening sequence contains im-

Figure 3.1. Low-angle shot from *La fórmula secreta* (Rubén Gámez, 1965).

ages of the Zócalo with low-angle shots created by placing the camera on a skateboard, Celestinos's Super 8mm shows the protagonist walking through the Zócalo from a similar low-angle shot, placing the camera on the ground to emphasize the student walking toward the spectator.

Countering the previous shots of the pair walking into the building from the back, this sequence moves the spectator to affectively engage with the student in his own process of politicization; in other words, instead of placing the spectator in the position of the voyeur, Celestinos places the viewer in the position of the communal, looking at the city he is exploring but also looking with, alongside, joining him. In this moment, the affective engagement is one of co-exploration of the city, especially the working- and lower-class spaces that the idealization of the youthful student from the middle-class in the central boroughs of Mexico City inadvertently silenced. As he walks across the city's edges, just as the experimental characters of Gámez come face to face with the urban chaos and stark class differences radicalized by the onslaught of consumerism, the student comes across a young boy attempting to tie a rope, whose efforts are literally unraveled. A visual reference to photographs of Rufino Tamayo and Tina Modotti, Celestinos repurposes the close-up of the hands and rope using low-angle shots to metaphorically critique the *crux* of student activism: how to bring together and maintain ties between the oppressed working classes and the politically inclined middle-class students.

The film then cuts back to the *jipiteca* student who remained within the space of art, isolated but nevertheless preoccupied by the same issues, as several shots show him surrounded by images of Che Guevara and Tlatelolco.[18] The sound montage in this moment allows for an understanding of the com-

Figure 3.2. *Mi casa de altos techos* (David Celestinos, 1970).

plex critique the film generates. While the rest of the film is musicalized with the Beatles and John Lennon and the Plastic Ono Band, the sequences with the artist isolated and tormented by "su propia existencia, la represión política, el amor" [his own existence, political repression, love] are accompanied by Mozart's *Requiem*.[19] This musical contrast signals the isolation this particular youth is choosing in response to the events experienced by the nation, a fact further emphasized by the metaphoric sequence (counterpointing the sequence of the boy and the rope) of the young man dressed in white walking in a lonely forest with a young woman, taking refuge in idyllic nature and art. The film ends with images of the other student, still walking through the city and playing in a fountain while the voiceover reiterates "Venceremos" [We will win], and the musical montage melds into Lennon's "Let's Give Peace a Chance." Given Celestinos's background as an art student, the film is a stark self-reflection on the role of art in political engagement. Two things must be underlined in this critique: first, the centralization of the figure of the student as the representative of society, and second, the use of global music, specifically the pop rock of the Beatles and John Lennon, as a way of giving shape to a soundscape that seeks to go outside the paradigms of both revolutionary nationalism (in the specific case of Mexico) and leftist aesthetics (in the case of protest songs of Latin America).

The second film I want to emphasize in these first years is *Víctor Ibarra Cruz* (Eduardo Carrasco Zanini, 1971). Responding to the general preoccupation that Celestinos's film makes visible how to use art (film) as a bridge between classes, *Víctor* follows a "real-life" character throughout a day of his existence as a street bum, accompanied by his faithful dog, Güero. Anticipating the aesthetics of *jodidismo*, the film shows Víctor sweeping streets, sharing food and cigarettes with fellow street-dwellers, scrapping a few coins used later to buy alcohol and bread, and ends with him celebrating his birthday with his dog. Exploiting the DIY potential of Super 8, the credits emphasize the individual production of Eduardo Carrasco as the sole director, producer, editor, and singer. The film opens with a fixed full shot of Víctor and the dog walking toward the camera, ending with a close-up of his eyes staring into the lens. As Víctor and Güero walk the streets of the Condesa neighborhood and the paths of Parque México, the soundtrack affectively engages the viewers in the register of Latin American protest songs; an acoustic guitar accompanies a melancholic voice that sings about the isolated and alienating experience

Figure 3.3. *Víctor Ibarra Cruz* (Eduardo Carrasco Zanini, 1971).

of life and the approach of death.²⁰ The film ends with Víctor and Güero celebrating his birthday in his impoverished room, drinking the bottle of tequila and blowing out a candle on a piece of bread while he hugs the dog.

Álvaro Vázquez Mantecón cursorily defines *jodidismo* as a cinematic style involving both form and content where "la constatación de la miseria se convertía en una prueba irrefutable de compromiso y militancia" [the verification of misery became the irrefutable proof of political commitment and militancy].²¹ Low-budget production coupled with storylines focused on a gritty, *engagé* approach make this cinema similar to the critical *pornomiseria* aesthetics that characterized some Colombian production, exemplified in the early work of Víctor Gaviria.²² *Jodidismo* (from the Mexican slang *jodido* meaning broken, messed up, or broke) was a style that defined some Mexican production of the 1970s and 1980s, focusing on (re)presenting poverty in a documentary-style format as proof of political commitment. In larger film formats, Gabriel Retes's *Chin chin el teporocho* (1975) can be seen as an exemplary film in this genre, as it focuses on a drunkard from the *barrio* of Tepito.

Highly celebrated by the critics of the time due to its freshness and intuitive approach, *Víctor* demonstrates the engagement of Super 8 with the *jodidismo* aesthetics that later became a marker of industry films during this decade, and precursor to the *pornomiseria* aesthetics that populated Latin American cinema in the latter decades. However, with lyrics such as "enséñame a ser feliz" [show me how to be happy], Carrasco Zanini delineates a viewer with a middle-class background looking *at* the lower-class urban subject as happy in spite of his alienation and economic despair. The various close-ups of Víctor's face underline this tension in the collaboration between the protagonist and filmmaker, when the smiling gestures contrast with the melancholic and deeply sad looks in his eyes. In this way, the *jodidismo* of Carrasco refuses to spectacularize (in the style of Ismael Rodríguez in *Nosotros los pobres* [1948], an antecedent of this aesthetics), while nevertheless not making a class critique nor providing an ideological or affective alternative to the social structures that produce and maintain this urban poverty. In foregrounding both the individual production behind the film and the isolated individualism of Víctor, the film constructs poverty as pedagogical, generating a representation of an urban space marked by class difference; the militancy of the film, however, is relegated to a making visible and not to a particular form of politics or political action.

Contrasting with this approach, the films of the Cooperativa de Cine Marginal form an archive that attempts to answer the problematics explored by Celestinos and Carrasco Zanini through collaborative and militant filmmaking. Active between 1971 and 1973, the Cooperativa became a gathering point for up to seventy members in its apogee and focused on renouncing film as a "cult of the author" to propose a collective film product that fulfilled a practical more than an artistic function; their filming ethics were, in large part, anti-cinematographic and sought to counter-inform what mass-media and other information sources showcase on workers' struggles.[23] Allying themselves with the Sindicato de Trajadores Electricistas de la República Mexicana (STERM) [Electrical Workers of the Mexican Republic Union], they produced and screened films with strikers and workers, recording images and sequences in their visits and raising funds through "boteo" (passing around a collections plate), a common practice inherited from the Student Movement. In total, they produced twenty-three films, four of which circulated in their distribution network that reached their intended audience of workers, peasants, and students coming together in various events, strikes, and militant gatherings.

Though motivated by increasing the participation of workers in the production process, with the ultimate goal of "giving" them the means of representation, the short-lived Cooperativa quickly realized the ultimate challenge to their approach to militant cinema: the needs of the strikers and workers went beyond cinematographic representation, which "stopped being a useful tool for the workers' struggle because other tools, which the students could facilitate, were needed—access to lawyers, petitioning to be heard in meetings, instructions on how to use mimeographs for producing leaflets, and so on."[24] The Cooperativa disbanded, with some members leaving to participate more fully in the workers movements (Paco Ignacio Taibo II, among them) and others heading to the film industry (Gabriel Retes, most notably). The 1972 short film/communiqué *Otro país* allows for an understanding of these tensions, captured in the several Comunicados de Insurgencia Obrera they collectively produced.

Following a series of strikes, union gatherings and political spaces, *Otro país* seeks to generate an alternative vision of the country. It opens with footage from an official parade on November 20, Day of the Revolution, in Monterrey, where a voiceover explains how the participation of the governor in this space is silenced by the irruption of students, workers, teachers, and residents who take over the parade. This "taking over" becomes a visual metaphor for the Cooperativa taking over the means of representation and dissemination of information; the film then cuts to the impoverished neighborhood of Topo Chico, where the voiceover explains how the members took over the land held legally by rich citizens of the northern state of Nuevo León.[25] The rest of the film shows scenes at Fundidora, a central foundry (now the biggest public park in Monterrey), where families are mourning workers who died in the steel factory, and focuses on various workers gathering in several symbolic spaces, ending with images of a strike at the Nopal Industrial Bakery, where the voiceover explicates the betrayal of the strikers by the Confederación de Trabajadores Mexicanos (CTM) [Mexican Workers Confederation], a national union closely aligned with the PRI leadership.

The film is exemplary in the catalog of Super 8 interventions as politically

Figure 3.4. *Otro país* (Cooperativa de Cine Marginal, 1972).

committed, especially in the bringing together of a multiplicity of struggles (land rights, poverty, workers' death, union co-optation, and corruption) into a singular cinematic space that constructs a vision of another country, one marked precisely by geographical displacement to the north, moving outside the urban space of Mexico City.[26] Mobilizing a Latin American revolutionary aesthetics, *Otro país* opens with a singer softly strumming a guitar and singing "ésta es mi tierra" [this is my land]. Thus, an affective alliance—one that mobilizes the shared affective vocabulary of protest music and anti-government sentiments—is generated between the middle-class production team and the workers represented, populating this *other country* with a multiplicity of bodies. As the film progresses, however, the shots of the tenants' and children's faces become accompanied by a slow piano music that progressively grows louder, creating an emotionally charged sequence. The images of class struggle are thus

Figure 3.5. *Otro país* (Cooperativa de Cine Marginal, 1972).

affectively signified with sympathy, and in doing so the film unconsciously reproduces a structure of representation where the middle-class production team holds the means and selects and orders the issue at hand. Thus, the cinematic assemblage generated in the productions of the Cooperativa de Cine Marginal rests upon this sympathetic affective charge; the militancy of the group demands a form of politics that must be enacted outside the screen.

It is within this particular context that Sergio García Michel's first short film circulated during the early 1970s. *El fin* (1970), like *Mi casa de altos techos*, returns to the themes of state violence but does so from a space of critical reflection, going beyond the figure of the student. The film opens with credits written on ruins as the opening chords of the Doors' "The End" play, and the sequence ends with a mustached man behind prison bars in the shape of Mexico, establishing the general sentiment of capture and imprisonment that troubled youth particularly. The camera cuts to a hippie couple running into the forest, their disappearance being both the idealization of escapism and the lack of political engagement that escapism entails, emphasized with the use of the Rolling Stones' "You Can't Always Get What You Want."[27] The forest reappears as an idyllic space but one that nevertheless harbors danger. Cut to two young men around a campfire who are chased down by a *charro* and four other nationalist figures (an armed soldier, a Catholic priest, a homely housewife, and a modern businessman) until one of them is killed by a soldier in a stone-ruin setting that indexes Tlatelolco, while the other flees to be captured later while smoking a cannabis joint. The man who captures him is dressed in a suit and substitutes the cannabis with a bottle of Coca Cola. Then, the film cuts to the final sequence of moving images of the urban landscape modified with a kaleidoscope effect that indexes a hallucinatory effect. In this sequence, the music returns to an accelerated soundbyte of "The End," which fades into a song by Armando Manzanero as the camera focuses on the young man, now suited and driving a car while adjusting the radio, presumably shifting from the foreign sounds to the domestic voice of Manzanero.

A lament of the situation experienced by youth across the nation, and going outside the paradigm of the student, the short film is also embedded with a series of insights and questions. Foremost, the film invites the viewer to ask herself what is it the end of, precisely? In the first context of distribution of 1973–1974, the answer to this question might have been, especially for the (male) youth viewers, the end of the dream of counterculture and youthful rebellion. In later contexts of distribution, however, such as screenings in the Foro Tlalpan that García Michel ran in the 1980s or its redistribution in the collected DVD of *Un toke de roc* released by the UNAM in 2006, the answer to that question changes as the film is viewed in retrospect alongside the other more female-centric films of García Michel. The question becomes layered with a class critique that reflects upon the centralization of a middle-class student body in its memorialization. In this multivalent way, *El fin* becomes a key node in the construction of countercultural nations in that it signals not only the power of the state and the market in eliminating and capturing the bodies of the (male) rebel youth but, most importantly, the limits of the particular countercultural assemblage of the student as a strategy for remembering. As such, in its first years of circulation, *El fin* marks a critical reflection on the power of institutions to capture youth and to reinsert them into capitalist society precisely through the use of commodities that induce some form of altered-states (pop music, new automobiles, sharp suits).

While it can be read as an abdication of the possibilities of radical change in the greater milieu of counterculture, within the corpus of Super 8 films, and especially within García Michel's oeuvre, *El fin* sets the basis for the visual vocabulary that will become the foundation of a utopian nationalism. The escapist youth couple figuratively blow up the fantasy of idyllic nature in their persecution by the Nation, embodied in the iconic *charro* who begins to track their trail. This figure, riding a horse, smoking a cigar, and sporting the eponymous moustache, is *mestizo* nationalism incarnate, a figure who collects the macho virility of the nation. In later years, the *guacarrock* musical aesthetics of Botellita de Jerez will play a central role in *Un toke de roc*, mutating this figure of *mestizo* nationalism into a female *charrocker*, a fusion of popular, nationalist, and countercultural aesthetics grounded in a series of subverted gendered subjectivities. In this initial moment of countercultural critique, García Michel nuances the material form this symbolic *mestizo* nationalism takes in the quotidian interactions of youth and the greater society. The *charro* cuts to a series of nationalist characters that substitute him in the hunt for the escapist youth: a mother wearing a white dress and holding a baby bottle, symbolizing the purity incarnate in the Mexican suffering mother and the infantilization of youth as non-adults in spite of their politicization; a soldier coming out from the trees with a rifle held in his arms, the military force of the state; a priest with a long frock and collar, swiftly running toward the camera; and a suited man, his clothes instantly marking him as a representative of "The Man." These figures each appear isolated, but quickly unite to run down a hill toward the couple. In this way, the nationalism that García Michel is critiquing is not simply an ideological construct that captures and subjectivizes youth but a series of specific social structures with embodied characters who perform this subjectification: the family, religion, the militarized state, and the capitalist market. *El fin* thus makes a poignant self-critique of the escapism associated with the countercultural movement, as well as to raise the alarm at the ease with which both state and market continue to capture and silence youth, either through violence and death or the forces of consumer capitalism.

As the film circulated during the decades—García Michel screened it over the years at Foro Tlalpan, and the short is included in DVDs—a more nuanced answer to the question of what ended can be reached by focusing on the gendered subjectivity of the bodies that experienced the violence of state and market; that is, the end of both the (male) student and the (male) *jipiteca* as the twin embodiments of the promise of revolution. A paradoxical effect of the stifling heteronormativity of *mestizo* nationalism upon the growing middle-class youth—especially in urban spaces—was the full absorption of these young men into normative consumer and nationalist subjectivities. In this sense, the male youth subjects that were produced by the media industries via the taming of rock and roll, as can be seen represented in the industry films scripted by José Agustín—*Cinco de chocolate y uno de fresa* (Carlos Velo, 1968), *Alguien nos quiere matar* (Carlos Velo, 1970), *Ya sé quién eres (te he estado observando)* (José Agustín, 1971), and the published but un-produced script *Ahí viene la plaga* (1985)—and the media-industry-produced singers in the likes of Armando Manzanero, Enrique Guzmán, or Johnny Laboriel. These male youth are mourned by García Michel as subjects who have been captured, literally, by a state allied with the market and social institutions who affect their everyday lives.

Continuing in the line of David Celestinos, García Michel focused his lens during this particular time on generating a self-critique of counterculture as a depoliticized social space. *El fin,* along with his later collaboration in the critical documentary *Avándaro* (Alfredo Gurrola, 1972), showcases a political position similar to the one taken in the rock chronicles of Parménides García Saldaña: a recuperation of a historical moment captured from a positioning *within* the marginalized group itself that activates a critical and valuing gaze looking inside.[28] What is noteworthy and unique about *El Fin* is its awareness of the role patriarchy is playing within counterculture itself. Whereas other Super 8 films such as José Agustín's *Lux externa* mobilize parody and humor as a way to critique the countercultural male youth, and in the process generate a representation of female *jipitecas* only as sexual objects, *El fin* removes itself from this tone and instead focuses on the ways in which the representatives of the nation were capturing, symbolically and materially, the young male *jipitecas*. In *El fin,* what matters is not only that the dream of a revolution is lost, but rather that the particular dream is specifically masculine and that the forces that crush it are embodied in *mestizo* state nationalism (i.e., the *charro*, the priest, the suffering mother, the soldier) and an expanding capitalist economy (i.e., the businessman in a suit and dark sunglasses).

After the apogee of Super 8 in the early years of the 1970s, and with the in-

Figure 3.6. *El fin* (Sergio García Michel, 1970).

creasing economic support of the Echeverrista government as a way to co-opt political dissidence, the majority of *superocheros* who continued producing moved on to larger formats or focused their use of the format into experimental aesthetics. By working to generate spaces of exhibition as spaces of socialization, free and accessible to youth across the urban centers where festivals popped up, García Michel extended the commitment of fourth cinema to youth culture onto a material level beyond the visual representations, bringing filmmakers together.[29] In the cinematic assemblages of these countercultural utopian nations, I understand youth and youth culture as a multifaceted population and phenomenon produced by the media industries as much as by the urban realities of class, education, ethnicity, and so forth. To expand on what Roger Bartra underscores as the "political necessity of the first order" contained in the definition and defense of Mexican "national" characters, the interventions of youth culture through the lens of García Michel underscore the ethical-political potential of counterculture to disrupt state nationalism by signaling the negative social and individual effects of nationalist icons defined exclusively by an authoritarian regime, and at the same time, redefining these nationalist icons through a playful, yet serious, parody.[30] Among the figures of the nation that are most redefined in García Michel's *oeuvre* is that of the mother, from the anguished and overbearing figure to representations of motherhood that rests upon the notions of fertility, caretaking, and home-building while rejecting the visual and ethical imagery associated with the suffering mothers constructed in mainstream film and other media.

This reconfiguration leads to the next step in the evolution of García Michel's critical *superochero* gaze, a focus on the figure of woman as a complex political, social, *and* sexual subject. Before the first generation of *superocheros* moved into larger format, García Michel released *Ah, verdá . . . ?* (1974), evidence of the greater reach of the movement as it first screened in the III Concurso Luis Buñuel held in Zacatecas. The film opens with an intertitle of a quote by Abbie Hoffman regarding theft and corruption, cutting to a young anarchist couple bombing national monuments and institutions, including the offices of a newspaper, *El Heraldo de México*. After cavorting merrily though the city, including holding a sexual tryst within a plush VW van, the young man is captured and murdered by undercover federal agents, and the young woman builds on her sexual and social autonomy by rejecting the violent sexual advances of an upper-class young man. In the final scenes of that sequence, the young woman placidly eats walnuts while holding a nutcracker in her mouth after a lightning-quick cut to the man's crotch and his grimace of pain. The film ends with the young woman fabricating LSD, joining and drugging a group of monks, and then collectively proceeding to infuse Mexico City's water supply with the substance. A playful and fantastical film, *Ah, verdá . . . ?* demonstrates a commitment to radical politics that seek to redefine militancy outside the paradigms of Third Cinema, particularly by focusing on the representation of female agency.[31] In this way, the cinematic subject generated on-screen challenges the limits of heteronormative nationalism and provides the viewer with an affective engagement that in turn allows for the reimagination of alternative cinematic and revolutionary subjects off-screen.

I underline this firmly gendered critique because it challenges the para-

Figure 3.7. Still from *Ah, verdá . . . ?* (Sergio García Michel, 1974).

digms of critiquing counterculture and political action. As an answer to the questions generated by *El fin*, *Ah, verdá . . . ?* converses directly with Rafael Montero's *Chuchulucos y arrumacos para burgueses* (1974), a film that also reflects on the shortcomings of middle-class political imaginaries, particularly those emanating from the students of the Centro Universitario de Estudios Cinematográficos (CUEC). With an iconoclastic gaze, Montero's film follows a revolutionary young man who seduces several young women, plans and carries out the kidnapping of a politician (played by film critic Jorge Ayala Blanco), and ends in a bizarre happening complete with aboriginal drums and ape-like sounds where onlookers gaze at a man performing a ritual to rid them of Octavio Paz, whose image represents the limits of leftist action contained within a liberal framework just short of revolution. Described as a self-reflexive critique of the position of the (male) filmmaker committed to revolutionary ideals, *Chuchulucos* nevertheless re-centralizes patriarchy and does not propose a clear position in terms of revolutionary praxis.[32]

Through a circularity emphasized by a montage of repeated sequences, Montero humorously underscores how politicized middle-class (male) youth were caught within a discourse with no clear exit.³³ Alongside José Agustín's *Lux externa* (1973), which focuses on making a critique of the limits of revolutionary change within the sphere of counterculture, Montero's film remains entrenched within the gendered definition of revolution that objectifies female citizens, as can be seen in the seduction sequences of *Chuchulucos*.

For the urban youth that García Michel represents in *Ah, verdá... ?*, political action is exhausted in the guerrilla tactics, from bombs to hallucinogenic drugs. When contextualized, the representation of female sexuality in the film is doubly striking. In previous work, I have referred to these female characters as countercultural heroines who resist the physical and psychical forces of patriarchy.³⁴ In representing the radically liberated sexuality of the female

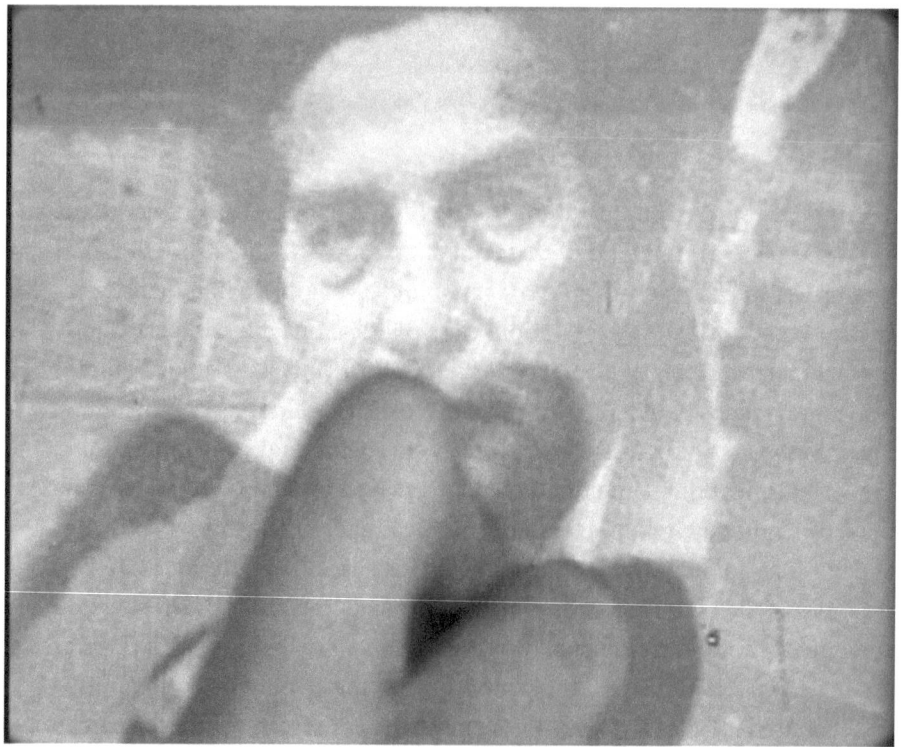

Figure 3.8. *Chuchulucos y arrumacos para burgueses* (Rafael Montero, 1974).

protagonist—in her relation with her fellow guerrilla fighter, her crushing of the upper-class man's genitals, and her planting of seeds in the monastery— García Michel tangentially but significantly engages with another avenue of Super 8 production taking place in those years, which coalesced with the Primer Festival de Cine Erótico organized precisely by Sergio García Michel, Alfredo Gurrola, and Héctor Abadie in 1974. With films by directors such as David Celestinos, Nicolás Echeverría, Miguel Ehrenberg, and Alfredo Robert, whose film *Materia nupcial* included moving images of a vagina dentata, the festival was criticized precisely due to its representation of female sexuality as a threat to be feared.[35] In this context then, the radical potentiality contained in the representation of female citizens participating in the construction of utopian nations in *Ah, verdá . . . ?* lies in what philosopher Rosi Braidotti has described as the "complex and multilayered embodied subject who has taken her distance from the institution of femininity."[36] The utopian nation that García Michel constructs rests upon these female figures whose sexuality represented on screen is not for the visual pleasure of the (male) viewer, and distanced even from the global sexual liberation movement referenced visually in the scene where the guerrilla couple have sex in the plush, carpeted interior of a van, which winks at the cult film *Barbarella* (Roger Vadim, 1968). Rather, the sexual existence of this guerrilla fighter is recognized, only to be dissolved into those forces that signify her, and with which she refuses to directly engage; her revolutionary and countercultural subjectivity is embodied in processes of becoming that ultimately will lead to the formation of an alternative community standing in for the countercultural nation that *might* be created in the Echeverría period of the 1970s.[37] The whimsical and humorous tone of the film indicates this possibility not as allegorical but as imaginative. In doing so, García Michel mobilizes the potential of the small format to generate other ways of imagining youth political activism by injecting it with a firmly gendered position that resists sexual objectification.

To conclude, after *Ah, verdá . . . ?*, much of the Super 8 production became either highly experimental and artistic, with the No Grupo collective and Silvia Gruner as the main exponents, or a product of school projects as the format began to be incorporated into the CUEC and the Centro de Capacitación Cinematográfia, with Luis Lupone as one of the main producers. In 1982, Sergio García released his first feature-length documentary, *Una larga experiencia*, which follows the trajectory of the rock band El Tri. It is in *Un toke de roc* (1988), however, when the utopic nationalism that García Michel had been developing in previous work coalesces into a feature-length rock opera musicalized with the rock bands of the moment, many of them led by female musicians. The film tells the story of four young women who form a series of communes while escaping the persecution of undercover federal agents in three acts. As they do so, they are aided in several moments by a caped superheroine whose appearance is coded as a gendered representation of the *guacarrock* aesthetics, the subversion of nationalist mythos led by the rock band Botellita de Jerez. Musicologist Guadalupe Caro Cocotle has developed how the musical milieu of Botellita, which appears in the film in various concerts, *tokines,* and communes, is better understood as an audiotopia, an imagined sonorous space that situates listeners in a specific time and space assembled from the pieces of a nationalist past, a capitalist present, and a utopic imagined future.[38] Whereas the utopic nationalisms of the 1970s were ephemeral imaginaries that dissipated in the moment of their screening, in *Un toke de roc* García Michel presents the viewer with a utopia grounded in the rock bands of the moment that continue to be heard outside the audiovisual space of the film and resignify the spaces of the city (Metro stations, public plazas, apartment buildings, 1985 earthquake spaces of solidarity).

The anonymous superheroine fuses the *charro* pants with a cannabis-printed shirt to become an embodiment of the city itself, as in the various scenes where she uses a bow and arrow similar to the statue of Diana Cazadora, repeatedly used in film as an urban reference, from Tito Davison's *La Diana cazadora* (1956) to Juan Ibáñez's *Los caifanes* (1967). In this latter example, the statue makes a central appearance in a key sequence where the female protagonist, played by pop star Julissa, "joins" the group of pachuco-inspired underdogs. By referencing this rich visual vocabulary, the superheroine becomes one more member of the collective of women who together subvert the nationalist opening of female sacrifice to found an alternative nation; the masculine isolated individuals that failed in the previous decade give way to the idea of a communal citizenship coalescing around women. Throughout the film, nationalist ideology (in the prologue), political reality (in the images of police violence and the persecution by the *per-judiciales* / federal police), and capitalist objectification (in the guise of the sexualization promoted by advertising) are resisted time and again by the collective of women.[39] The use of graffiti signals not only a growing urban counterculture

Figure 3.9. *Un toke de roc* (Sergio García Michel, 1988).

taking over the streets but also defines these utopian countercultural nations as processes of becoming; when the nun paints "el roc ha muerto, viva el roc" [rock is read, long live rock], she defines rock as ever-changing, mutating, and adapting, placing these graffiti as public conversations between multiple voices. After three of the women are kidnapped and tortured by the police forces and rescued by the superheroine, they reunite with their companion at a rock concert, and the film ends with them walking against traffic with various cars swerving to avoid them. This final image coalesces the political message that García Michel, as a main producer of Super 8 and a key figure in the maintaining of screening spaces, festivals, and projection tours, embeds within the format.

Thus, within the context of the lost decades of Mexican cinema, small-format production served as a medium where filmmakers found and developed a space of alternative cinema. Their production, extremely diverse in themes and approaches, is marked by a commitment to political action whose expressions explored a diversity of action, from collective filmmaking in the Cooperativa de Cine Marginal to the representations of female sexuality as subjects of their own personal and political existence. In this corpus, the *superocheros* (and García Michel especially) appropriated the visual culture of *mestizo* nationalism in order to subvert it by fusing it with rock and urban culture. Their creative networks, which managed to break outside the centralization of culture so prevalent in Mexican arts and film especially, anticipated the video production networks of the 1990s and later. As Jesse Lerner and Álvaro Vázquez Mantecón have signaled, their production, short-lived and forgotten by film criticism for decades, is not only of historical value but above all of cultural and filmic value, as their explorations set the basis for later cinema, video, musical, and artistic production of the century.

## Notes

1. Álvaro Vázquez Mantecón, *El cine Super 8 en México (1970–1989)* (Mexico City: UNAM, 2012), 307.

2. Referring to the presidency of Miguel Alemán (1946–1952), *alemanismo* describes the historical period of economic growth sometimes referred to as the Mexican Miracle. Through state-supported industrialization, large-scale public works (particularly the National University and highways), and subvention and protection of cinema through the writing of the Law of the Cinematographic Industry, this period promoted an idea of a Mexican economy and society independent from foreign intervention and influence. Paradoxically, this not only created a bureaucratic society that counterculture critiqued sharply but also did not impede the advancement of consumer capitalism as the decades progressed.

3. Teresa Rizzo, *Deleuze and Film. A Feminist Introduction* (New York: Continuum Books, 2012), 93.

4. It is important to signal the previous work carried out by Jesse Lerner in the *Wide Angle* special issue of 1999, which focused on the *superocheros* and historian Álvaro Vázquez Mantecón. Without the labor of these critics, this chapter could not have been written.

5. Susana Draper, *1968 Mexico: Constellations of Freedom and Democracy* (Durham: Duke University Press, 2018), 95.

6. García Michel's Foro Tlalpan was a venue where Super 8 and rock coexisted, not only in the screening of important historical documentaries like *Avándaro* that kept alive the memory of the fatidic rock festival, but also in the conjoining of live music with film projections. Vázquez Mantecón, *El cine Super 8*, 303.

7. Jesse Lerner and Rita González, *Mexperimental Cinema. 60 Years of Avant-Garde Media Arts from Mexico* (Michigan: Smart Art Press, 2015), 85, 89.

8. Rosi Braidotti, *Metamorphoses: Towards a Materialist Theory of Becoming* (Cambridge: Polity Press, 2002), 2.

9. Rizzo, *Deleuze and Film*, 57–69. The film theorist explains cinematic assemblages as open, in the sense that assemblages break with the divide between representation and an "outside" world that is being represented. In other words, film as assemblage not only in the technical understanding (sound, image, montage, editing, viewer-position) but also in terms of how from the outset film connects itself and the viewer with a multiplicity of assemblages existing outside the filmic experiences, such as the economic, political, legal, medical, cultural, etc. In this way, García Michel's interventions in the Super 8 film space are countercultural assemblages in technical terms but, more importantly, in how they mobilize characters and scenes that generate lines of flight, especially for the national viewer whose subjectivity is interpellated through the visual and audial cues of cultural nationalism.

10. José de la Colina, "El cinito ha muerto, ¡Viva el cine!" *El Heraldo de México*, Mexico, August 29, 1971, reprinted and translated in *Ism, Ism, Ism: Experimental Cinema in Latin America*, eds. Jesse Lerner and Luciano Piazza (Oakland: University of California Press, 2017), 50–55.

11. Jonathan Gunter, *Super 8: The Modest Medium* (Switzerland: UNESCO, 1976), 85.

12. Sergio García Michel, "Toward a Fourth Cinema," trans. Jesse Lerner, *Wide Angle* 21, no. 3 (1999): 169.

13. Draper, *1968 Mexico*, 124.

14. García Michel, 170. Emphasis in original.

15. García Michel, 171.

16. Lerner and González, *Mexperimental Cinema*, 83.

17. Christopher Dunn, *Contracultura. Alternative Arts and Social Transformation in Authoritarian Brazil* (Chapel Hill: University of North Carolina Press, 2016), 9.

18. A portmanteau of *hippie* and *azteca*, jipiteca quickly became and remains a popular term used to describe a specifically Mexicanized counterculture that fuses Orientalized native traditions—mainly Nahuatl—with global hippie aesthetics and ethics.

19. Vázquez Mantecón, *El cine Super 8*, 64.

20. Vázquez Mantecón, *El cine Super 8*, 87. Although the critic notes the character composed the songs, the credits mark Carrasco Zanini as composer of the music.

21. Vázquez Mantecón, *El cine Super 8*, 90.

22. Sayak Valencia and Sonia Herrera Sánchez, "Pornomiseria, violencia machista y mirada colonial en los filmes *Backyard: El traspatio* y *La mujer del animal*," *Anclajes* 24, no. 3 (2020): 9.

23. Vázquez Mantecón, *El cine Super 8*, 204.

24. Draper, *1968 Mexico*, 106.

25. The voiceover reads: "Era tierra de nadie que tenían guardada para cuando la ciudad creciera, para construir sus residencias, para venderlas. Pero nosotros no tenemos nada, nada que perder, por eso la tomamos."

26. Draper, *1968 Mexico*, 105.

27. This theme and critique of counterculture will reappear in García Michel's second short film *Aquí, allá, en todas partes* (1971), which tells the story of another countercultural couple who escape to an isolated island only to die as the US government tests nuclear bombs in the vicinity. Firmly entrenched within the counterculture of rock and roll, sexual liberation, and communal life, García Michel nevertheless is one of its strongest critics.

28. Iván Eusebio Aguirre Darancou, "Parménides García Saldaña en la escritura pública del rock en México post-1968," *Romance Notes* 16, no. 1 (2016): 107–17.

29. Lerner and González, *Mexperimental Cinema*, 85.

30. Roger Bartra, *The Cage of Melancholy* (Michigan: University of Michigan Press, 1992), 64.

31. In this, *Ah, verdá . . . ?* dialogues with Sara Gómez's *De cierta manera* (1974) in centralizing female experiences within the context of revolution and social change.

32. Vázquez Mantecón, *El cine Super 8*, 155.

33. A similar self-critique of the limits of bourgeoisie revolutionary attitudes can be seen in Montero's previous films *Enamorado fantástico de plástico* (1972), *Esperanza* (1973), and *La libertad es un hombre chiquito con ganas de darle en la madre a todo el mundo, la soledad es el mismo hombre un poco menos politizado* (1973).

34. Iván Eusebio Aguirre Darancou, "*El roc ha muerto, viva el roc*: Countercultural Heroines in Sergio García Michel's Super8mm Production (1967–1989)," in *The Routledge Companion to Gender, Sex and Pop Culture in Latin America,* ed. Frederick Luis Aldama (New York: Routledge, 2018), 187–95.

35. Vázquez Mantecón, *El cine Super 8*, 180–83.

36. Braidotti, *Metamorphoses*, 12.

37. Braidotti, *Metamorphoses*, 81.

38. Guadalupe Caro Cocotle, "Complejos o acomplejados?: Del *Guacarock de la Malinche* a *Alármalade Tos*, Botellita de Jerez y la metáfora de lo colonial," *Arizona Journal of Hispanic Cultural Studies* 16 (2012): 153. Caro Cocotle uses the term coined by Josh Kun to describe the specific counternational audiotopias that Botellita de Jerez construct in their various albums and video participation.

39. *Per-judicial* refers to a wordplay made famous by rock band Three Souls in My Mind in their song "Ratero." The *policia judicial federal* were an infamously corrupt police branch active until 2002, referred to commonly on the street as *perjudiciales* due to their violent and extortionary attitude toward the general population. Of all the police/military branches, the *judiciales* was the most feared and used in undercover/covert operations.

## Bibliography

Aguirre Darancou, Iván Eusebio. "Parménides García Saldaña en la escritura pública del rock en México post-1968." *Romance Notes* 16. no. 1 (2016): 107–17.

———. "*El roc ha muerto, viva el roc*: Countercultural Heroines in Sergio García Michel's Super 8mm Cinema." In *The Routledge Companion to Gender, Sex and Pop Culture in Latin America,* ed. Frederick Luis Aldama, 187–95. New York: Routledge, 2018.

Bartra, Roger. *The Cage of Melancholy*. Michigan: University of Michigan Press, 1992.

Braidotti, Rosi. *Metamorphoses: Towards a materialist theory of becoming*. Cambridge: Polity Press, 2002.

Caro Cocotle, Guadalupe. "Complejos o acomplejados? Del *Guacarock de la Malinche* a *Alármala de Tos*, Botellita de Jerez y la metáfora de lo colonial." *Arizona Journal of Hispanic Cultural Studies* 16 (2012): 149–60.

de la Colina, José. "El cinito ha muerto, ¡Viva el cine!" *El Heraldo de México*. Mexico, August 29, 1971, reprinted in *Ism, Ism, Ism: Experimental Cinema in Latin America*, edited by Jesse Lerner and Luciano Piazza, 50–55. Oakland: University of California Press, 2017.

Draper, Susana. *1968 Mexico: Constellations of Freedom and Democracy*. Durham: Duke University Press, 2018.

Dunn, Christopher. *Contracultura. Alternative Arts and Social Transformation in Authoritarian Brazil.* Chapel Hill: University of North Carolina Press, 2016.

García Michel, Sergio. "Entrevistas," *Un Toke de Roc*. DVD, directed by Sergio García Michel (Mexico: Filmoteca de la UNAM, 2005).

Gunter, Jonathan. *Super 8: The Modest Medium.* Switzerland: UNESCO, 1976.

Lerner, Jesse, and Rita González. *Mexperimental Cinema. 60 Years of Avant-Garde Media Arts from Mexico.* Michigan: Smart Art Press, 2015.

Rizzo, Teresa. *Deleuze and Film. A Feminist Introduction.* New York: Continuum Books, 2012.

Valencia, Sayak, and Sonia Herrera Sánchez. "Pornomiseria, violencia machista y mirada colonial en los filmes *Backyard: El traspatio* y *La mujer del animal*." *Anclajes* 24, no. 3 (2020): 7–27.

Vázquez Mantecón, Álvaro. *El cine Super 8 en México (1970–1989).* Mexico: UNAM, 2012.

# 4

## THE MEXICAN CHILI WESTERN AND CRISIS MASCULINITY

CHRISTOPHER CONWAY

The Hollywood Western has represented American masculinity in different ways throughout its history. The juvenile Western, which found its apotheosis in television programs of the 1950s and 1960s, highlighted shallow male heroes who seemed custom designed to ride through the small screen and the pages of Dell comics, a publishing company known for its sanitized storytelling and television crossovers. A different kind of masculinity, one that was complex, contradictory, and alienated, appeared in adult-themed Hollywood Westerns after World War II. One popular formula was to tell stories about outsiders who put their machismo to the service of protecting domesticity and town life. The character of Shane, from the 1953 film of the same title, or John Wayne's groundbreaking turn as a racist antihero named Ethan Edwards in John Ford's *The Searchers* (1957), are two of the most iconic examples of the paradoxical archetype of a solitary man of violence who eliminates threats to the family and "civilized" life without becoming domesticated himself.[1] In Mexican film history, this progression from formulaic family-values Westerns to grittier tales did not begin until the 1960s and did not take definitive shape until 1968, when Alberto Mariscal's *Todo por nada* was released, inaugurating the genre of the Chili Western.[2] There had been Mexiwesterns, or *caballitos*, before but nothing like *Todo por nada* and the films that followed.

Chili Westerns foreground a psychological and traumatized brand of masculinity defined by impotence, despair, and abandonment. They challenge the worn-out revolutionary and modernizing clichés of the Mexican state, reflecting a broader mood of disenchantment and powerlessness also evident in 1970s auteur films. This chapter explores three representative Chili Westerns to examine their portrayal of broken and symbolically castrated men. The first is Alberto Mariscal's *El tunco Maclovio* (1970), arguably the most ambitious and anarchic Chili Western ever made. The second is René Cardona Sr.'s *La mula de Cullen Baker* (1971), an eloquent attempt to create a psychological Western, and the third is *Las víboras cambian de piel* [*Guns and Guts*] (René Cardona Jr., 1974). These Chili Westerns emphasize the dialectic between the traumatic past of its protagonists and their neurotic present. In contrast to other popular genres of the 1970s, like *fichera* films, which toy with male impotence only to restore it, Chili Westerns are pessimistic in depicting the disintegration of masculinity and insistent in framing Mexican masculinity through psychology rather than specific and easily identifiable social or political frames.[3] As I show in the pages that follow, Chili Westerns use rape, homosociality, and Oedipal themes to present their damaged male protagonists as neurotics who cannot overcome their past and find a place in productive society. In this regard, the films dialogue with the popularity of psychoanalysis in mid-twentieth-century Mexico, as well as with a rhetoric and poetics of defeat.

## Mexican Masculinities and the Western, 1940–1968

It is a commonplace in the field of Mexican studies that masculine and feminine archetypes are foundational to the study of Mexican film. Beginning in the 1970s, the influential cultural critic Carlos Monsiváis argued that the Mexican melodramas of the 1940s taught Mexicans how to behave and how to feel in a threatening modern world.[4] His view of cinematic machismo was subtle because it acknowledged both its monolithic cultural stature and its ambiguity. Although machismo might have had some kind of authentic meaning during the Revolution, he argued, afterwards it became a compensatory, artificial, and contradictory performance of bravado.[5] One of Monsiváis's contemporaries, Jorge Ayala Blanco, pointed to the same ambiguity when he observed that the homoerotic tension between Pedro Infante and

Jorge Negrete in the classic *ranchera* comedy *Dos tipos de cuidado* [*Two Careful Fellows*] (Ismael Rodríguez, 1953) undermined their otherwise exaggerated heterosexual posturing.[6]

More recently, scholars have continued to build upon the centrality and ambiguities of celluloid masculinity. Charles Ramírez Berg argued that during Mexico's Golden Age, the cultural regime of gender was relatively binaristic and homogenous, whereas the political crisis of 1968 brought about its collapse and destabilization.[7] Robert McKee Irwin proposed a cultural history of Mexican masculinity centered on the interrogation of gendered binaries, arguing that masculinity, heterosexuality, and homosexuality were multiple, performative, and contradictory, rather than rigid categories.[8] Like Ramírez Berg, both Sergio de la Mora and Héctor Domínguez-Ruvalcaba posit the centrality of machismo to twentieth-century cultural nationalism and to the symbolic legitimacy of the Mexican state. De la Mora emphasizes contradictions in cultural representations of masculinity while Domínguez-Ruvalcaba applies the concept of "homosociety" to the interrelationship between gender, nationalism, and state power.[9] Homosociety is a hegemonic cultural construct that promotes patriarchal heroic narratives and regulates gender binaries, while linking homosexuality, homosociality, and homophobia.[10] These and other studies substantiate the monolithic standing of Mexican masculinity in cultural nationalism while also acknowledging its contradictions and instability.[11]

Masculinity in Mexican Westerns has received little or no commentary because the genre has received scant attention in critical literature.[12] Since the 1940s, Mexicans have produced film Westerns of various types. By "Westerns" I mean films that emulate Hollywood Westerns in recognizable ways and which contrast with neighboring "Mexican" genres like *comedias rancheras,* rural melodramas, or films about the Mexican Revolution. What makes a Mexican Western a Western are the shopworn commonplaces of the one-street clapboard town, short-brimmed cowboy hats, masked avengers, Winchester rifles and Colt revolvers, and saloons with swinging doors. In the 1940s, Raúl de Anda's four *Charro Negro* films popularized elements of the US Western formula, despite the specifically Mexican *charro* identity of its titular hero. This dandy on horseback, distinguished by his signature wide sombrero and lushly embroidered costume studded with silver buttons and chains, originally descended from Mexico's colonial rural aristocracy.

Figure 4.1. Still from *La venganza del Charro Negro* (1942), featuring Raúl de Anda as the titular hero.

After the Revolution, the Mexican state co-opted the icon and enshrined it as a nationalist symbol. At the same time, filmmakers made *charros* the non plus ultra of Mexican masculinity and glamour.[13] In *El peñón de las ánimas* (Miguel Zacarías, 1942), Jorge Negrete immortalized the credo of the *charro* by singing "Mi orgullo es ser charro, valiente y bragado / traer mi sombrero con plata bordado, / Que nadie me diga que soy un rajado" [My pride is in being a *charro* / brave and energetic / wearing my sombrero embroidered with silver, / may nobody say that I am a coward].[14] Raúl de Anda's *Charro Negro* series was a bit of an outlier in the canon of Negrete-style charromania because of his character's mournful and reserved nature. (He is, after all, a chaste, disguised avenger who does not sing or pursue women.) Yet, de Anda's series canonized three elements that become central to Mexican Westerns of the 1950s: the theme song, the avenger or crime-fighting motif, and the use of sidekicks for comic relief.

The most successful Western star to follow Raúl de Anda was Antonio Aguilar, who starred in twelve *Mauricio Rosales* and *El Norteño* films between 1955 and 1964. In these films, Aguilar is a genial, clean-cut government agent who dresses in black, wears a short-brimmed cowboy hat, sings songs, and bests rivals in anodyne fist fights. Sometimes, because he occasionally goes undercover as a *charro*, his films blend Hollywood and Mexican archetypes. Aguilar's Westerns were a product of their time and politics, specifically the administrations of Miguel Alemán and his successors (1946–1968), who steered the revolutionary state rightward after the nationalist populism of President Lázaro Cárdenas (1934–1940). Very much in alignment with the state-run political culture of the time, Aguilar's Westerns enshrined "law and order" and political centrism against rural underdevelopment. As I have written elsewhere, his missions were always about restoring order, combating *caciquismo*, and defending the state's right to wield violence in the name of peace and progress.[15] Aguilar's masculine persona is controlled, cheerful, and largely asexual: he's a walking, breathing, wholesome cartoon hero. He represents paternalistic power and is ready made for wide-eyed children to identify with and accept. His only discernible joys are his love of family, his devotion to la Virgen de Guadalupe, and his friendship with his older sidekick, Emeterio Berlanga (Agustín Isunza), with whom he shares a dorm in Mexico City, as well as vacation time.

The Aguilar formula, which echoed across other series such as *El Látigo Negro* and *El Justiciero Vengador,* began to break down in the 1960s.[16] Toothless, matinee Westerns gave way to a transitional formula that distanced itself from masked avengers and statist, law-and-order narratives. Rodolfo de Anda's *El solitario* (Arturo Martínez, 1964) and its sequel *Duelo en el desierto* (Arturo Martínez, 1964) sparkled with moments of adult intensity and rage. (Rodolfo de Anda was Raúl de Anda's son and began his film career with two sequels to the *Charro Negro* series in which he played the hero's son.) Although films like *El solitario* might seem tame in comparison to US Westerns, they detached their likeable hero from a state-sponsored role and cast him as a mournful loner. In the arena of prestige or mainstream filmmaking, the maturation of the Mexican Western flowered in Ismael Rodríguez's critically acclaimed *Los hermanos del Hierro* [*My Son, the Hero*] (1960) starring Columba Domínguez, Antonio Aguilar, and Julio Alemán. The film retells both *The Gunfighter* (Henry King, 1950) and *Shane* (George Stevens, 1953), and foreshadows Chili

Figure 4.2. Still from *El rayo justiciero* (1955), Antonio Aguilar's first outing as the titular cowboy avenger. In this scene El rayo rebuffs the advances of a villainess, played by Elda Peralta.

Westerns because of its fatalistic pessimism and psychological bent.[17] Another prestige adult Western was Arturo Ripstein's *Tiempo de morir* [*Time to Die*] (1966), which was based on a screenplay by Gabriel García Márquez and Carlos Fuentes. Like Rodríguez's Western, Ripstein's was a classical tragedy about revenge and the inescapability of fate and death.

Inspired by the example of grittier Hollywood Westerns of the 1950s, as well as by the example of Rodríguez and Ripstein, a director named Alberto Mariscal began to push the boundaries of the family-values Western formula by remixing *The Gunfighter* in *Pistoleros de la frontera* (1967) and *Shane* in *El Silencioso* (1967). In *El Silencioso,* Mariscal opens with blood swirling around a dead man's head in a mountain stream. Later, he leeringly plunges his camera into his female protagonist's cleavage. Mariscal's breakthrough came in 1968 with his revenger *Todo por nada*, which starred Mario and Fernando

Figure 4.3. Title panel from *El solitario* (1965), which helped to recast the Mexican Western along grittier lines before the emergence of Chili Westerns.

Almada, who in the film play brothers named Mario and Fernando. After a band of gunfighters brutally massacres their family, the brothers embark on a mission to kill the murderers at any cost, evoking John Ford's *The Searchers* (1956). Influenced by the "dirty" aesthetic of Spaghetti Westerns, *Todo por nada* is arguably the first Chili Western.[18]

The Chili Western emerged at a key moment in the political and cultural history of Mexico. On October 2, 1968, the Mexican state under the leadership of President Gustavo Díaz Ordaz massacred hundreds in the Plaza de las Tres Culturas, traumatizing the body politic and wounding the legitimacy of the ruling PRI party. Díaz Ordaz's successor, Luis Echeverría (1970–1976), reoriented state discourse and foreign policy leftward while continuing to wield state violence against protestors and rivals. He installed his brother, Rodolfo, as director of the Banco Cinematográfico, which funneled state monies into the film industry. The bank's new director formed state-sponsored production companies to support adventurous auteur filmmaking (the so-called *Nuevo Cine*) while private-sector filmmaking languished.[19] It was in this sexennium and under this system that Chili Westerns had their fleeting "Golden Age," especially thanks to the films of Alberto Mariscal. In 1976, the incoming administration of José López Portillo moved to privatize film financing and triggered a boom in low-budget Mexploitation-genre films that made the Chili Western recede. Spaghetti Westerns had also begun to wane in popularity around the world, and Hollywood Westerns were practically dead.[20] Chili Western stars, like the Almada brothers and Rodolfo de Anda, appeared in fewer Westerns and found a new home in crime and narco capers. The age of the Chili Western had passed.

## The Psychology of Chili Westerns: Three Case Studies

Scholars like Charles Ramírez Berg and Sergio de la Mora have amply demonstrated that post-1968 films parodied and undermined the monumentalist icons of machismo and heterosexuality. The genre of the Chili Western did the same but its treatment of masculinity in crisis was grimmer than in other "trashy" genres, like *fichera* films. Chili Westerns used trauma to explain the paralysis or castration of men and sank their unsympathetic protagonists into the psychological quicksand of confusion, shame, and rage. Psychoanalysis, in particular, can provide us with concepts that illustrate the construction and deconstruction of masculinity in these self-consciously "psychological" films. Psychoanalysis has been vital to foundational arguments in feminism, cultural studies, and film studies by Gayle Rubin, Eve Kosofsky Sedgwick, and Laura Mulvey.[21] In their studies, Freud is not a boundary nor a sacred totem but a springboard and an interlocutor to challenge and revise. Psychoanalysis is also helpful to our inquiry because of its prestige and ubiquity in the middle of the twentieth century, when psychologists, writers, and filmmakers commonly infused Freudian topics into their work. In the case of Mexico, psychoanalysis became a prominent cultural force in the 1950s during the so-called "Milagro Mexicano" [Mexican Miracle], a period of rapid industrialization and modernization that promoted the growth and social capital of the urban middle class. In Carlos Monsiváis's wry formulation, the Mexican bourgeoisie of the 1950s delighted in the acquisition of the unconscious as a commodity to validate its maturity and social aspirations.[22] Octavio Paz's seminal psycho-mythological study of Mexican identity, *El laberinto de la soledad* [*The Labyrinth of Solitude*] (1950), is the most notable and influential Mexican book to embrace Freudian themes. Inspired by Freud's *Moses and Monotheism* (1930), Paz wove the topics of trauma, repression, and the unconscious into a fatalistic theory of the Mexican mind and helped to propagate and preserve traces of psychoanalysis among the intelligentsia and in cultural conversation.[23] Other books, such as *El mexicano: su dinámica psicosocial* by Francisco González Pineda, and Ismael Rodríguez's Western film *Los hermanos del Hierro* foreground the centrality of psychoanalytic questions to Mexican national identity.[24] Rodríguez's Western, which Alberto Mariscal remade in 1971 as *El sabor de la venganza* [*Eye for an Eye*],[25] sought to explain Mexico's culture of violence in terms of childhood trauma, neurosis, parricide, and the trope of the fallen woman. These formulations and the film's fatalistic point of view aligns it loosely with Paz's landmark essay and underlines the stylistic ease with which psychology could be joined with some of the commonplace themes of the Western, such as revenge, solitude, and empty landscapes. The ubiquity of these kinds of formulas in twentieth-century Mexican intellectual history was so great that Roger Bartra sarcastically called Mexico "un paraíso de las expediciones psicoanalíticas" [a paradise for psychoanalytic expeditions], and Carlos Monsiváis attributed the cultural construction of Mexican machismo to the "Freudianization" of Mexican culture at midcentury.[26]

Although most of Alberto Mariscal's Chili Westerns could function as paradigms for a short introduction to the genre, *El tunco Maclovio* (1970) is probably the best one to cite because of its baroque texture and thematic density. In the film, a fearsome female landowner named Laura Montaño summons a legendary one-handed killer, Tunco Maclovio (Julio Alemán), to come to town to kill a young gunfighter who is courting her daughter, Sara (Barbara Angely). Like the archetypal character of Doña Bárbara, Laura Montaño is intent on dominating all the men around her, and on destroying the man who, through her daughter, might threaten her property and wealth. The one-handed gunfighter rides into town after Montaño has left on business and, having killed Sara's boyfriend in a chance encounter, comes into her orbit and falls in love with her. Tunco also meets a young, orphaned boy named Marcelo (Julián Bravo) and starts to believe that he can leave behind the gunfighter life and

Figure 4.4. Julio Alemán in the title role of *El tunco Maclovio* (1970). His costuming and persona are reminiscent of the Man With No Name immortalized by Clint Eastwood in Sergio Leone Spaghetti Westerns.

become a rancher with Sara and Marcelo. When Tunco and the boy show up at her hacienda, Sara has her gunfighters ambush and kill him. Before this denouement, the film fills in Tunco's background and introduces a mysterious antagonist named Juan Mariscal (Mario Almada). As a boy, Tunco accidentally shot his best friend Martín Mariscal, a crime for which he atones by axing off his right hand and fleeing society. The dead boy's father, Juan Mariscal, has been shadowing Tunco, waiting for the right time to have his revenge. When Tunco shows up at the Montaño hacienda at the end of the film, Mariscal interrupts them, but before he can take Tunco's life, Sara's men kill the gunfighter. The film closes with Juan Mariscal and Marcelo riding out of town at nightfall as Laura Montaño returns to town with her men.

Emilio García Riera considers *El tunco Maclovio* to be a ridiculous work patched together from echoes of other films.[27] In contrast, Jorge Ayala Blanco admires its absurdist symbolism, irrationalism, and iconoclastic destruction of the commonplaces of the Western. He writes "ya era tiempo de que a algún cineasta nacional se le ocurriera, y lo dejaran, filmar en fiebre, aunque estuviera en múltiples ocasiones en el abismo del ridículo o al borde de jodorowskysmo" [it's about time that some national filmmaker decided to, or was allowed to, film in the heat of the moment, even though on multiple occasions in the abyss of ridiculousness or on the border of Jodorowsky-ism].[28] The comparison to Alejandro Jodorowsky, whose *Fando y Lis* [*Fando and Lis*] (1968) and *El Topo* (1969), are deliberately and intensely surreal and experimental, is useful here. Jodorowsky envelops us in carefully crafted and beautifully finished absurdist and surrealist narratives while Mariscal's disordered film makes it hard for us to determine if we are watching art or recycled schlock. *El tunco Maclovio* has a messy aesthetic, but it's also exhilarating and original because of its excess.

The film showcases symbolism about trauma and masculinity that resists conventional binaries and simplistic definitions. For one thing, Tunco is an Oedipal figure because he amputates his own hand to atone for the unintentional killing of Martín. In "The Uncanny," Freud underlined that the terrible fear of blindness or injury to the eye is linked to the male's fear of castration.[29] Tunco's symbolic castration and self-exile, however, is not linked to incestuous desire but rather to remorse for killing his friend. Moreover, his castration is paradoxical because his missing hand is replaced with a stump that acquires the metonymic or symbolic power of a legendary nickname: "Tunco" (which means one-handed). Since Tunco is a well-known killer, the stump functions as both a phallic substitute for his hand as well as a reminder of its absence. In other words, Tunco's persona as a fearsome gunfighter is phallic (masculine power) while also being rooted in the loss of his hand (lack or castration). Sean Homer's explanation of how Lacan understood the phallus helps us understand this paradox. Lacan built his definition of the phallus on Freud's theory of castration anxiety, in which the child must wrestle with the anatomical differences between Mother and Father, with his desire for the Mother, and his fear of the Father. Homer writes: "Castration involves not just an anxiety about losing one's penis but simultaneously the recognition of lack or absence. The idea of the penis, therefore, becomes metonymically linked to the recognition of lack. It is in this sense that Lacan argues that the phallus is not simply the penis; it is the penis plus the recognition of absence or lack."[30]

The film's vengeful father (Juan Mariscal) is a melancholy and indecisive figure who does not punish, whereas Laura and Sara are angry figures of authority that threaten, subjugate, and destroy men. What is certain is that when we first meet Tunco he's a threatening and hardened killer. As the film progresses and he becomes humanized through the revelation of his sadness and foolish optimism, our perception changes and we realize he's a wounded male. Before he is shot, he tells Sara that she was his first, disclosing a lifetime of sexual impotence or denial. Such details underline Tunco's ambiguity: he's a threatening macho and a lonely virgin, a barren soul and a childlike dreamer, a heartless gunfighter and a prospective farmer. These paradoxes encapsulate an unstable version of masculinity riven with trauma and confusion that the film does not ultimately resolve. Is it redemptive for Tunco to have fleetingly rediscovered his lost humanity before being killed? Or does the realization, in that final instant of life, that Sara has murdered him and shattered his newborn hope, simply reinforce defeat and existential solitude?

Like *El tunco Maclovio* and Mariscal's other Westerns, René Cardona Sr.'s *La mula de Cullen Baker* has high production values and high-minded psychological pretensions. It also returns to the theme of the phallus and castration. Cardona's film opens when eight-year-old Cullen is crossing some desert dunes on a donkey with his father, who is on foot. A sniper fires at father and son, killing the boy's ride. Another gunshot wounds Cullen's father, who implores his son to leave him behind and flee. As the fleeing boy crests a dune, we see riders coming over the horizon toward the fallen father. Then the film abruptly cuts to the narrative present, with a close-up of a fist smashing into Cullen's face, sending the young man sprawling out of a saloon onto a dusty street. In the savage fight, Cullen (Rodolfo de Anda) bests his rival by pinning the man's wrist to a post with a bowie knife and pummeling his face and stomach until his foe begins to vomit blood and beg for mercy. The frenzied beating only stops when a sheriff's deputy knocks Cullen unconscious. Cardona now quickly sketches other scenes of violence to establish his out-of-control and murderous protagonist: Cullen confronts an unarmed man in a barn and murders him by shooting him with a shotgun in each leg at point-blank range, and later, while fleeing a posse, Cullen kills and robs a boatman. Most memorably, Cardona depicts Cullen's savagery when the young man dispatches two killers who have tortured and murdered a band of Indians. The suspicious men train their rifles on Cullen when he approaches them on foot and asks them for food and coffee. The men agree to the request

Figure 4.5. Still from *La mula de Cullen Baker* (1971) in which the titular hero holds a strip of meat in his mouth in a shootout when he kills two men.

in exchange for his mule and gear, to which Cullen meekly assents. He tears off a chunk of meat from a spit that's over the fire pit, puts it in his mouth, and quickly knifes one of his two antagonists, sweeping his victim's rifle into his arms and shooting down the other. During this burst of lethal violence, a rag of thick meat hangs from Cullen's mouth like a bloated, oversized tongue, if not a bloodied, male member.

The core of the film's plot is Cullen's lustful desire to possess Colt Dragoon revolvers that officers from the US cavalry are carrying on the frontier. He ambushes two officers one night and steals their guns, after which he starts robbing banks and saloons, killing anyone who gets in his way. In the film's third act, Cullen tries to reinvent and camouflage himself as the foppishly dressed "Henry Foster." He befriends a bank teller named Jane Patterson (Ana Elena Noreña Grass, known as "Anel") and her fiancé Bill Miller, the local schoolteacher. When Cullen in the guise of Foster indignantly buys out the mortgage of a local widow to save her ranch from repossession, Jane befriends the outsider and soon asks him to walk her down the aisle, in the place of her father, at her wedding with Bill. Cullen, who has fallen in love with Jane, hires an assassin named Collum to murder Bill, without knowing that the would-be killer is a government agent who is hunting him. In the ambush, Collum fires at Cullen rather than at Bill, wounding and knocking him down. As Collum approaches, Cullen improbably comes alive and shoots him dead before passing out. When the authorities discover Cullen's true identity, the wounded outlaw shoots his way out of town with Jane as a hostage. A pursuit and more shoot-outs ensue until Bill kills his rival and frees Jane.

The film is packed with allusions to failed masculinity, neuroticism, and rage, beginning with the title: *La mula de Cullen Baker*. The film alludes to the title in a scene in which the camera looks over a man's shoulder at Baker's wanted poster, which says that he always rides a mule. From the outset then, the protagonist is framed within the theme of sterility, as a reproductive end of the line. As Cullen lies wounded in a hotel after Collum's ambush, with Jane sitting by his side, he tells her a cryptic story about the outlaw Cullen Baker. When the killer was a boy, he explains, some men killed his father and then tortured him. In previous scenes of peril, the film cuts away from Cullen's face to show his father's killers cresting over a sand dune toward him, alluding to an unspecified but impending traumatic event. Is it literally a rape or just a terrible beating that functions as an analogous violation? Regardless, the murder of Cullen's father and the boy's capture by his killers is a traumatic brutalization of a child. He grows up to be bestial in his amorality and ease with killing. His childlike wonder at the Colt revolvers of the upright, nononsense cavalry officers, underlines the symbolic charge of these weapons as both a fetish and a status symbol. The guns take Cullen from being a lethal nobody to a legendary outlaw and ultimately to the persona of Henry Foster, a rich man about town. In short, the revolvers compensate for Cullen's lack.

In the psychoanalytic tradition, fetishism is a function of a male child's traumatic realization that his mother does not have a penis. To disavow this threatening realization, he substitutes the missing organ with another body part or object, assigning to it the value of the penis. Freud writes that for the male child the substitute object, or fetish, "is usually something that he in fact saw at the moment at which he saw the female genitals" and that it functions to "destroy the evidence for the possibility of castration, so that fear of castration can be avoided."³¹ As a model for thinking about Cullen's trauma, and his subsequent lust for the Colt Dragoon revolvers, the concept of fetishism can clarify the dialectic between loss and compensation. Cullen's nebulous origin story is haunted by the absence of a mother figure, the murder of his father, and his brutalization by men with guns. Although his inaugural trauma is not the literal sighting of woman's genitals, the horror and ramifications of his trauma resonate with that disquieting perception because the men with guns symbolically castrate him. They slay Cullen's father and either rape or violently beat him, instilling in him a sense of the precariousness of his own masculinity. The guns of his attackers are the witness, instrument, and symbol of his violation. In this context, Cullen's desire for a weapon with a name (*dragón*) that evokes a mythical, *reptilian* monster, makes phallic, compensatory sense. Possessing the guns not only allows him to become rich through killing, but to take on a more self-confident persona. The guns restore something that was taken from him.

The film returns to hints of rape and motifs of trauma, neurosis, and castration in various scenes. When a sheriff wearing a pink scarf aims a shotgun at Cullen, the outlaw momentarily flashes back to the sight of his father's killers coming over a dune to get him. The limp scarf of the sheriff drapes over the stock of the shotgun, evoking an image of phallic penetration that Cardona links directly to a traumatic flashback. Cullen's killing of two men as a thick tear of flesh hangs from his mouth emphasizes the link between lethal contests between men and phallic symbolism and status. As Robert McKee Irwin writes: "Contests of wit, authority, or brute force produce symbolic relations of sexual penetration, in which the loser cracks, gets fucked, and is feminized by the winner, who, in this way, enhances his masculinity."³² In this particular scene, the dialectic between demure submission and the fury with which Cullen suddenly becomes a destroyer of men, symbolically reenacts a violent interruption of fellatio. Put another way, Cullen meekly agrees to submit to the men who point guns at him, promises to give them everything they want, and goes through the motions of surrender and submission, but at the very same moment that he tears off a strip of meat from over the fire to put into his mouth, he turns on the men and destroys them. Cullen's first on-screen murder is also symbolically linked to the motif of castration. He shoots an unarmed man in both legs because he wants to permanently cripple him ("te quiero dejar lisiado") [I want to cripple you].

The introduction of Jane and Bill in the film's second half creates a symbolic family romance, with Jane playing the role of the desired Mother, while Bill plays the role of Father and rival. Cullen fixates on Jane and competes with Bill to possess her, but the schoolteacher, who embodies the structures of parental authority and dominance over children, finally tames the rebellious man-child by killing him. Cullen's end, in which he stands legs apart and takes two gunshots—one to each side of his torso—with a slow, theatrical kind of composure, evokes the iconography of Saint Sebastian looking upward at his maker with arrows sticking out of his sides. The Oedipal triangle on which the story ends is skewed because the boy is supposed to yield to the Law of the Father and ally himself with Him. But Cullen's childhood trauma has not allowed him to know the Law of the Father. He's lived his short life trying to recapture the power that his father's killers tore from him. Instead, the tragically neurotic Cullen is killed by a father substitute who is intent on wresting Cullen's mother substitute from him.

*Las víboras cambian de piel*, directed by René Cardona Jr., the son of the director of *La mula de Cullen Baker*, is arguably the best-known Chili Western among non-Mexican aficionados of Spaghetti Westerns. In the US, it circulates on DVD under the title *Guns and Guts*, and its claim to fame is a strip poker scene and a climactic shoot-out reminiscent of the ending of Sam Peckinpah's *The Wild Bunch* (1969), in which the titular Anglo-American antiheroes use a machine gun to kill Mexican *federales* en masse. In Mexico City, *Las víboras cambian de piel* was a sensation, playing for fifteen weeks in Cine Variedades; by comparison, *La mula de Cullen Baker* played for only two weeks.[33] The film is largely exempt from the tragic and psychological overtones of the two preceding films we have seen, until one of the final scenes when the last of the three protagonists dies with a gunshot to the forehead.

The plot of *Las víboras cambian de piel* is so elementary and hackneyed that we can summarize it minimally. Three men band together to assassinate the sheriff of Santa Fe, a corrupt killer who resides in an old hacienda with a small army of armed henchmen. The motives of the would-be killers vary. One of them (Rogelio Guerra) is a fugitive who wants to kill the sheriff because he betrayed and landed him in jail. Another (Pedro Armendáriz Jr.) is the sheriff's brother and the cuckolded husband of the sheriff's mistress. The third avenger (Jorge Rivero) is a professional gunfighter and gigolo, whose only motive is money and perhaps, to some degree, the companionship he feels with the other two men. In the end, after various twists and turns, the three men assault the hacienda with guns and machine guns firing. The cuckolded husband kills the sheriff and his malevolent-looking mistress, and the other two massacre many of the sheriff's men. The last survivor of the gunfight is the gigolo, who jumps over a wall to flee before being shot in the forehead by one of the sheriff's henchmen.

At one point, the sheriff holds the men captive and gloats over defeating them. It is at this point that we hear about a terrible form of "torture" to be inflicted on the cuckolded husband, one that cannot be named (or seen) on screen. The sheriff condemns his brother to this punishment and when his henchmen later release the brother in a forest, one of his captors tells him to not say anything about what was done to him. Nothing else in the film or in the victim's demeanor clarifies the meaning and repercussions of this unnamed act of torture, but it's significant because it casts some light on the unnamed trauma that Cullen survives in *La mula de Cullen Baker*. Yet, in contrast to the films discussed above, *Las víboras cambian de piel* dispenses almost entirely with the pretense of psychology, trauma, flashbacks, and symbolism. It is a well-oiled formula flick that undresses women's bodies and delights in the spectacle of men convulsing as they're drilled with bullets. That said, the film does develop, to some degree, the motif of homosocial bonding, which speaks to the deconstruction of heteronormative narratives about men.

Homosociality relates to same-sex relationships and makes itself manifest in same-sex institutions or spaces (the locker room, a military barracks, etc.) and storytelling conventions (buddy heroism, police or superhero partnerships, etc.). Homosociality might appear to turn away from heterosexual relationships but on a deeper level, it is a form of desire that is structurally linked to heterosexuality and its prohibitions. In her landmark study *Between Men: English Literature and Male Homosocial Desire*, Eve Sedgwick argued that homosexuality and homosociality are distinct from each other while also being conceptually linked. "To draw the 'homosocial' back into the orbit of 'desire,'" she writes, "is to hypothesize the potential unbrokenness of a continuum between homosocial and homosexual—a continuum whose visibility, for men, in our society, is radically disrupted."[34] Homosocial relationships are also defined through the negotiation of heterosexual desire rather than its negation. In particular, Sedgwick shows how literary representations of male desire are primarily directed toward male bonding and negotiation and only nominally about women or heterosexual desire, which function as pretexts and catalysts for attachments between men. In this, Sedgwick built on the work of Gayle Rubin, who linked culture, the interaction between kinship groups, and the very definition of gender to how men exchange women.[35]

*Las víboras cambian de piel* commences with ridiculously drawn-out fist fights between the fugitive avenger and three separate men he's pushing around to get information about his target, the sheriff. The fights are lumbering, slow and ritualistic, and punctuated by heavy breathing, as if they were hard work or sensual rather than the enactment of damaging or dangerous aggression. The apotheosis of the fist fighting is when the fugitive and the gigolo tangle with each other after meeting for the first time in a saloon. The fight comes about because the gigolo boisterously claims to own all the women in the establishment, which alienates the cocky fugitive who picks a fight with him. When, after wrecking the saloon with their blows and thrown chairs, the two panting and bruised men eventually realize that they are evenly matched, they declare a truce and drink to seal their newborn friendship. The gigolo now agrees to lend the fugitive one of his prostitutes, who accompanies the battered man to his room, where she does a striptease for him. By the time she has stripped off her clothes, her exhausted would-be partner has fallen asleep with a smile on his face. He has had his tiring fun already. In other words, the film's insistence on highlighting panting men falling over each other as they throw slow-motion punches overshadows heterosexual desire, even as the male gaze tries to capitalize on disrobing women's bodies. Whatever heterosexual desire those bodies might instill in the film's protagonists is broken down by the surprisingly intimate yet clumsy (and even sensual) ballet of the fist fight. Another example of homosociality can be found in one of the film's most famous scenes, in which the gigolo plays strip poker with some prostitutes. After the women lose some hands and begin to strip, the gigolo falters and follows suit. Just as he sheepishly drops his pants, the fugitive bursts in and interrupts him from what would have certainly become an orgy. Male bonding and homosociality divert the men from fully embracing their pursuit of women.

Figure 4.6. The gigolo (Jorge Rivero) and the fugitive (Rogelio Guerra) reconcile after an exhausting fight scene in *Las víboras cambian de piel* (1974).

The film diminishes or rejects heterosexual desire in other ways as well. The fugitive and the cuckolded husband exhibit little to no heterosexual libido throughout the film. The gigolo operates as an exaggerated embodiment of that desire, although the film ultimately portrays him as a tragic figure who, like the titular protagonist of *El tunco Maclovio*, is struck down just as he begins to envision a more hopeful and procreative way of living. At the outset at least, the gigolo's entire existence revolves around being with "his girls" without forming any lasting attachments to them. The enthusiasm he exhibits for this way of life is explained by the fact that his mother was a prostitute and he was raised in a brothel. In the film's final act, he reunites with an older, more experienced prostitute and falls under her spell. The gigolo becomes the titular snake that sheds its old skin to become something different. The two lovers conspire to elope together after his last job, which he does not survive. The film cuts from his shocked expression at being shot in the head to the forlorn woman in her traveling clothes waiting for him at their rendezvous point in town. The one possibility of meaningful heterosexual union in the film is canceled. The protagonists have succeeded in their mission, but they have killed themselves in the process. The brotherhood of fist fighting and killing is strong, while marriage, motherhood, and family bonds are ruined.

## Conclusion: The Enigma of the Chili Western

The men in extremis who appear in Chili Westerns challenge the definition of masculinity that we glimpse in so many Golden Age Mexican films, as well as in Mexican Westerns of the 1950s and 1960s. I'm referring to men who wield violence to protect the family, or repair injury to it, while also promoting an idealized definition of masculinity. Chili Westerns, in contrast, paint a darker picture, one that strips masculinity of its referential power and meaning. Although their protagonists go on blood-soaked journeys to punish villains or do right, their traumatized psyches make it impossible for them to achieve release or relief. They cannot recover the women they once loved, nor learn how to love again. They have no family structure to validate their heroics or sacrifice and to help define their social role. They might get their revenge, but they remain on the outside of civilization and its familial and social bonds. Some of this fatalism is a function of the influence of Spaghetti Westerns on Mexican directors. As Álvaro Enrigue writes in his Western novel *Ahora me rindo y eso es todo* (2018), Spaghetti Westerns invert the optimistic contours of the genre to emphasize defeat: "Una película de vaqueros italiana es un canto al fracaso de cualquier esfuerzo civilizatorio, y Sergio Leone un existencialista" [An Italian cowboy movie is a song in homage to the failure of any civilizing effort, and Sergio Leone is an existencialist].[36] But Chili Westerns differ from Spaghetti Westerns because of the intensity of their representation of psychology and failure. In this regard, Chili Westerns belong to a Mexican narrative tradition known as the Cult of Defeat, which, as Brian Price shows, can function variously "to revise history, to explain failed utopian ideals, to undermine opposing political ideologies, to promote platforms of social change, to consecrate messianic missions with martyrdom, or to express pessimism about the future."[37]

In light of the grimness of Chili Westerns, it's fair to ask what kind of pleasure and lessons Mexican audiences might have derived from them. One attraction was that Chili Westerns provided audiences with Spaghetti-style Westerns while also foregrounding Mexican stars. Performers like Antonio Aguilar, Julio Alemán, and the Almada brothers inflected the Chili Western with an attractive dose of Mexicanness and familiarity, even when the films were not set in Mexico. Furthermore, since Chili Westerns are also an example of exploitation culture, their appeal was also linked to graphic depictions of violence and sexuality. The pro forma murder of innocents, the leering depictions of rape, a primal delight in violent revenge, and the undressing of women's bodies define the genre as a stereotypically "masculine" entertainment. In a scene from *El sabor de la venganza*, to cite one example, Alberto Mariscal depicts the protagonist raping his girlfriend. As he tears off her clothes, Mariscal briefly trains his camera on the man's eyes, with a camera-like shutter sound effect that conflates the filming and viewing of the scene with the viewpoint of the rapist. The shock value alone of such scenes made Chili Westerns appealing to some viewers.

Audience identification can also be political and historical. Although reading national allegories into Chili Westerns is difficult because of their formulaic and derivative construction, it is important to acknowledge that a genre about traumatized men coincided with the period of profound national trauma that followed the Tlatelolco Massacre of 1968. In a landscape of political corruption and broken institutions, in which crimes against humanity are committed with impunity, and the rhetoric of progress does not track with reality, the heroic narratives of the past fall away to be replaced by cynicism and the horror of loss.[38] Chili Westerns chronicle the inner lives of men whose heroism and violence cannot reconstruct the wholeness of a violated home and family unit. In *Todo por nada,* for instance, the villains take over a town and gloat about using the discourse of progress to justify their crimes and self-enrichment. In *Los marcados* (Alberto Mariscal, 1971), the good guy succeeds in killing the "degenerate" outlaws, but the grief and loneliness that blankets him and his world stays the same. What is broken cannot be put back together. Chili Westerns do not pose a solution, or an escape, but in their own way they reinforce the sanctity of the home through the depiction of its destruction or the psychological aftermath of its loss.

Understanding the messages and appeal of Chili Westerns is challenging because of their paradoxes. For example, the psychological arguments of these films are often told in shorthand and are outweighed by rote generic and formulaic storytelling devices. Secondly, the psychological pretensions of the genre might grow out of the same Freudian mood that inspired psychopathological studies of Mexican identity like Octavio Paz's *El laberinto de la soledad,* but the genre does not code its imaginary world in a specifically Mexican or historical key. The traumatized male heroes of the Chili Westerns are outcasts, exiles, or traumatized neurotics, but they are not represented as prototypically Mexican. As characters, they move in a fictional world that is often North American, or in a landscape that might be nominally Mexican, but which does not evoke Mexican imagery or symbols. Another paradox is that Chili Westerns, while specifically "Mexican" films, are also transnational because many of them recycled, adapted, or riffed on Italian and US films and capitalized on the same exhibition circuits and marketing tropes as Spaghetti Westerns.

Like other understudied genres of Mexican film, Chili Westerns are something of an enigma. At first glance, they seem like derivative "trash." But their ubiquity in Mexican film history, coupled with a persistent popularity both then and now, demands that we take a second look to ask what they are really about and how they engage with the broader arc of Mexican cultural and film history. As the preceding pages have shown, the traumatized male psyche is a vital cornerstone for linking the genre to well-established critical conversations about gender in Mexican culture and film. Let's bring the serape-covered, scowling gunfighter in from the desert and into dialogue with other characters and trends, like singing *charros*, wrestling superheroes, menacing vampires, tragic revolutionaries, and fast-talking comedians.

## Notes

1. Thomas Shatz, *Hollywood Genres: Formulas, Filmmaking, and the Studio System* (New York: Random House, 1981), 57.

2. Christopher Conway, *Heroes of the Borderlands: The Western in Mexican Film, Comics, and Music* (Albuquerque: University of New Mexico Press, 2019), 119–21. As is common with many Chili Westerns, corroborating the correct English-language release title is difficult. According to IMDB, the UK release for *Todo por Nada* was *Bullet for a Dead Man,* but no American release title is listed. According to the Spaghetti Western Database, the American release title was *Everything in Vain,* whereas Bowker's *Complete Video Directory* uses *All for Nothing* (2584).

3. For discussion of how *fichera* films regulate gender codes, see Sergio de la Mora, *Cinemachismo: Masculinities and Sexuality in Mexican Film* (Austin: University of Texas Press, 2009), 114.

4. Carlos Monsiváis, *Amor perdido* (Mexico City: Ediciones Era, 1977), 76; Carlos Monsiváis, "Notas sobre la cultura mexicana en el siglo XX," *Historia general de México* vol. 2, ed. Daniel Cosío Villegas (Mexico City: El Colegio de México, 1976): 1375–548.

5. Monsiváis, *Amor perdido,* 31; Monsiváis, "Notas," 1516.

6. Jorge Ayala Blanco, *La aventura del cine mexicano: en la época de oro y después* (Mexico City: Editorial Grijalbo, 1993), 67.

7. Charles Ramírez Berg, *Cinema of Solitude: A Critical Study of Mexican Film, 1967–1983* (Austin: University of Texas Press, 1992), 44–45.

8. Robert McKee Irwin, *Mexican Masculinities* (Minneapolis: University of Minnesota Press, 2003), 2–3, 130.

9. de la Mora, *Cinemachismo,* 4–5, 88–89; Héctor Domínguez-Ruvalcaba, *Modernity and the Nation in Mexican Representations of Masculinity: From Sensuality to Bloodshed* (New York: Palgrave Macmillan, 2007), 77.

10. Domínguez-Ruvalcaba, *Modernity,* 4–5, 67–68.

11. Other studies include Andrea Noble, *Mexican National Cinema* (London & New York: Routledge, 2005.); Michael Schuessler, "Vestidas, Locas, Mayates and Machos: History and Homosexuality in Mexican Cinema," *Chasqui* 34, no. 2 (2005): 132–44; and Claudia Elizabeth Puente Vázquez, "Masculinidad y violencia en el Nuevo Cine Mexicano. Las películas de Luis Estrada," *La Palabra* 28 (2016): 59–72.

12. Besides essays on a few landmark films (*Los hermanos del Hierro, Tiempo de morir*) there are brief references to the genre of Mexican Westerns in Monsiváis, "Notas," 1529; Rafael Aviña, *Una mirada insólita: temas y géneros del cine mexicano* (Mexico City: Océano, 2004), 159–62; Norma Iglesias Prieto, *Entre yerba, polvo, y plomo: lo fronterizo visto por el cine mexicano* (Tijuana: Colegio de la Frontera Norte, 1991), 37–38; and the essays in Bernd Hausberger and Raffaele Moro, *La revolución mexicana en el cine: Un acercamiento a partir de la mirada ítaloeuropea* (Mexico City: El Colegio de México, 2013). My book, *Heroes of the Borderlands: The Western in Mexican Film, Comics, and Music* (Albuquerque: University of New Mexico Press, 2019), provides a lengthier overview of Mexican film Westerns.

13. Christopher Conway, "Charros: A Critical Introduction," in *Modern Mexican Culture: Critical Foundations,* ed. Stuart A. Day (Tucson: University of Arizona Press, 2017), 68–70.

14. The word rajado comes from "rajarse," a gendered term relating to splitting, cracking, or opening oneself, to not be manly and phallic. In *The Labyrinth of Solitude,* Octavio Paz famously theorized about the historical meanings of this term. See Paz, 30.

15. Conway, *Heroes of the Borderlands,* 70–72.

16. Conway, *Heroes of the Borderlands,* 80.

17. Conway, *Heroes of the Borderlands,* 102–104.

18. It would be imprecise to apply the Chili Western label to earlier Mexican Westerns. The spicy connotation of "Chili" accents the genre's cruelty and violence, helping to distinguish 1970s Westerns from the matinee ones that preceded them. For further discussion, see Conway, *Heroes of the Borderlands,* 122–23.

19. This period in the history of the film industry is discussed in, among others, Ramírez Berg, *Cinema of Solitude,* 44–46 and de la Mora, *Cinemachismo,* 119–120.

20. John G Cawelti, *The Six-Gun Mystique Sequel* (Bowling Green: Bowling Green State University Popular Press, 1999), 2; Edward Buscombe and British Film Institute, *The British Film Institute Companion to the Western* (London: Da Capo Press, 1991), 48.

21. Gayle Rubin's "The Traffic in Women: Notes on the Political Economy of Sex" in *Femi-*

*nism and History*, ed. Joan Wallach Scott (Oxford and New York: Oxford University Press 1996) is a classic study of how women function as objects of exchange in male-dominated kinship systems. Eve Kosofsky Sedgwick drew from Rubin's work in her groundbreaking studies *Between Men* (New York: Columbia University Press, 2016), which examined how the exchange of women in nineteenth-century Victorian literature was a pretext for binding men together. Laura Mulvey defined and theorized the concept of the "male" gaze in "Visual Pleasure and Narrative Cinema," *Screen* 16, no. 3 (1975): 6–18.

22. Carlos Monsiváis, *Historia mínima: la cultura mexicana en el siglo XX* (Mexico City: El Colegio de México, 2010), 192.

23. Rubén Gallo, *Freud's Mexico: Into the Wilds of Psychoanalysis* (Cambridge: MIT Press, 2015), 93–95; Maarten Van Delden, *Carlos Fuentes, Mexico, and Modernity* (Nashville: Vanderbilt University Press, 1998), 165. Sigmund Freud, *Moses and Monotheism; An Outline of Psycho-Analysis, and Other Works: (1937–1939)* (London: Hogarth Press, 1995).

24. Francisco González Pineda and Asociación Psicoanalítica Mexicana, *El mexicano: su dinámica psicosocial* (Mexico City: Editorial Pax-México, 1961).

25. The difficulty in determining variant titles and translations for Mexican Westerns is amply illustrated by *El sabor de la venganza*. Mariscal's film should not be confused with Joaquin Luis Romero Marchent's *El sabor de la venganza* (1963), which, according to Michael Pitts's *Western Movies: A Guide to 5,105 Feature Films*, was titled in English *Gunfight at Nigh* [sic] *Noon* (137). The Spaghetti Western Database lists *Eye for an Eye* as the English translation for the American release of the film, but this is almost identical to the title of Michael Moore's Western *An Eye for an Eye* (1966). The Italian title of Mariscal's film, according to the Spaghetti Western Database, is *Occhio per occhio dente per dente sei fregato Cobra!*, which literally means *An Eye for an Eye a Tooth for a Tooth You're Screwed Cobra!*

26. Roger Bartra, *La jaula de la melancolía: identidad y metamorfosis del mexicano* (Mexico City: Penguin Random House, 2016), 191; Carlos Monsiváis, "Ortodoxia y heterodoxia en las alcobas (hacia una crónica de costumbres y creencias sexuales en las alcobas," *Debate Feminista* 6, no. 11 (1995): 193.

27. Emilio García Riera, *Breve historia del cine mexicano, primer siglo, 1897–1997* (Mexico City: CONACULTA, 1998), 280–81.

28. Jorge Ayala Blanco, *La búsqueda del cine mexicano (1968–1972)* (Mexico City: Editorial Posada, 1986), 1999.

29. Sigmund Freud, *The Uncanny*, trans. David McLintock (New York: Penguin Classics, 2003), 140.

30. Sean Homer, *Jacques Lacan* (New York: Routledge, 2004), 56.

31. Sigmund Freud, *An Outline of Psycho-Analysis. Authorized Translation by James Strachey* (London: Hogarth Press, 1949), 117.

32. Irwin, *Mexican Masculinities*, xxiii.

33. García Riera, *Breve historia*, vol. 15, 91–92.

34. Eve Kosofsky Sedgwick and Wayne Koestenbaum, *Between Men: English Literature and Male Homosocial Desire* (New York: Columbia University Press, 2016), 1–2.

35. Sedgwick, *Between Men*, 25–26.

36. Álvaro Enrigue, *Ahora me rindo y eso es todo* (Barcelona: Editorial Anagrama, 2018), 220.

37. Brian L. Price, *Cult of Defeat in Mexico's Historical Novel: Failure, Trauma, and Loss* (New York: Palgrave Macmillan, 2014), 4.

38. Conway, *Heroes of the Borderlands*, 126–128; 132.

# Bibliography

Ayala Blanco, Jorge. *La aventura del cine mexicano: en la época de oro y después*. Mexico City: Editorial Grijalbo, 1993.
Aviña, Rafael. *Una mirada insólita: temas y géneros del cine mexicano*. Mexico City: Océano, 2004.
Bartra, Roger. *La jaula de la melancolía: identidad y metamorfosis del mexicano*. Mexico City: Penguin Random House, 2016.
———. *La búsqueda del cine mexicano (1968–1972)*. Mexico City: Editorial Posada, 1986.
Bowker, R. R. *Bowker's Complete Video Directory 2000*. R. R. Bowker Company, 2000.
Buscombe, Edward, and British Film Institute. *The British Film Institute Companion to the Western*. London: Da Capo Press, 1991.
Cawelti, John G. *The Six-Gun Mystique Sequel*. Bowling Green: Bowling Green State University Popular Press, 1999.
Conway, Christopher. *Heroes of the Borderlands: The Western in Mexican Film, Comics, and Music*. Albuquerque: University of New Mexico Press, 2019.
———. "*Charros*: A Critical Introduction." In *Modern Mexican Culture: Critical Foundations*, edited by Stuart A. Day, 66–83. Tucson: University of Arizona Press, 2017.
de la Mora, Sergio. *Cinemachismo: Masculinities and Sexuality in Mexican Film*. Austin: University of Texas Press, 2009.
Domínguez-Ruvalcaba, Héctor. *Modernity and the Nation in Mexican Representations of Masculinity: From Sensuality to Bloodshed*. New York: Palgrave Macmillan, 2007.
Enrigue, Álvaro. *Ahora me rindo y eso es todo*. Barcelona: Editorial Anagrama, 2018.
Freud, Sigmund. *An Outline of Psycho-Analysis. Authorized Translation by James Strachey*. London: Hogarth Press, 1949.
———. *The Uncanny*. Translated by David McLintock. New York: Penguin Classics, 2003.
———. *Moses and Monotheism; An Outline of Psycho-Analysis, and Other Works: (1937–1939)*. London: Hogarth Press, 1995.
Gallo, Rubén. *Freud's Mexico: Into the Wilds of Psychoanalysis*. Cambridge: MIT Press, 2015.
García Riera, Emilio. *Breve historia del cine mexicano, primer siglo, 1897–1997*. Mexico City: CONACULTA, 1998.
González Pineda, Francisco, and Asociación Psicoanalítica Mexicana. *El mexicano: su dinámica psicosocial*. Mexico City: Editorial Pax-México, 1961.
Hausberger, Bernd, and Raffaele Moro. *La revolución mexicana en el cine: Un acercamiento a partir de la mirada ítaloeuropea*. Mexico City: El Colegio de México, 2013.
Homer, Sean. *Jacques Lacan*. New York: Routledge, 2004.
Iglesias Prieto, Norma. *Entre yerba, polvo, y plomo: lo fronterizo visto por el cine mexicano*. Tijuana: Colegio de la Frontera Norte, 1991.
Irwin, Robert McKee. *Mexican Masculinities*. Minneapolis: University of Minnesota Press, 2003.
Monsiváis, Carlos. *Amor perdido*. Mexico City: Ediciones Era, 1977.
———. *Historia mínima: la cultura mexicana en el siglo XX*. Mexico City: El Colegio de México, 2010.
———. "Notas sobre la cultura mexicana en el siglo XX." In *Historia general de México* vol. 2, edited by Daniel Cosío Villegas, 1375–548. Mexico City: El Colegio de México, 1976.
———. "Ortodoxia y heterodoxia en las alcobas (hacia una crónica de costumbres y creencias sexuales en las alcobas." *Debate Feminista* 6, no. 11 (1995): 183–210 .

Mulvey, Laura. "Visual Pleasure and Narrative Cinema." *Screen* 16, no. 3 (1975): 6–18.
Noble, Andrea. *Mexican National Cinema*. London & New York: Routledge, 2005.
Paz, Octavio. *El laberinto de la soledad*. Madrid: Cátedra, 1995.
Pitts, Michael R. *Western Movies: A Guide to 5,105 Feature Films*. Jefferson, NC, and London: McFarland and Company, 2013.
Price, Brian L. *Cult of Defeat in Mexico's Historical Novel: Failure, Trauma, and Loss*. New York: Palgrave Macmillan, 2014.
Puente Vázquez, Claudia Elizabeth. "Masculinidad y violencia en el Nuevo Cine Mexicano. Las películas de Luis Estrada." *La Palabra* 28 (2016): 59–72.
Ramírez Berg, Charles. *Cinema of Solitude: A Critical Study of Mexican Film, 1967–1983*. Austin: University of Texas Press, 1992.
Rubin, Gayle. "The Traffic in Women: Notes on the 'Political Economy' of Sex." In *Feminism and History*, edited by Joan Wallach Scott, 105–51. Oxford and New York: Oxford University Press, 1996.
Shatz, Thomas. *Hollywood Genres: Formulas, Filmmaking, and the Studio System*. New York: Random House, 1981.
Schuessler, Michael. "Vestidas, Locas, Mayates and Machos: History and Homosexuality in Mexican Cinema." *Chasqui* 34, no. 2 (2005): 132–44.
Sedgwick, Eve Kosofsky, and Wayne Koestenbaum. *Between Men: English Literature and Male Homosocial Desire*. New York: Columbia University Press, 2016.
Van Delden, Maarten. *Carlos Fuentes, Mexico, and Modernity*. Nashville: Vanderbilt University Press, 1998.

# 5

## BLACKNESS AND RACIAL MELODRAMA IN 1970S MEXICAN CINEMA

CAROLYN FORNOFF

In the 1970s, a quantitative and qualitative shift occurred in the representation of Black subjects in Mexican cinema. Black characters were given more screen time and leading roles, often in films thematizing interracial romance. These films came packaged in a variety of genres: the majority melodramas, but also in the form of comedies, Westerns, historical dramas, and *lucha libre* films. In tandem with this surge in protagonism, the long-standing practice of using blackface to perform Black subjectivity was largely abandoned, and instead, Black talent was hired. These actors were not recruited from the domestic Afro-Mexican population but from the United States, the Caribbean, and other Latin American countries.

In this chapter, I dig into this shift and its implications for the enactment of Black subjectivity in Mexican cinema. I consider a corpus of approximately a dozen films produced in the 1970s that feature Black actors and thematize the question of race.[1] Attending to this small but conspicuous surge helps us better understand this moment of rupture in the representation of Blackness on screen. The repudiation of blackface and move toward casting foreign ethnic actors indicated a growing awareness about the politics of casting practices, while simultaneously reinforcing the notion that "authentically" Black people could not be found in Mexico. The upswing in Black characters and topics centered on Black subjectivity—such as discrimination, Black power, and Black beauty—signaled that filmmakers were invested in ongoing hemispheric debates about anti-Black racism, and how these conversations translated to the Mexican cultural context. The inclusion of Black characters and racial ideologies that diverged from *mestizaje* also evidenced a strategic diversification of content that aimed to capture transnational markets where Mexican productions circulated and recuperated costs.

Mexican cinema in the 1970s ascribed divergent meanings to Black subjectivity. Several films situated Black leads in tired tropes (the humble mammy, the angry Black woman, the supernaturally strong man), while others depicted them as talented professionals who suffered discrimination. Racism against Black people was narrated and visualized in contradictory ways: both as a legitimate societal problem and as one that wasn't as "bad" as in other places and could, therefore, be gently corrected. The assertion that racism did not exist in Mexico was somewhat paradoxically intoned in films that staged a conflict originating in race-based prejudice. Moreover, anti-Black sentiment was presented as a problem that had nothing to do with other iterations of racism such as colorism. The specter of indigeneity, for instance, was rarely raised. These films thus functioned as a safe cultural space where viewers could ponder racial bias from a sanitized distance. In sum, the presence of Black leads in 1970s Mexican cinema was a complicated phenomenon; one that undeniably reflected the rise in interest in Black peoples—who were increasingly visible in international political and cultural spheres—but one that also fell back on clichés, was told from non-Black perspectives, and glossed over connections to other forms of discrimination.

## Context and Casting

People of African descent have been present in Mexico since the earliest expeditions of colonial conquest. Historians estimate that before 1640, over 150,000 enslaved Africans were forcibly brought to Mexico, second in number only to Brazil.[2] Forced to work as domestic servants, agricultural laborers, or in urban spaces like textile mills, convents, and markets, the presence of enslaved Africans in colonial Mexico was a prerequisite for the accumulation of Spanish wealth; they were active participants "in all areas of colony-building."[3] The growing Black population inspired constant fears of revolt; to manage this "threat," the colonial administration passed legislation that barred Blacks from group gatherings and carrying arms.⁴ Other measures of control, like the caste system, reinforced racial theories that naturalized the supposed "inferiority" of Black and indigenous subjects and buttressed the privileged status of white Spaniards as "uniquely capable of making rational decisions."⁵

In spite of this foundational presence, the role of Black peoples in Mexico has been downplayed in national retellings, and Afro-Mexicans have been infrequently included within its imagined community. It wasn't until 2014 that Mexico's Instituto Nacional de Estadística y Geografía [National Institute of Statistics and Geography] (INEGI) recognized Afro-Mexican as an ethnic identity; the 2015 preliminary census was the first time that citizens were able to formally identify themselves as such. While places like Veracruz and the Costa Chica of Guerrero are more recognizable locales of African heritage, in other regions this legacy has been forgotten. Residents of Puebla, Pablo Miguel Sierra Silva notes, are surprised to learn that a sizable population of enslaved African descendants lived there throughout the colonial period.⁶

Although Afro-Mexicans have been "dismissed as culturally irrelevant" by the state—unrecognized until recently as an ethnic category or as autochthonous communities—they have nonetheless been frequently invoked by the arts.⁷ In *Mexico's Nobodies,* Christine Arce elaborates that Mexico's relationship with Blackness is paradoxical: Black subjects are erased by official discourse yet assert a gravitational force within the popular imaginary. Cultural interest in Afro-Mexicanness crystallized in the twentieth century around several reductive tropes, including the dangerously sensual *Mulata de Córdoba,* and her inverse, the comically ignorant and asexual *mulato,* embodied by the comic book character Mimín Pinguín. Like other Western countries, Mexican culture has depicted Black subjects through a delimited number of stereotypes associated with rhythm, animal impulsivity, and unbridled sensuality—or inverse traits such as docility, naivety, and asexual maternalism. These racist tropes were often framed in a purportedly positive light, as a welcome corrective to other racialized forms of being. In *The Cosmic Race,* José Vasconcelos wrote that "the infinite quietude" that Mexicans inherited from their indigenous ancestors was advantageously complemented by "the drop put in our blood by the Black, eager for sensual joy, intoxicated with dances and unbridled lust."⁸

In his comprehensive study of Mexican cinema, Carl Mora explains that racism is a subject rarely treated by Mexican filmmakers. According to Mora, this is because racial tensions between those of lighter and darker skin "is a subject that most Mexicans prefer to ignore (or rather sublimate), categorically stating that there is no racial prejudice in their country."[9] The belief that racism is negligible in Mexico can be attributed to the robust ideological project of *mestizaje*. Central to the discourse of revolutionary and post-revolutionary nation building, *mestizaje* articulated racial mixing as a positive phenomenon that produced a stronger, more capable "cosmic" race. In contrast to the scientific racism propounded by neighboring regions, *mestizaje* celebrated the hybridity that emerged from cultural blending. Framed as the common denominator that united all Mexicans regardless of class, *mestizaje* proposed that to be Mexican was to be *mestizo*. Race was removed from the census in 1921, a decision that communicated to the public that race was irrelevant—since everyone was *mestizo*—and also meant that the government did not have to decide "how to measure or define the mixed-race population."[10]

At the same time that *mestizaje* was celebrated as the shared Mexican condition, whiteness has nonetheless been preferred. Juliet Hooker sums up this tension, writing that depictions of "the region as racially harmonious" have long coexisted with "the reality of racial hierarchy."[11] Even for Vasconcelos, the promise of the cosmic race was its ability to eradicate Blackness, which he characterized as an "inferior race" that "could be redeemed . . . by voluntary extinction."[12] Mexico is a pigmentocracy, or society in which class distinction maps onto skin color: those with lighter skin are concentrated in the upper classes, and those with darker in the lower. The association of whiteness with wealth and power is inherently to the advantage of those with lighter skin.[13]

Mexican cinema registers and perpetuates this privileging of whiteness; most Mexican film stars of the twentieth century reflected the beauty standards established by Hollywood and European cinemas. In her study of early Mexican cinema, Mónica García-Blizzard demonstrates that throughout Mexican film history, whiteness has been presented as the "aspirational model for the nation."[14] The frequent use of phenotypically white actresses to play indigenous or *mestiza* characters functioned to erase ethnic difference and fossilize ideal Mexican femininity within the white body.[15]

The casting of white actors to depict non-white characters extended to Golden Age productions that featured Black protagonists, such as *Angelitos negros* (Joselito Rodríguez, 1948), *La negra Angustias* (Matilde Landeta, 1950), and *Mulata* (Gilberto Martínez Solares, 1953), all of which starred light-skinned actresses garbed in theatrical make-up.[16] Unlike the use of blackface in the parodic context of Cuban popular theater or Mexican political cabaret, these films were melodramas that deployed it as a tool to extend the viewer's sympathy to racial others.[17] While the purported intention of featuring darker characters was to enact the space occupied by Blacks in Mexico, the use of blackface worked against this aim by subsuming Blackness into the *mestiza* body and transforming it into a spectacle for the enjoyment of non-Black viewers. Arce elaborates this point, writing that blackface "separates the body from the person, and the person from the reality of the social conditions that surround them . . . [it] becomes a 'vehicle' for white self-exploration; it stops being about Black people at all."[18] The decision to use white actors to protagonize Black characters demonstrated the extent to which the industry was dominated by white beauty standards.

By the 1960s, the use of blackface for lead roles had fallen from favor, a trend that echoed its abandonment a decade earlier by Hollywood, thanks to the burgeoning Civil Rights Movement. Instead, Mexican films interested in showcasing Black characters often set these films in foreign contexts. The Mexican-Brazilian coproduction *Rumbo a Brasilia* (Mauricio de la Serna, 1961), for instance, depicted Brazil as a post-racial paradise, where people of all shades interacted harmoniously.[19] Alternatively, domestic features cast Black actors recruited from the United States or the Caribbean. Perhaps no role exemplified the shift away from blackface more than the casting of African American actress Juanita Moore to play the role of Nana Mercé in Joselito Rodríguez's 1969 remake of *Angelitos negros,* a marked contrast with the part's original performance in blackface by light-skinned Cuban actress Rita Montaner in 1948.

Several Caribbean, Latin American, and North American Black actors became recurrent fixtures in the Mexican scene in the 1970s, finding employment in the small wave of films focused on topics like anti-Black racism and interracial romance. Actors cast in at least two Mexican features in the 1970s included Dominican actor Julio César Imbert as a dashing leading man, Cuban actor and former Mr. Universe Sergio Oliva as a humble *luchador,* Cuban actress Eusebia Cosme as a stereotypical mammy, and actresses Robertha and Shandira, respectively from Peru and Uruguay, as romantic heroines cum sexy vixens circulating in the *cine de ficheras* (sexploitation comedy genre).[20] African American actors were also recruited for specific roles in Mexican films, including Playboy model Jeannie Bell, model/singer Steve Flanagan, and actor Philip Michael Thomas, who later hit it big as Detective Ricardo Tubbs on the TV series *Miami Vice.*

While the move toward diverse casting practices was a positive recognition of the importance of societal casting—in which actors are "cast in roles that they perform in society"—the absence of Afro-Mexican actors indicated that in spite of representational gains, the troubling assumption that "authentic" Blackness could only be found outside of Mexico continued to flourish.[21] The casting of foreign actors (and only occasionally an Afro-Mexican actor) to protagonize Black characters suggested there was no Black domestic talent readily available, indicating the industry's entrenchment in the privileging, cultivating, and promotion of whiteness.

When director Roberto Gavaldón was looking to cast the lead role of Gaspar for the film *El hombre de los hongos* (1976), he auditioned Black actors in New York, Puerto Rico, and Los Angeles. He ultimately cast Philip Michael Thomas, an African American actor who had yet to appear in any Spanish-language films. In a recent email exchange, Thomas recounted that Gavaldón told him that he was cast for his muscular physique, green eyes, and ability to speak Spanish without a heavy accent.[22] A Mexican-Spanish coproduction, the historical drama featured a transnational cast made up of actors from Spain and Mexico alongside Thomas. Within the logic of the film, all of the characters are presumably from the same place: a plantation set in Veracruz, shortly after Mexican Independence, while slavery was still legal. Casting Thomas in the role of Gaspar (an oblique reference to Gaspar Yanga, an enslaved African who led a band of escaped slaves to found a maroon colony in Veracruz in 1570) illustrates that even when Blackness was recognized as part of Mexico's historical makeup, visually identifiable Black people continued to be thought of as only originating outside of the nation.

Thus, in order to thematize racial injustice, and specifically the injustices suffered by Blacks in Mexico in a way that was immediately recognizable to Mexican audiences as being *about Blackness* (rather than about *mestizaje* or racial ambiguity), talent was recruited from countries where this was understood to be organically located: the United States and the Caribbean. Filmmakers and audiences expected Blackness to be unmistakably identifiable in its embodiment, manifest in a way that left no question in the viewer's mind. This visual certainty was linked to specific phenotypic traits, like kinky hair, dark skin, and full lips. Casting practices followed these visual imperatives, and rejected or avoided racial ambiguity at all costs.

Bizarrely, this imperative that the character's African heritage be immediately identifiable meant that blackface continued to be a recurrent tool used for supporting roles. Many films utilized a blended approach: ethnic actors were cast in leading roles, and extras were garbed in blackface to interpret secondary characters representing the protagonist's community. For example, the Mil Máscaras *lucha libre* film *El poder negro* [*Black Power*] (Alfredo B. Crevenna, 1975), a Mexican-Venezuelan coproduction, starred the Afro-Cuban bodybuilder Sergio Oliva in the titular role of dockworker Pedro, who becomes a *luchador* and fights under the name Black Power. However, the role of Pedro's mother, who is featured in multiple scenes, was performed by a light-skinned extra (María José Picado) in heavy blackface and afro wig. His love interest Mariela is interpreted by the Venezuelan singer Lila Morillo, who although herself a light-skinned *mulata,* dons heavy bronzer to more closely approximate Mariela's diegetic description as "la diosa de ébano" [the goddess of ebony]. This performative racial modification from *mulata* to Black exemplifies what Alison Fraunhar terms "mimicry by degree," an effort "that relies on the legibility of exaggerated racialized stereotypes."[23]

The use of blackface for supporting characters was certainly a cost-saving measure that minimized the need to recruit Black extras abroad, but again reinforced the notion that identifiably Black people did not readily exist in Mexico. Given that most working actors matched the racialized aesthetic of whiteness historically privileged by the industry, the continued recurrence to blackface "out of necessity" reflected the industry's colorist history. To seek out racial diversity would have been to undertake a costly talent search beyond the industry's unionized nucleus in Mexico City and toward coastal regions. Furthermore, the use of theatrical makeup to foreground a character's Blackness—rather than, say, to cast actors with darker coloring but whose traits were not stereotypically Black—underscored filmmakers' desire to avoid racial ambiguity when thematizing anti-Black racism, a visual decision that stressed the distinctiveness of the Black experience relative to that of other brown peoples.

## Transnational Audience and Cultural Translation

This leads to a perplexing question: why the surge in cinematic interest in Black subjects, interracial romance, and racism in a country where these populations and problems presumably did not exist? Who was the intended audience? As noted before, these topics were not sui generis to the 1970s but prefigured by hits like *Angelitos negros* and *La negra Angustias*. And yet, the increase in Mexican films across genres featuring Black protagonists in the 1970s was a novel phenomenon, one that we can attribute to the tastes of the ever-important transnational markets where Mexican films circulated and recuperated costs. Filmmakers seized upon global interest in political and cultural debates spearheaded by Black groups in the United States and the Caribbean and explored the extent to which these current events resonated with Spanish-speaking audiences. Diversified casting practices also recognized the commercial possibilities of catering to ethnically heterogenous transnational distribution markets, where audiences were responsive to the formulation of Black characters as protagonists.

The centrality of transnational audiences for the fiscal health of Mexican productions was not idiosyncratic to the era. Since the Golden Age, Mexican cinema has actively appealed to audiences that stretched far beyond its borders. According to Marvin D'Lugo, by the 1940s, Mexico enjoyed a dominant regional market position as the *de facto* "Mecca of [the] transnational Latin American film industry." Unlike Hollywood's failed attempts to appeal to Latin American audiences, Mexico was successful in this endeavor because of its crucial interstitial location in between the United States and Latin America. The Mexican film industry served as a "buffer" between the two regions, a rich inventive space where "North American modernity" could be translated "into a Hispanic idiom."[24]

By the 1970s, transnational markets had become an indispensable source of revenue. The domestic market was less profitable due to a confluence of factors, including a dip in quality and cinema's displacement by the growth in television ownership.[25] So filmmakers sought out audiences abroad. However, as Seraina Rohrer has observed, many South American countries that had previously operated as reliable distribution networks were troubled by political and economic instability, prompting Mexican producers to look for more profitable markets.[26] One massive pool of viewers was located to the north. Producing material of interest to Spanish-speaking viewers based in the United States was fiscally advantageous, given the region's higher ticket prices. By 1981, the US Spanish-speaking public constituted 75 percent of Mexican film revenues.[27]

Numerous Mexican films featuring Black protagonists tapped into viewers' interest in topical debates about equality that permeated political conversations in the United States. Several thematized the Civil Rights Movement or the Black Power Movement and decoded them for Mexican viewers. Sometimes these references were implicit, like the enchained pet black panther that helps Gaspar fight back against his oppressors on the plantation in *El hombre de los hongos*. This reference drew a parallel between the Black Panther Movement and anti-colonial efforts in Latin America, likening the two causes and generating sympathy for the self-defense tactics employed by the Black Panthers through the domestic analogue.

Other times, references to US Black culture were more explicit and even didactic. In *Negro es un bello color* (Julián Soler, 1974), Joyce (Jeannie Bell), an African American diva who is working in Mexico as a back-up singer, gestures to a wall in her house adorned with photos of Black icons, including Ray Charles and Angela Davis, while describing the reasons she is proud to be Black. These references surely inspired nods of recognition from US-based viewers (it was screened in nine Spanish-language theaters in New York), while simultaneously contextualizing North American racial dynamics to non-US viewers (it was also released in Mexican theaters).[28] The film's theme song, "Negro es un bello color," echoed sentiments popularized by the "Black Is Beautiful" cultural campaign in the US that sought to counteract the notion that Black features were unattractive. Joyce embodies the ideals of Black power and beauty that were of the moment in the States: a soulful and glamorously dressed diva, a strong advocate for herself (verging on the trope of the angry Black woman), both an object of desire and a nurturing mother. The film culminates with the success of Joyce's campaign for acceptance: in the final scene her racist mother-in-law (Libertad Lamarque) turns over a new leaf, embracing her *mulata* granddaughter (and by proxy, her African American daughter-in-law) while reprising the song, "Negro es un bello color."

The potent purchase power of Chicano and Latino viewers in the United States helps explain interest in films that represented racism in North American cultural terms, like the binary Black/white paradigm. Filmic narratives thematizing anti-Black discrimination provided Hispanic viewers (located in the US or elsewhere) a visual and affective means to grasp the discrimination experienced by Black people as an experience distinct from their own. They didactically encouraged audiences to advocate for the fair treatment of Black people—at times presenting them as passive victims worthy of pity (Roberta in *Rosas blancas para mi hermana negra*; Yaira in *Lo blanco, lo rojo, y lo negro*; and Dolores in *Mamá Dolores*) or alternatively as agents fighting back against their victimization (Gaspar in *El hombre de los hongos,* Jeannie in *Negro es un bello color,* and Manuel in *Fuego negro*). Simultaneously, the majority of these films perpetuated an idealized view of Mexico as less afflicted by race-based tensions. To this end, multiple films parsed the distinction between the forms of racism found in the US, depicted as purposeful and malicious, in contrast with more benevolent racism in Mexico, represented as unintentional and consequently easier to overcome.

Some films presented anti-Black racism as a North American problem that trickled into Mexico as an unwelcome import. In this subset, characters espousing racist beliefs were exaggerated caricatures of US bigotry, like Mr. Cotton in *La amargura de mi raza* (Rubén Galindo, 1972). In this film, Afro-Caribbean protagonist Alfonso (Julio César Imbert) migrates to Mexico in order to make it big as a racecar driver. He is hired by a team that is owned by the not-so-subtly-named Mr. Cotton (Arthur Hansel), who tries to fire Alfonso after finding out that he is Black. The team's Mexican manager intervenes on Alfonso's behalf, cautioning him that if he makes even the smallest mistake, he will lose his job. This warning is actualized: Cotton fires Alfonso after he crashes his racecar to avoid hitting a dog. In a racist tirade, Cotton calls Alfonso a "maldito negro" [damned Black] and accuses him of being uppity. Alfonso objects and is slapped by Cotton, who threatens to kill him. Racist beliefs and discriminatory practices are thus situated in *La amargura de mi raza* as unequivocally linked to the US. Meanwhile, the Mexican manager (with whom the Chicano or Mexican viewer would identify) acts as Alfonso's advocate, and yet is separate from him, never the target of Cotton's white supremacist violence. The resulting racial grid places the Chicano or Mexican spectator in a comfortable viewing position, neither a racist nor the victim of racism, able to extend empathy to the Black victim while not feeling victimized themselves.

While the Chicano or Mexican viewer is not made to feel personally responsible for Alfonso's plight, *La amargura de mi raza* endeavors to educate viewers curious about the Black Power Movement. It justifies why the Civil Rights Movement did not simply dissipate in the wake of its legal victories. Alfonso's unjust firing illustrates that, in spite of the Civil Rights Act of 1964 prohibiting employment discrimination, Black people continued to face prejudice in the workplace and were held to impossible standards. It extends this critique beyond the borders of the US to suggest that, contrary to the widespread belief that anti-Black racism did not exist in Mexico, racial bias structures the professional realm throughout the hemispheric Americas.

Second, *La amargura de mi raza* argues that the Black subject's identification of discrimination is not an overreaction or an imagined harm. In an early scene, Alfonso's light-skinned Mexican friend (Andrés García) insists that Alfonso is overly sensitive to racial slights. Alfonso responds that his anger is justified: "No es complejo, es coraje contra la gente que nos quiere hacer menos. Ya ves lo que está pasando en Estados Unidos" [It is not a complex, it is anger at the people who want to diminish us. You see what is happening in the United States]. Alfonso's friend retorts that they are not in the United States but Mexico, where the situation is different: "Aquí estamos en México. No hay discriminación racial. Además, en el mismo Estados Unidos hay muchas personas que están de lado de las personas de color" [We are in Mexico. There is no racial discrimination here. Plus, even in the United States there are many folks that are on the side of people of color]. The common refrain that Mexico is untouched by the racism that plagues the United States is discredited by Alfonso's later troubles—which, while caused by an Anglo businessman, unfold in Mexico. The script juggles inconsistent messages about anti-Black racism: it exists and should not be chalked up to heightened sensitivity, and yet it is qualitatively different than other forms of colorism, which divorces the struggles of Black and brown peoples. While the film acknowledges and stages instances of anti-Black racism in Mexico, its source is always deferred and distanced from the national body, displaced onto the white supremacy of the United States.

Like its title reflects, *La amargura de mi raza* ends in tragedy. In the final scene, after Alfonso has proved his worth as a racecar driver by winning a pivotal race, his wife Carla (Cotton's estranged daughter) dies during childbirth. Unlike in other films, Carla's death does not bring about racial reconciliation. The Cottons refuse to speak to Alfonso, who is now totally alone. In the final shot, he leaves the hospital dejected, with an enormous trophy in hand, his isolation underscored through a dramatic zoom-out that frames him as a solitary speck. This conclusion debunks Alfonso's initial assertion that money and success are the avenues for overcoming racism, as he told his parents in the opening scene, "Es la única forma en que tomen en cuenta a los negros" [It is the only way they will take us Black people into account]. The film's pessimistic outlook is that there is no escape from racism, which is expansive and pernicious and cannot be resolved through climbing the social ladder.

The casting of Julio César Imbert, a well-known Dominican baseball player turned actor, was a move meant to draw in Caribbean audiences. Many Mexican films featuring Black actors in the 1970s targeted transnational audiences in the Caribbean, where racial difference was marketable as a narrative hook. The melodrama *Rosas blancas para mi hermana negra* (Abel Salazar, 1970) thematized the fraught nature of interracial friendship and romance, and premiered to great success in Puerto Rico. However, as Roberto Ortiz has noted, in spite of its popularity on the island, the film flopped in Mexico, where it did not generate the same draw.[29] We can speculate that its success in the transnational context is precisely what portended its failure domestically: it featured a wide-ranging international cast (Argentine star Libertad Lamarque, Afro-Cuban actress Eusebia Cosme, Afro-Peruvian pop star Robertha, African American actor-model Steve Flanagan, and only two Mexican actors: Irma Lozano and Roberto Cañedo). Its convoluted plot—which involves unrequited love, racism, terminal illness, a car accident, and a heart transplant—is only tied to the Mexican setting in the loosest of senses. Even though *Rosas blancas* did not fare well in Mexico, its strategy of assembling an international cast and a generically Latin American milieu increased its potential to be successfully exported, since recognizable stars from other countries made it more likely that their home audiences would come out to see them on the big screen.

Many of these films were coproductions that aspired to global commercial success by sharing costs and guaranteeing a film's circulation abroad. Such was the case of *El derecho de los pobres* (René Cardona, 1973), a Mexican-Ecuadorian coproduction set in Guayaquil and starring Afro-Cuban actress Eusebia Cosme, and *El poder negro*, the aforementioned Mil Máscaras coproduction by Mexico and Venezuela. Other films partnered with European producers. These took up themes that riffed on popular conceits in contemporaneous

Hollywood Blaxploitation, an exploitation subgenre that emerged in the early 1970s and featured Black casts. The most common subtype of Blaxploitation adapted by Mexican coproductions was the slave revenge drama, made iconic in Hollywood by the box office hit *Mandingo* (Richard Fleischer, 1975). In Mexico, the narrative formula of slave revenge meets steamy interracial sex was reworked in the aforementioned Mexican-Spanish coproduction *El hombre de los hongos* and the Mexican-Italian coproduction *Fuego negro* (Raúl Fernández, 1979). These transgressive, low-budget flicks trafficked in racialized violence and sex.[30] *Fuego negro* includes scenes of voodoo, slave whippings, beheaded white people, and erotic interracial lovemaking. Dubbed in English, it was released in Finland, the Netherlands, and West Germany.

## Performing Interracial Romance

With the exception of *Mamá Dolores* (Tito Davison, 1970), a spin-off of *El derecho de nacer* (Tito Davison, 1966) starring Afro-Cuban actress Eusebia Cosme as a stereotypical mammy and *El derecho de los pobres,* all of the Mexican films that featured Black protagonists in the 1970s included plot lines thematizing interracial romance. This narrative node channeled spectators' fears and fantasies about racial mixing and constituted the driving conflict to be resolved. Marriage was framed as a limiting case that tested societal tolerance for racial difference. Love and desire were depicted as modes of racial reconciliation, and interracial marriage as a form of assimilation of Blackness into the *mestizo* nation.

Somewhat surprisingly, interracial desire was not overwhelmingly gendered by this corpus in one direction or another. It went both ways, expressed by white male characters for Black female characters, or white female characters for Black male characters, and vice versa. But the pairing was always between very dark and light-skinned actors, never an ethnically ambiguous brown. The striking visual contrast between the lovers' pigmentation was pointedly used as a marketing tactic; promotional posters prominently displayed images of tightly embracing interracial couples to attract audiences.

The decision to stage interracial romance as a binary pairing of Black and white purposefully elided the discourse of *mestizaje* to maximize drama and highlight engagement with provocative content. Whereas the ideology of *mestizaje* presented racial mixing as socially acceptable (even if this was not the case), the more radical encounter between racial "opposites" was presented as qualitatively different: no longer a question of degree, but an anomaly that brought with it the baggage of a different racial ideology altogether, inherited from North American paradigms of miscegenation and slavery. Cinematic romances between Black and white characters were presented in a schizophrenic manner. On the one hand, they asserted that (unlike in the United States) racial prejudice did not exist in Mexico because of *mestizaje*, and therefore these unions were not problematic. Yet, on the other hand, the interracial coupling was marketed as a source of fascination and conflict—the hook whose abnormality drove the plot and enticed viewers with the promise of melodramatic strife. In other words, the films counted on viewers' racial bias in selling the strangeness of interracial romance, while simultaneously diegetically asserting that such racial bias did not exist.

The on-screen coupling promised by the films' promotional materials was delivered to varying degrees depending on genre and projected audience. In chaste melodramas, characters were simply shown kissing and subsequently marrying. At the other end of the spectrum, films dabbling in sexploitation included nude scenes: usually pre- or post-copulation with full frontal female nudity and full-body male nudity that was captured from behind, never revealing male genitalia. Exploitation films with Black protagonists objectified the female body (regardless of race) and the Black body (regardless of gender). The only body that was not captured in this objectifying way was that of the white male. The exploitation Western *Lo blanco, lo rojo, y lo negro* (Alberto Mariscal and Alfredo Salazar, 1979) illustrates this dynamic in a post-copulation shot. The white male character (Hugo Stiglitz) is tastefully covered with sheets from the waist down. Next to him, his Black lover (Shandira) reposes totally exposed, including full pubic bush. As in other exploitation films of the era, the camera operates as the white gaze, objectifying the Black body as an exotic source of hypersensuality.

Exploitation films overtly used Black male nudity in their promotional materials. The poster for *El hombre de los hongos* includes a muscular illustration of the naked Black protagonist from behind. More perturbingly, the VHS box art for the slave revenge exploitation flick *Fuego negro* depicts its Black protagonist (Julio César Imbert) hanging naked from a tree, grimacing and bleeding while being whipped by a white overseer.[31] All of the other (non-Black) characters are fully dressed, in stark contrast to the centered, exposed

Black body. This promotional image of lynching collapses Black sexuality and victimization into torture porn, presenting Black subjugation as a sadistic and titillating spectacle. Other artwork for this same film marketed its content in a radically different manner. The poster for the German release of *Fuego negro* is a low-angle shot of Imbert with a rippling torso and a phallic firearm, an image that suggests that the content focuses on Black power, rather than oppression. Oscillating back in the other direction, the poster for its release in Mexico depicts Imbert kneeling next to his white lover, who stands, her hand cupping his face beneath her bare breasts. This image objectifies both characters while underscoring the Black partner's submissive stance. As the varied promotional images for *Fuego negro* demonstrate, representations of Black protagonists within Mexican iterations of Blaxploitation swung mercurially from trope to trope: from supernatural strength to helpless victim, sexual conqueror to submissive lover.

While undertaken in highly problematic ways, several films in this corpus actively endeavored to trouble the presumed universality of white aesthetic ideals and present Blackness as desirable. This gesture was nonetheless articulated through a white lens, justifying Black beauty through clichés or in relation to whiteness. Such is the case of *Vidita negra* (Rogelio González, 1973), a Mauricio Garcés comedy about Enrique (Garcés), a struggling writer living in Paris, and his relationship with Vidita (Robertha), who arrives to work for him and his fiancée as their domestic employee. Vidita is a Black aborigine from a fictional island in the Indian Ocean who has moved to Paris to study sociology. Jokes pour forth from this apparent paradox: she is both primitive (clad in animal prints, a practitioner of witchcraft) and far more advanced that Enrique (she speaks ten languages and has read all the classics, from Unamuno to Dostoevsky). The duo's dynamic is reminiscent of the contemporaneous TV show *I Dream of Jeannie* (1965–1970), in which a beautiful genie shows up to serve Captain Tony Nelson as her "master," to whom she brings good fortune. Vidita also immediately falls for Enrique, for no apparent diegetic reason. Like Jeannie, Vidita is totally "other" to the Mexican expats, she happily works as their servile maid, and yet possesses a monetary fortune that she uses to help pay off Enrique's debts.

Vidita mysteriously appears after Enrique describes the "ideal woman" that he hopes will inspire his next novel. In this comedic exchange, his light-skinned fiancée suggests that this perfect specimen will be just like her: a thin blonde with blue eyes. But Enrique invokes a different type, a woman with raven hair and dark, black eyes, "una boca con los labios carnosos, sensual . . . Envolviéndolo todo como con magia . . . una cosa así como hechicería" [a mouth with thick lips, sensual . . . Covering everything as if with magic . . . something like witchcraft]. Blackness is preferred over whiteness to comedic effect and valorized through the white male gaze for its mystical sensuality. This point is later reinforced in a long comedic monologue where Enrique breathlessly lists all the sex acts that he would like to perform on Vidita, an inventory that he wraps up by saying, "qué cosa cochinísima, pensó" [what a disgusting thing, he thought]. *Vidita negra* underscores that traits coded as Black are not only desired by white men but also by white women when Vidita affirms: "Las mujeres blancas, cuando van a las playas, solo llevan una idea: ¡volverse negras!" [When white women go to the beach, they are motivated by one idea: becoming Black!]

Yet, while the film presents Black femininity as desirable, these sexualized fantasies are unidirectional, expressed solely from the white male perspective toward the Black female body. Like other films of the era, *Vidita negra* presents itself as anti-racist thanks to its portrayal of Black subjects as desirable partners who can be legitimately chosen over lighter-skinned options. By the film's conclusion, Enrique leaves his fiancée for Vidita, declaring, "la amo tanto, que la amaría aunque fuese blanca" [I love her so much, that I would love her even if she were white]. On the surface, the comedy's culmination in marriage suggests that love for Black women is not just borne of lust or passing fetish but is enduring, underscoring the message that love supersedes racial identification. However, this racial identification must be articulated and said aloud in order for it to be overcome. Enrique's declaration that her race is not consequential to their love is immediately undone by a joke made by an onlooker, who joshes, "Otra vez, se llevó el Cortés a la Malinche!" [Once again, Cortés has made off with La Malinche!]

As illustrated by *Vidita negra*, racial difference is framed as a problem that must be overcome in order for romance to flourish. The "success" of the interracial pairing is typically presented by these films as a matter of assimilation, dependent upon the Black partner's acceptance by and absorption into the light-skinned majority. This dynamic is never reversed: the white partner's favorable reception by the Black protagonist's community is never in question. This is unsurprising given that few of these films depict the Black protagonist's community in the first place, usually utilizing one ancillary character—often the mother—as a stand-in for the entire ethnic group (and in blackface, as we have seen). This shortcut was due to budgetary and casting constraints, but also revealed the extent to which these films did not actually account for the Afro-Mexican or Black experience. The lopsided development of the white partner's point of view and social milieu relative to that of the Black partner reinforced the imaginary of the Black experience in Mexico as atypical and rootless, without history or interiority. The non-Black point of view was assumed to be the diegetic status quo and the viewpoint shared by the audience.

Not all of the films culminated in the "happy" assimilation of the Black partner into the dominantly light-skinned culture. Several films (*La amargura de mi raza*, *Negro es un bello color*, and *Fuego negro*) articulated the pairing's impossibility by tragically killing off one or more of the partners, an end that implied that there was no conceivable future for interracial couples. In other films, the happy ending of assimilation and acceptance came at a heavy cost. In *Rosas blancas para mi hermana negra*, interracial marriage is only viable thanks to the untimely demise of the Black female protagonist, whose heart is then transplanted into the body of her white female friend, allowing her to overcome her illness and happily marry her Black doctor.

When racial difference was presented as a potentially insuperable obstacle, this problem was at times enacted as internal, located in the protagonist's psyche, and other times external, the result of societal ill will. When the focus was on racism as an internal dilemma, or a question of mentally "getting over" racial difference, it was always expressed by the Black character, never the white character, as a manifestation of their anxiety that their race was a deal-breaker. This anxiety was often presented as illogical—as if it were an invented fear or complex—even in the face of evidence to the contrary. Because these films presented race and racial identification in simplistic terms, the white lover pursuing an interracial romance was always depicted in a positive light, totally unaffected by the phenotypically darker partner's race, never giving it a second thought. In films that expressed this internal conflict, the climax is inevitably articulated via the white partner's declaration that love is colorblind (as in *Vidita negra*). In *Lo blanco, lo rojo, y lo negro*, the damsel-in-distress Yaira asks her white lover Cris whether it bothers him that she is Black. In response, he drolly returns the question, asking whether it matters that he is white. Without waiting for her response, he proclaims: "Yo pienso que todas las razas son iguales. Solo hay gente que me agrada y otra que no" [I think that all races are equal. There are only people that I like and people that I don't]. This sort of response is typical. It addresses what the audience is thinking, while simultaneously dismissing the query as if it were unreasonable (as if it were the same to ask the question in reverse) and culminates in a heroic declaration of tolerance.

Other films complicated the facile notion that anti-Black racism was nonexistent in Mexico. In *Negro es un bello color*, the maternal protagonist Eugenia (Libertad Lamarque) grapples with prejudice when her son Mario declares his intention to marry Joyce, the African American diva. Eugenia reacts with dismay and insists that her reluctance is not grounded in bigotry, but out of fear that he will be unhappy: "Tú no vas a cambiar el mundo. Piensa en qué clase de vida tendrán ustedes y sus hijos" [You are not going to change the world. Think about what sort of life you and your children will have]. In this line of argumentation, happiness is framed as the successful ascription to the racialized status quo, which holds within it the promise of normalcy. Interracial marriage and mixed-race offspring, by contrast, have no futurity. Eugenia's construction of "happiness" excludes Joyce altogether, whose Blackness forecloses that aspiration. The film treats Eugenia's objections as well intentioned (rather than racist), and as correctable. Like other melodramas tracking interracial romance, the characters dramatically evolve: Joyce softens from the hardened trope of the angry Black woman into a nurturing mother, and Eugenia's disapproval melts away, changes that are hastened by the *deus ex machina* car crash that kills her son Mario, which brings the two women together.[32]

The melodrama *Rosas blancas para mi hermana negra* similarly instructs non-Black viewers to face their prejudicial attitudes. It debunks the classic myth that having Black friends signals a lack of bigotry. Laura (also played by Libertad Lamarque) has a best friend who is Black (Eusebia Cosme), but when her daughter wants to marry a Black man, she reacts with horror. Her opposition echoes Eugenia's: "Tal vez lo entenderías si pensaras en los hijos de una unión así. No, no quiero para ti, ni para los tuyos, ese dolor . . . Entiéndame, yo solo quiero que seas feliz . . . Tú no vas a resolver una situación que lleva siglos de preocupar el mundo" [Perhaps you would understand my concerns if you thought about the children of a mixed-race union. No, I don't want that pain for you, or for yours . . . Understand me, I only want you to be happy . . . You won't solve a situation that has been bothering the world for centuries]. While Laura eventually gets over these objections, her fears are first made more comprehensible to the audience in a dream sequence in which Laura imagines that her *mulata* grandchild wants to play with other children, who run away, laughing at her. This access to Laura's interiority grants her greater sympathy and understanding from the audience so that she is not seen in a bad light but as having concerns worth considering. At the same time, Laura's bald prejudice reveals the hypocrisy of an earlier scene in which she assured the Black character Roberta that her romantic problems were unrelated to her race, insisting, "No te atormentes con esas ideas. En nuestros países, el racismo no existe . . . Nada tiene que ver con tu color este problema amoroso" [Don't torment yourself with those ideas. In our countries, racism doesn't exist . . . Your color has nothing to do with your romantic troubles].

To recapitulate, the societal casting of Black actors to represent Black characters in Mexican films in the 1970s had several contradictory effects. In a positive sense, it gave greater visibility and embodied shape to the existence of Black peoples in Mexican society. Even when interpreted by non-Mexican actors, this recognition was notable, particularly for a country where cultural representations of Blackness circulated within what Ben Sifuentes-Jáuregui has described as "a rather limited set of spaces."[33] Furthermore, in contrast with the stereotypical Black figures that were most visible in Mexican culture in the first half of the twentieth century like the suffering *mulata* servant and the happy *negrito*, the Black characters in these films were not ancillary, but protagonists with agency who, within the robust tradition of Mexican melodrama, fought for love and equality.

However, while the move to feature Black subjects in leading roles was positive, their depiction was uneven: complex in some films, flat and cliché-ridden in others. The casting of non-Mexican actors who were immediately identifiable as "Black" had the counter-productive effect of communicating that the racism experienced by these characters was reducible to a Black-and-white binary and not a more complicated question of degree. The elision of *mestizaje* collapsed notions of racial oppression into easily digestible terms that did not require Mexican-based audiences to critically reflect on the domestic status quo.

Sentiments about interracial relationships in these films were simultaneously discriminatory and inclusionary. Fears about racism expressed by Black characters tended to be portrayed as overreactions—even in spite of evidence to the contrary—allowing lighter-skinned characters to occupy the heroic role of declaring race a non-issue. Likewise, societal disapproval of interracial marriage was articulated as a generational problem, which optimistically presented discrimination as a problem on its way out. The characters that objected to these unions were configured in sympathetic ways that asked audiences to identify with and understand their qualms, even if they were ultimately shown to be incorrect. The absence of supporting characters representing the communities of these Black protagonists reinforced the overall sensation of their rootless and atypical presence in Mexican society.

The small boom of Mexican films that prominently featured Black protagonists died out in the 1980s, with Black characters waning to secondary and supporting roles. As Mexican cinema embraced the representation of middle-class concerns in the 1990s, Afro-Mexican and foreign Black characters receded further from view. It was not until recently—over forty years after the films analyzed in this chapter—that a Mexican feature-length fiction featured an entirely Afro-Mexican cast. *La negrada* [*Black Mexicans*] (Jorge Pérez Solano, 2018), composed of non-professional actors from Oaxaca's Costa Chica, announced from the outset its intention to make visible a community that had long been glossed over. Yet even *La negrada*, a social realist film that fleshes out the dramas of an Afro-Mexican community, illustrates the continued struggle to define what an "authentically" Black Mexican looks like on screen. In an interview with *La Jornada*, director Jorge Pérez Solano mentioned that his Afro-Indigenous cast members were not quite Black enough for his taste, noting, "El tono de piel que utilizo en la película no llega a lo totalmente negro que yo hubiera querido" [The skin tone that I use in the film isn't as totally Black as I would have liked].[34] The ambition to make Blackness legible for Mexican audiences accustomed to thinking about Blackness in phenotypically reductive ways, defined by national and transnational cinematic traditions, continues to be a vexed and unsettled question.

## Notes

1. The corpus of feature-length Mexican films with a Black lead in the 1970s includes: *Mamá Dolores* (Tito Davison, 1970), *Rosas blancas para mi hermana negra* (Abel Salazar, 1970), *Vidita negra* (Rogelio A. González, 1973), *El derecho de los pobres* (René Cardona, 1973), *La amargura de mi raza* (Rubén Galindo, 1973), *Negro es un bello color* (Julián Soler, 1974), *Poder negro* (Alfredo B. Crevenna, 1975), *El hombre de los hongos* (Roberto Gavaldón, 1976), *Los temibles* (Alfredo B. Crevenna, 1977), *Lo blanco, lo rojo, y lo negro* (Alberto Mariscal and Alfredo Salazar, 1979), and *Fuego negro* (Raúl Fernández, 1979).

Other films that include a Black actor in a secondary role: *Paraíso* (Luis Alcoriza, 1969), *Vuelo 701* (Raúl de Anda Jr., 1971), *Abejas asesinas* (Alfredo Zacarías, 1978), *Hilario Cortés el rey del talón* (Javier Durán 1980), and *Ilegales y mojados* (Afredo B. Crevenna, 1980).

I would like to thank Raúl Miranda López of the Cineteca Nacional de México, James Spinks of DAARAC (Department of Afro American Research, Arts & Culture), and Olivia Cosentino for their invaluable assistance locating copies of these films.

2. Frank Proctor III, *"Damned Notions of Liberty": Slavery, Culture, and Power in Colonial Mexico, 1640–1769* (Albuquerque: University of New Mexico Press, 2010), 15.

3. Matthew Restall, *The Black Middle: Africans, Mayas, and Spaniards in Colonial Yucatan* (Stanford: Stanford University Press, 2009), 15.

4. Ben Vinson III, *Before Mestizaje: The Frontiers of Race and Caste in Colonial Mexico* (Cambridge: Cambridge University Press, 2018), 13.

5. Vinson, *Before Mestizaje*, 2.

6. Pablo Miguel Sierra Silva, *Urban Slavery in Colonial Mexico* (Cambridge: Cambridge University Press, 2018), 5.

7. Christine Arce, *Mexico's Nobodies: The Cultural Legacy of the Soldadera and Afro-Mexican Women*, (Albany: State University of New York Press, 2016), 2.

8. José Vasconcelos, *The Cosmic Race/La raza cósmica: A Bilingual Edition*, trans. Didier Jaén (Baltimore: Johns Hopkins Press, 1997), 22.

9. Carl Mora, *Mexican Cinema: Reflections of a Society, 1896–2004. 3rd Edition* (Jefferson: McFarland, 2005), 83. These beliefs may be shifting. The 2017 Encuesta Nacional sobre Discriminación found that more than 50 percent of the population reported experiencing discriminatory treatment for the color of their skin; it is yet to be seen whether this societal awareness of racism will translate into sustained cinematic treatment. *Encuesta Nacional Sobre Discriminación* (Mexico: CONAPRED, 2017).

10. Christina Sue, "Negotiating Identity Narratives among Mexico's Cosmic Race," in *Global Mixed Race*, eds. Rebecca C. King-O'Riain, Stephen Small, Minelle Mahtani, Miri Song, and Paul Spickard (New York: New York University Press, 2014), 145.

11. Juliet Hooker, *Theorizing Race in the Americas: Douglass, Sarmiento, DuBois and Vasconcelos* (Oxford: Oxford University Press, 2017), 156.

12. Vasconcelos, *The Cosmic Race*, 32.

13. Christina Sue, *Land of the Cosmic Race: Race Mixture, Racism, and Blackness in Mexico* (Oxford: Oxford University Press, 2013), 106.

14. Mónica García-Blizzard, "Whiteness and the Ideal of Modern Mexican Citizenship in Tepeyac (1917)," *Vivomatografías* 1 (2015): 77.

15. Joanne Hershfield, *Mexican Cinema/Mexican Woman, 1940–1950* (Tucson: University of Arizona Press, 1996), 103. *María Candelaria,* in which the titular indigenous protagonist is

depicted by the phenotypically white actress Dolores del Río, exemplifies this dynamic. See Adriana Zavala, *Becoming Modern, Becoming Tradition: Women, Gender, and Representation in Mexican Art* (State College: Penn State Press, 2010), 250.

16. While some Golden Age films included ethnically Black actors, they were often background characters, like Afro-Cuban male musicians frequently included in *rumbera* films, who functioned more as local color or backdrop than as characters with narrative importance.

17. Alison Fraunhar, *Mulata Nation: Visualizing Race and Gender in Cuba* (Jackson: University of Mississippi Press, 2018), 98. For more on Blackface in Mexican political cabaret, see Laura G. Gutiérrez, "*El derecho de re-hacer*: Signifyin(g) Blackness in Contemporary Mexican Political Cabaret," *Arizona Journal of Hispanic Cultural Studies* 16 (2012): 163–76.

18. Arce, *Mexico's Nobodies*, 209.

19. See Carolyn Fornoff, "Musical Interludes in 1960s Mexican Melodrama: Crafting a Sonic Space of Exclusion," *Romance Notes* 58, no.3 (2018): 507–18.

20. For more on Eusebia Cosme's career trajectory see Antonio López, "Re/Citing Eusebia Cosme," in *Unbecoming Blackness: The Diaspora Cultures of Afro-Cuban America* (New York: New York University Press, 2012), 61–111.

21. Angela C. Pao, *No Safe Spaces: Re-casting Race, Ethnicity, and Nationality in American Theater* (Ann Arbor: University of Michigan Press, 2011), 4.

22. Philip Michael Thomas, email message to author, Feb. 6, 2018.

23. Fraunhar, *Mulata Nation*, 97–98.

24. Marvin D'Lugo, "Aural Identity, Genealogies of Sound Technologies, and Hispanic Transnationality on Screen," in *World Cinemas, Transnational Perspectives*, eds. Natasa Ďurovičová and Kathleen Newman (New York: Routledge, 2010), 175.

25. Eduardo de la Vega Alfaro, "The Decline of the Golden Age and the Making of the Crisis," in *Mexico's Cinema: A Century of Film and Filmmakers*, eds. Joanne Hershfield and David R. Maciel (Lanham: SR Books, 1999), 176.

26. Seraina Rohrer, *La India María: Mexploitation and the Films of María Elena Velasco* (Austin: University of Texas Press, 2017).

27. Emilio García Riera, *Breve historia del cine mexicano: primer siglo, 1897–1997* (Mexico: Conaculta, 1998), 305.

28. "Movie Ad of the Week: Negro es un bello color," *Temple of Schlock* (blog), October 14, 2012, http://templeofschlock.blogspot.com/2012/10/movie-ad-of-week-negro-es-un-bello.html.

29. Roberto Ortiz, "Performing Blackness in Mexican Cinema: Eusebia Cosme, Rita Montaner and Juan José Laborier," *Mediático* (blog), March 9, 2018, http://reframe.sussex.ac.uk/mediatico/2018/03/09/performing-Blackness-in-mexican-cinema-eusebia-cosme-rita-montaner-and-juan-jose-laboriel/.

30. For more on exploitation cinemas in Latin America, see Victoria Ruétalo and Dolores Tierney, eds., *Latsploitation, Exploitation Cinemas, and Latin America* (New York: Routledge, 2009).

31. Interestingly, the VHS box art provides an alternative title for the film, referring to it as *Casta indomable* [Indomitable Caste].

32. The poster advertising the film's run in the Teatro Plaza in Queens, New York, included the racist tagline: "Su color la hace agresiva, amargada . . . Su maternidad, comprensiva y humana" [Her skin color makes her aggressive, bitter . . . Her maternity, understanding and human].

33. Ben Sifuentes-Jáuregui, "*El derecho de responder:* Reactions to Laura Gutiérrez's '*El derecho de re-hacer:* Signifyin(g) Blackness in Contemporary Mexican Political Cabaret': Melodrama of Race," *Arizona Journal of Hispanic Cultural Studies* 16 (2012): 178.

34. Sergio Raúl López, "*La negrada*, filme de ficción que aborda el tema de la tercera raíz en México," *La Jornada*, August 10, 2018, https://www.jornada.com.mx/2018/08/10/espectaculos/a07n1esp. Pérez Solano went on to say, "Me dijeron que si me metía más iba a encontrar más negros, pero son más salvajes" [They told me that if I went deeper inland (for casting) I would find blacker people, but they are more savage]. Afro-Mexican advocacy groups, including Afrodescendencias, México Negro, and Colectiva de la Costa de Oaxaca, among others, signed a letter denouncing his use of the word "salvaje" to describe Black people as well as to decry the filmic representations of Blacks as stereotypical.

## Bibliography

Arce, B. Christine. *México's Nobodies: The Cultural Legacy of the Soldadera and Afro-Mexican Women*. Albany, NY: State University of New York Press, 2017.

de la Vega Alfaro, Eduardo. "The Decline of the Golden Age and the Making of the Crisis." In *Mexico's Cinema: A Century of Film and Filmmakers*, edited by Joanne Hershfield and David R. Maciel, 165–91. Lanham: SR Books, 1999.

D'Lugo, Marvin. "Aural Identity, Genealogies of Sound Technologies, and Hispanic Transnationality on Screen." In *World Cinemas, Transnational Perspectives*, edited by Natasa Durovičová and Kathleen Newman, 160–85. New York: Routledge, 2010.

Fornoff, Carolyn. "Musical Interludes in 1960s Mexican Melodrama: Crafting a Sonic Space of Exclusion." *Romance Notes* 58, no. 3 (2018): 507–18.

Fraunhar, Alison. *Mulata Nation: Visualizing Race and Gender in Cuba*. Jackson: University of Mississippi Press, 2018.

García-Blizzard, Mónica. "Whiteness and the Ideal of Modern Mexican Citizenship in *Tepeyac* (1917)." *Vivomatografías* no. 1 (2015): 72–95.

García Riera, Emilio. *Breve historia del cine mexicano: primer siglo, 1897–1997*. Mexico: Conaculta, 1998.

Gutiérrez, Laura G. "*El derecho de re-hacer:* Signifyin(g) Blackness in Contemporary Mexican Political Cabaret." *Arizona Journal of Hispanic Cultural Studies* no. 16 (2012): 163–76.

Hershfield, Joanne. *Mexican Cinema/Mexican Woman, 1940–1950*. Tucson: University of Arizona Press, 1996.

Hooker, Juliet. *Theorizing Race in the Americas: Douglass, Sarmiento, DuBois and Vasconcelos*. Oxford: Oxford University Press, 2017.

López, Antonio. "Re/Citing Eusebia Cosme." In *Unbecoming Blackness: The Diaspora Cultures of Afro-Cuban America*. New York: New York University Press, 2012, 61–111.

López, Sergio Raúl. "*La negrada*, filme de ficción que aborda el tema de la tercera raíz en México." *La Jornada*, August 10, 2018, https://www.jornada.com.mx/2018/08/10/espectaculos/a07n1esp.

Mora, Carl. *Mexican Cinema: Reflections of a Society, 1896–2004*. Jefferson, NC: McFarland & Company, 2005.

"Movie Ad of the Week: Negro es un bello color." *Temple of Schlock* (blog). October 14, 2012. http://templeofschlock.blogspot.com/2012/10/movie-ad-of-week-negro-es-un-bello.html.

Ortiz, Roberto. "Performing Blackness in Mexican Cinema: Eusebia Cosme, Rita Montaner and Juan José Laborier." *Mediático* (blog). March 9, 2018. http://reframe.sussex.ac.uk/mediatico/2018/03/09/performing-Blackness-in-mexican-cinema-eusebia-cosme-rita-montaner-and-juan-jose-laboriel/.

Pao, Angela C. *No Safe Spaces: Re-casting Race, Ethnicity, and Nationality in American Theater.* Ann Arbor: University of Michigan Press, 2011.

Proctor, Frank T., III. *"Damned Notions of Liberty": Slavery, Culture, and Power in Colonial Mexico, 1640–1769.* Albuquerque: University of New Mexico Press, 2010.

Restall, Matthew. *The Black Middle: Africans, Mayas, and Spaniards in Colonial Yucatan.* Stanford: Stanford University Press, 2009.

Rohrer, Seraina. *La India María: Mexploitation and the Films of María Elena Velasco.* Austin: University of Texas Press, 2017.

Ruétalo, Victoria, and Dolores Tierney, eds. *Latsploitation, Exploitation Cinemas, and Latin America.* New York: Routledge, 2009.

Sierra Silva, Pablo Miguel. *Urban Slavery in Colonial Mexico.* Cambridge: Cambridge University Press, 2018.

Sifuentes-Jáuregui, Ben. "*El derecho de responder:* Reactions to Laura Gutiérrez's '*El derecho de re-hacer:* Signifyin(g) Blackness in Contemporary Mexican Political Cabaret': Melodrama of Race." *Arizona Journal of Hispanic Cultural Studies* 16 (2012): 177–80.

Sue, Christina. *Land of the Cosmic Race: Race Mixture, Racism, and Blackness in Mexico.* New York: Oxford University Press, 2013.

———. "Negotiating Identity Narratives among Mexico's Cosmic Race." In *Global Mixed Race*, edited by Rebecca C. King-O'Riain, Stephen Small, Minelle Mahtani, Miri Song, and Paul Spickard, 144–64. New York: New York University Press, 2014.

Vasconcelos, José. *The Cosmic Race / La raza cósmica: A Bilingual Edition.* Translated by Didier Jaén. Baltimore: Johns Hopkins Press, 1997.

Vinson, Ben, III. *Before Mestizaje: The Frontiers of Race and Caste in Colonial Mexico.* Cambridge: Cambridge University Press, 2018.

Zavala, Adriana. *Becoming Modern, Becoming Tradition: Women, Gender, and Representation in Mexican Art.* State College: Penn State Press, 2010.

# 6

## UN CINE FAMILIAR

Recovering the 1980s Mexican Family Film

OLIVIA COSENTINO

President José López Portillo's nepotistic appointment of his sister, Margarita, as director of the newly established Dirección General de Radio-Televisión-Cinema (RTC) in 1976 was the literal embodiment of a transformation that was beginning to take shape: the centrality of the "family" in 1980s Mexican filmmaking. After the hands-on Echeverría era, the López Portillo administration dramatically bowed out of film production, creating space and incentives for privatized filmmaking in hopes that it would "propiciar un retorno a la llamada 'época de oro' del cine mexicano, y a un cine 'familiar'" [foster a return to the so-called "Golden Age" of Mexican film, and to a "family" cinema].[1] Reflecting on the post-Echeverría film industry, Tomás Pérez Turrent writes, "The auteur cinema and the so-called critical approach to reality were put back in the closet. Family cinema was the new watchword of the cinema authorities."[2]

Indeed, we could classify a significant body of 1980s film production as *cine familiar,* loosely translated as "family cinema," which envisioned families—adults and children alike—as their target audience and whose narratives centered on families and their problems. My notion of *cine familiar* accounts not only for narrative content and intended audience, but also for the changing production structures of the era, thus expanding upon what Margarita López Portillo initially implied with the term. In the industrial shift from state-sponsored cinema to privately funded, largely commercial production, making movies became, quite literally, a family affair. To varying degrees, the largest media companies at the time were dynastic ventures run by members of the same family—the Azcárragas, the Galindos, the Agrasánchez, and the Calderóns—which often functioned as a strategy for cost-effectiveness given the tantamount goal of profit.[3]

Despite the centrality of *cine familiar* to 1980s Mexican cinema, this group of films has slipped through the cracks in part due to the pejorative connotation of *cine familiar* and its connection to Margarita López Portillo. Never forgiven for her role in the 1982 Cineteca Nacional fire that destroyed films and archival materials alike, López Portillo has been lambasted by critics and filmmakers over the past thirty years for her "disastrous" management of Mexican cinema.[4] Alejandro Pelayo, the current director of the Cineteca Nacional, calls her appointment to the RTC "imperdonable" [unforgivable], given that Margarita "carecía de la experiencia, los conocimientos, de la sensibilidad y el carácter necesario para esta responsabilidad" [lacked the experience, the knowledge, the sensibility, and the necessary character for this responsibility].[5] Anger toward the administration, combined with deep-rooted elitist tendencies to disdain commercial cinema, has prevented scholars from identifying this multifaceted familial phenomenon that unfolded throughout the 1980s and into the early 1990s.

In this chapter, I first situate my analysis of *cine familiar* within recent, revisionist Anglo and Mexican critical engagement with 1970s–1980s Mexican cinema and how it dialogues with larger debates on "family films" in the Hollywood and global context. Then, I trace the context from which *cine familiar* arose, paying particular attention to family-centered industrial production practices, with special attention to those used by the Galindos due to the availability of archival information. Building upon Colin Gunckel's recent call for "an historical industry histories approach to Mexican and Latin American cinema that incorporates while departing from more text-centric approaches," my definition of *cine familiar* emphasizes the relationship between industrial conditions and the genesis of the genre.[6] I explore how the "doubleness" of these films' hybrid appeals to adults and children affects aspects of distribution (marketing strategies), production (youth stars, *actuación especial*, popular music), and the text (shared narrative tropes) through salient trends seen across *cine familiar*. While this chapter is not exhaustive, it pulls a plethora of examples from a *cine familiar* corpus.[7] My conclusion proposes a new direction for Mexican film studies: the thriving YouTube afterlife of 1980s *cine familiar* and the contemporary comment-section communities it fosters.

English- and Spanish-language scholarship have only begun to revitalize debates on commercial, non-auteur 1970s–1980s Mexican film within the past ten years. Seraina Rohrer's *La India María* draws critical attention to this time period by mapping La India María's (María Elena Velasco) films within "Mexploitation" production. Though Rohrer points to comedies, sexy films, wrestler hits, and border cinema as subcategories, she overlooks the family film phenomenon.[8] In my own previous work on multiplatform youth star Lucerito and Televisa's cross-promotion strategies, I identified some *cine familiar* as "Televisa youth star films."[9] Yet, *cine familiar* goes beyond Televisa and Lucerito with a more refined understanding of media players, production companies, and the family film as a genre. Mónica María González Saravia Peña's thesis on Mexican "cine infantil" [children's films], which spans 1939–2009, is the first scholarship published in Mexico that takes the family film seriously. For González, *cine familiar* functions as an umbrella term solely related to the rating system—"aptas para todo público" [suitable for all audiences]—yet she claims that some A-rated films "contienen temas, lenguaje o escenas no recomendables para niños" [contain subjects, language, or scenes that are unsuitable for children].[10] González classifies feature-length children's films into "Adaptaciones literarias, Melodrama infantil, Cine de aventuras y Cine de animación" [Literary Adaptations, Children's Melodrama, Adventure Films and Animation], largely discussing discursive content.[11] Most of what I consider *cine familiar,* González categorizes as children's melodrama, which she in fact views as the "género donde la línea entre el cine familiar y el cine infantil es más delgada" [genre where the line is thinnest between family films and children's films].[12]

## *Cine familiar* vs. the Hollywood Family Film

Extant Hollywood-centric scholarship of the "family film" helps guide our approach to understanding *cine familiar*. Robert C. Allen explains that "the 'family film' emerged in the late 1980s and early 1990s as Hollywood's attempt to exploit the profit potential of the video markets."[13] Allen hesitates tying the "family film" to subject matter; instead, he claims the term "became the discursive marker for a set of narrative, representational and institutional practices designed to maximise marketability and profitability across theatrical, video, licensing and merchandising markets by means of what we might call cross-generational appeal."[14] Despite the fact that Mexican family films never had licensing deals, Allen's methodological focus on practices and markets shapes my own.[15]

The introduction to Noel Brown and Bruce Babington's volume *Family Films in Global Cinema: The World Beyond Disney* theorizes a system for identifying the (global) family film, pulling from Brown's *The Hollywood Family Film*. Uniting factors include: one, "suitability for children;" two, "recurrent themes and situations, including the reaffirmation of nation, kinship and community; the exclusion and/or defeat of disruptive social elements; the minimization of 'adult' themes," and "upbeat, morally and emotionally straightforward" endings that are "supportive of the social status quo;" and three, the centrality of "a literal or symbolic child figure," often "child stars."[16] Importantly, Brown and Babington also gesture toward "non-textual manufacturing processes which collectively inform a film's 'family' identity: i) marketing and distribution strategies; ii) suitability ratings; iii) critical responses; iv) merchandising; and v) television broadcast strategies," all of which contribute to "a film's playability to 'family' audiences."[17] Most critical to the analysis I undertake in the following sections is what Brown and Babington call "child/adult doubleness," a term they use to refer to the ways in which family films attempt to widen their appeal to "the parents/guardians accompanying young children to the cinema."[18]

Although Brown and Babington's volume attempts to treat the family film "beyond Hollywood," chapters on other cinemas (Brazil, India, and Japan) are limited to the framework of "the relationship between cinema and state," often equating them to studies of national identity.[19] The disproportionate focus on the national in cinemas other than Hollywood in the field of film and media studies contributes to Mexican film scholarship's deep-rooted obsession with *mexicanidad*, or Mexicanness, and results in critical absences.[20] This fixation with national identity is one reason why the Mexican family film is overlooked in much of canonical Mexican film criticism and would never be included within a global film history. *Cine familiar* does not promote specific forms of *mexicanidad*, perhaps with the exception of the popular music that draws from traditional Mexican styles. This lack of didactic *mexicanidad* distinguishes the 1980s *cine familiar* from the Golden Age classics, to which Margarita López Portillo hoped to return. While national identity is an unproductive lens for *cine familiar*, the particularities of national context are critical to understand the genesis of this genre.

## Situating *Cine familiar* and the Family in 1980s Mexico

*Cine familiar* emerges at a very specific moment, both within Mexican film history and the socio-historic, economic, and political context of Mexico. With highly popular and explicit *ficheras* and *sexycomedias* flooding theaters, the market for family-friendly cinema was wide open. The guaranteed safeness of *cine familiar* can be read as reactionary to the fervently racy films that targeted adult-only audiences. *Cine familiar* also revives the discursive figure of the family, which disintegrated on-screen in the post–Golden Age era, as seen in canonical productions like *Mecánica nacional* [*National Mechanics*] (Luis Alcoriza, 1972) and *El castillo de la pureza* [*The Castle of Purity*] (Arturo Ripstein, 1973) that show the Mexican family at its lowest point.[21] A 1978 issue of *fem,* a feminist magazine published in Mexico, critiqued "the family" and its role in exploiting women and reproducing sexism. Among articles like "¿para qué sirve la familia?" [what is the family for?] and "la crítica feminista a la familia" [feminist critique of the family], by Marta Lamas, the magazine collectively declares in its editorial: "*fem* no está contra los lazos afectos y la solidaridad de la familia, sino contra su forma patriarcal y opresiva, consecuencia de la función económica e ideológica que cumple en este sistema" [*fem* is not against the affective ties and solidarity of the family, but rather is opposed to its oppressive, patriarchal form, a consequence of the economic and ideological function that it fulfills in this system].[22] This dissatisfaction, bubbling to the surface within public discourses of the late 1970s, is indicative of a larger questioning of the institution of the family.

While the state's response to this discursive crisis was to instate El Sistema Nacional para el Desarrollo Integral de la Familia (SNDIF) in 1977, *cine familiar* was a parallel attempt to culturally reclaim the family. As Eric Zolov notes, "Discipline must start within the family, for the nation was a reflection of this basic social unit."[23] Thus, the resemanticization of the "family" is equivalent to the reimposition of the cultural order and further accompanied by a figurative reconsolidation of the parent-child relationship where the alienated, rebellious 1960s–1970s youth are reincorporated into kinship structures that are microcosms of the nation. As I explore later in the chapter, cinematic narratives no longer focus on intergenerational conflict like 1950s–1960s teen rock and roll films, but now pit established family structures against external threats like exploitative bosses and cruel landlords or insidious, internal problems typically related to health. *Cine familiar* functions as an escape mechanism during the difficult 1970s and 1980s economic crises as well as the devastating 1985 Mexico City earthquake, which shook citizens' already waning confidence in the state. By presenting solvable problems, *cine familiar* helps families envision a better tomorrow, specifically through uniting with other families, as well as offering temporary avoidance of real-world struggles that lack clear solutions.

## Family Filmmaking as Industrial Practice

My conceptualization of *cine familiar* goes beyond narrative content and intended audience to gesture toward a larger shift in industrial practices. Rohrer confirms that "the Calderón, Galindo and Agrasánchez families" were the "prolific producers of Mexploitation films."[24] I utilize the Galindo family as a case study because, unlike the Agrasánchez or the Calderóns, the majority share of the *cine familiar* treated here was produced by the Galindos. Likewise, the Galindos dominated the available archival information. I do tread carefully in this section given that a history of producers and/or film production companies in Mexico has yet to be written and most production companies' archives are closed to the public.[25] As Rohrer's study demonstrates, interviews seem to be the most fruitful method for researching these otherwise undocumented familial filmmaking practices, although we then must account for potential biases and intermittent false information. With this in mind, I cautiously draw from sources like Norma Iglesias Prieto's 1988 interview with Rubén Galindo Jr., included in her monograph, *Entre yerba, plomo y polvo*, to sketch out some of the familial dynamics at play in the 1980s Mexican film industry.

First, we need to disentangle some of the Galindo family relations and confusion about their production holdings.[26] In figure 6.1, I offer a Galindo family tree, containing members who were/are involved with various aspects of the filmmaking process, most frequently scriptwriting or adaptation, di-

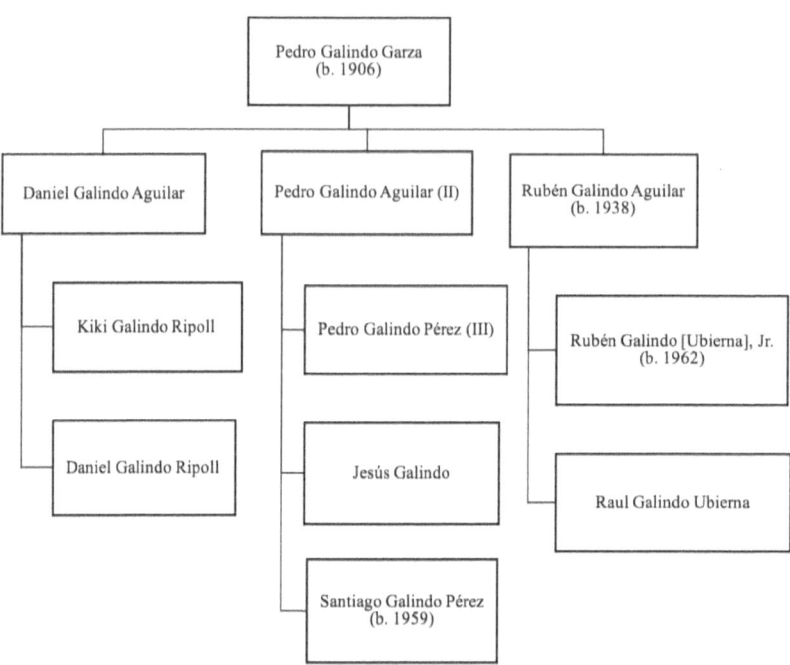

Figure 6.1. An (approximate) Galindo family tree, compiled by Olivia Cosentino.

recting, and executive producing. While Rubén Sr. and Pedro II were largely involved with *cine fronterizo,* Daniel (I) was behind the Pedrito Fernández-Lucerito films.[27] I have been unable to verify how Eduardo Galindo (I) and Eduardo Galindo Pérez (II, III?) are related to the family, but given the temporality of their activity in the film industry, it is likely that Eduardo Galindo Pérez is the same age as Pedro (III) and Rubén Jr. and that Eduardo Galindo (I) is his father. Notably, the Galindo family discussed here is *not* related to Golden Age director (Héctor) Alejandro Galindo Amezcua, who worked primarily for the Agrasánchez family. The Galindo family ran a multitude of companies, including Filmadora Chapultepec, Producciones Galubi/Galubi Films, Galmex, Casa Blanca Producciones, S.A. and Cinematográfica Tabasco, specifically run by Daniel (I).[28]

Family filmmaking in 1980s Mexico for the Galindos takes a web-like structure, which offered "ventajas económicas y organizativas" [organizational and economic advantages].[29] Family members worked together as a team, taking on multiple roles and handling various stages of the film production process as a strategy for more cost-effective filmmaking. Iglesias Prieto explains the Galindos streamlined the often complicated filmmaking process "por la participación laboral y empresarial de los distintos miembros de la familia . . . desde el argumentista, el guionista, los operadores, técnicos y músicos, hasta los actores y empresas que rentan equipo, estudios, salas de montaje y laboratorios" [via the industrial and managerial participation of distinct family members . . . from the storywriter, the screenwriter, the camera operators, crew and musicians, to even the actors and the businesses that rent equipment, studios, editing rooms and labs].[30] The Galindo team became a well-oiled machine, "con muy poco margen de error" [with a very small margin of error].[31] They produced so many films that, given the delays in exhibition, at times their own films went head-to-head at the box office. *Niño pobre, niño rico* (Sergio Véjar, 1983) and *Cementerio del terror* (Rubén Galindo Jr., 1985) both screened on December 12, 1985, but were released in vastly different theaters in Mexico City and targeted distinct audiences.[32] While *Niño pobre* aimed for a family audience, the bloody horror film *Cementerio*, which ultimately did better at the box office, sought teen and adult spectators.

Money was a central concern for the Galindos and other industry families. In 1988, Rubén Galindo Jr. implicitly reveals the priority behind *cine familiar* practices:

> La ventaja de hacer cine familiar es la confianza. No es lo mismo, darle X cantidad de dinero a tu hermano y decirle, contrata un barco, tráite [sic] una ambulancia, y cómprate vidrio, a decírselo a un empleado que a la hora de las cuentas se gastaron efectivamente 50% del dinero y el otro 50% se desparramó en cosas que no sabes.
>
> [The advantage of making *cine familiar* is trust. It is one thing to give X amount of money to your brother and tell him, "hire a boat, bring an ambulance, and buy some glass," and another to send an employee who, when all is said and done, spent 50 percent of the money and squandered the other 50 percent on who knows what.][33]

Galindo's remark is noteworthy for two reasons. First, it shows that industry members took up Margarita López Portillo's term *cine familiar* to refer to their own strategic familial operations on an industrial level, rather than meaning narrative content or intended consumers. Second, Galindo's implicit understanding of "confianza" [trust] demonstrates the importance of profit. The main advantage of *cine familiar* is that family members could be trusted to spend funds efficiently and not embezzle money because, logically, doing so would cut into their own profits. Another important money-saving strategy employed by both the Galindos and the Agrasánchez was to move their filmmaking operations to Brownsville, Texas, in the 1970s. Iglesias Prieto explains that this allowed the families to evade the high cost of the unionized technical crew in addition to pricey studio rentals.[34] This practice continued (and thrived) until 1985, when the US began to require that some of the crew was from the US, a condition that would have cut into profits.[35]

And yet, it seems that these family production units were not solely driven by profits. While the "recognizable low-budget aesthetic" of Mexploitation productions can be attributed to the practice of "keeping shooting times as short as possible," this was not always the case for the Galindo family's films.[36] Whereas *Niño pobre, niño rico* was shot in twenty-five days, the shoot for *Delincuente* (Sergio Véjar, 1984) lasted approximately two months, from November 22, 1984, to January 25, 1985.[37] In November 1984, *El Heraldo* reported that Daniel Galindo had invested 35 million pesos in his film *Delincuente*.[38] Galindo told the press, "Cuando tenemos una buena historia no nos importa invertir un poco más de dinero" [When we have a good story, we do not mind investing a bit more money] for Lucerito, Pedrito, and Chico Che and the musical arrangements.[39] While Galindo makes obvious his desire to "recuperar al público familiar" [recover family audiences] with this "historia tierna" [tender story], the investment is still quite risky from a business perspective given that by November 1984, Galindo's first Pedrito-Lucerito film, *Coqueta* (Sergio Véjar, 1983), had yet to screen in Mexico.[40] When asked "si esos retrasos en la exhibición no lo hacen mejor invertir su dinero en valores bancarios" [if these delays in exhibition make it better to invest your money in banking securities], Galindo responds in a surprising way: "Lo he pensado, pero tenemos el cine en las venas, por lo menos yo . . . Seguiremos en este medio hasta que el cuerpo aguante" [I've thought about it, but we've got cinema in our blood, at least I do . . . We'll continue this way as long as possible].[41] This expression of love and devotion for cinema, a connecting factor for the family, makes me doubt that profit was the only motivation in these *cine familiar* ventures. After this sentimental remark, Galindo quickly notes that despite some box office failures, all of his films eventually get back the initial investment, revealing that "La American General, que distribuye películas mexicanas en EU, ya me pidió 'Delincuente,' y en seis meses se estrenará" [American General, who distributes Mexican films in the US, already asked me for *Delincuente,* and it will be released in six months].[42] There is not room here to sufficiently explore the complexity of *cine familiar*'s (transnational) distribution, yet this anecdote supports Rohrer's claim that many Mexploitation films made the majority of their profits on the other side of the border.[43]

A discussion of *cine familiar*'s industrial practices would be incomplete without a word on the well-known, yet highly secretive, Televisa dynasty. Many Galindo family members now work as producers for Televisa, after their *cine familiar* and other cinematic ventures faded out in the 1990s. While the Azcárraga family has always been at the top of Televisa's operations—including Televicine, a film production branch that produced *cine familiar* in the 1980s and 1990s—a much more pernicious notion of family has pervaded the company. Raúl Trejo Delarbe writes that "entre las principales trabas que encuentran los trabajadores de Televisa están la ideología colaboracionista y despolitizadora que imponen en la empresa (la idea de que todos forman parte de una sólida y exclusiva familia)" [among the main obstacles faced by Televisa employees is the collaborationist, depoliticizing ideology instilled by the company (the idea that everyone is part of a strong, exclusive family)].[44] In other words, the idea of family allows Televisa to exploit, silence, and disenfranchise workers who are discouraged from questioning or turning their back on their "family."

## Child/Adult Appeals

My understanding of 1980s *cine familiar* also addresses how targeting a cross-generational family audience shaped advertising and marketing strategies and dictated certain diegetic features, like utilizing multilayered plots and casting recognizable adult actors alongside youth star protagonists to create what Brown and Babington call "child-adult doubleness" or "double address."[45] One of the biggest reasons that *cine familiar* was so popular for private production companies was that bringing in an entire family to the theater would sell more tickets and generate greater box office receipts. Thus, *cine familiar* made its family friendliness known at every opportunity, beginning with the rating of "Clasificación A: Apta para toda la familia" [Classification A: Suitable for the entire family]. Marketing materials for films specifically targeted family moviegoers. *Tele Guía* published a handwritten letter from Pedrito Fernández, cut and pasted over images of the fourteen-year-old star posing shirtless in a speedo. His letter tells readers, "Hace aproximadamente un mes y medio terminé una película que por título lleva 'Coqueta.' Ojalá que cuando se esté exhibiendo, no dejen de ir a verla, es para toda la familia y tiene un mensaje muy bonito" [Approximately a month and a half ago I finished a movie called *Coqueta*. I hope that, when it comes out, you don't forget to go see it, it's for the whole family and it has a nice message].[46] Likewise, a radio spot for *Delincuente* enticed potential family audiences: "DELINCUENTE. ¡Emotiva! ¡Conmovedora! DELINCUENTE por robar un cariño . . . Por robar el amor de una familia" [*DELINCUENTE*. Touching! Moving! DELINCUENTE for stealing your heart . . . For stealing the whole family's heart].[47] VHS marketing was especially interested in helping families identify the movies that they should rent or purchase. On the back cover of the VHS packaging for *Un corazón para dos* (Sergio Véjar, 1989), potential spectators are interpellated with the following: "Vea este drama de la vida real junto con su familia, y disfrute una vez mas [*sic*] de sus artistas preferidos" [Watch this real-life drama together with your family and once again enjoy your favorite artists]. The back cover of the box for *Fiebre de amor* (René Cardona Jr., 1985) functions similarly, promising "*Fiebre de Amor* es una película para toda la familia, llena de amor y acción en uno de los escenarios más bellos del mundo: ACAPULCO" [*Fiebre de Amor* is a film for the whole family, full of love and action in one of the world's most beautiful settings: ACAPULCO] and approving a consumer's choice to show the film to their family.

The two VHS back cover blurbs gesture toward key aspects of the "double address," or the ways in which *cine familiar* speaks to both children and adult audiences. *Fiebre de amor* contains both love and action, meaning that its multilayered plot allows for the narrative to be understood in a multiplicity of ways by different viewers. (And, if not, viewers will appreciate the beauty of Acapulco.) González critiques movies marketed as "películas familiares" [family films] that "resultan demasiado complicadas para niños de 3 a 7 años" [turned out to be too complicated for children ages 3 to 7], specifically pointing to *La niña de los hoyitos* (Rubén Galindo, 1984) and *Coqueta*.[48] What González seems to miss is the central issue of suitability for children; while three- to seven-year-olds may not engage with the narrative like older children, youth, or adults, the content overall is not inappropriate. These narrative insufficiencies, however, do suggest that other appeals beyond the story itself make up this child/adult doubleness.

One critical aspect to cross-generational appeal are multiplatform youth stars, bouncing between acting, singing, and other commercial ventures. Multiplatform youth stars, including Lucerito, Luis Miguel, Pedrito Fernández, Paquito Cuevas, Anahí, María Rebeca, and Usi Velasco, repeatedly appear in *cine familiar*. Brown and Babington suggest that "child stars" are "obvious identification figures for children, while remaining objects of fascination, nostalgia and objectification for adults."[49] Youth stars, usually pre- to mid-teens in *cine familiar*, tend to serve a similar purpose in Mexico with the critical distinction that, unlike in Hollywood, the popular music of these young actor-singers was a huge draw for spectators of all ages.[50] A small advertisement in a Colombian newspaper for a double showing of *El Sargento Capulina* (Alfredo Zacarías, 1983) and *La niña de los hoyitos*, both films rated suitable for all, even dedicates valuable print space to listing all the songs that Pedrito performs in the film.[51] This intermedial cinema-music-television connection in *cine familiar* is predicated by the fact that nearly every aforementioned Mexican youth star started their nationally-recognized singing careers on Televisa's televised variety show, *Siempre en Domingo*, in the late 1970s or early 1980s.

Laura Podalsky underscores how 1960s Argentine youth films synergistically borrowed from other cultural industries—"íconos musicales; la música nuevaolera; y cierta organizacion episódica caracteristica de los programas televisivos" [musical icons; new wave music; and a certain episodic organization characteristic of television shows]—as a tactic for tapping into, or maybe even creating, an incipient youth market while maintaining existing older audiences.[52] Podalsky describes how the ending of *Fiebre de primavera* (Enrique Carreras, 1965), with six brief musical performances by the young singer-actor stars, "parece seguir la gramática de *los shows musicales de la televisión argentina del momento*" [seems to follow the grammar of music shows from Argentine television at the time].[53] In this way, cinema echoes the episodic style of popular televised music shows, often at the expense of narrative coherence.

We see these strategies at work in 1980s Mexican *cine familiar*, where semi-diegetic musical numbers feature the young stars' singing talents. Pedrito Fernández performs classic *rancheras* in *Niño pobre, niño rico*, an appeal to adult audiences who grew up with this form of popular music. In a musical sequence that acts as the film's finale, the families gather around at a party to watch a performance by Mario (Pedrito Fernández), accompanied by a full mariachi band. Mario sings, "Allá en el rancho grande," a tune from the most important, successful, and nostalgia-inducing Golden Age *comedia ranchera*. The lyrics to the classic song have no connection to the narrative of *Niño pobre*. Other *cine familiar* films, like *Fiebre de amor, Coqueta*, and *Delincuente*, include performances of pop music by Luis Miguel and Lucerito that, at best, connect loosely to the films' themes.

The centrality of popular music to *cine familiar* becomes even more evident with the common practice of releasing films and soundtrack albums with the same name. Unlike the merchandising and licensing of the Hollywood family film, soundtracks were usually the only product promoted alongside films. Given their holdings in television, cinema, and music production in the 1980s, Televisa best exemplifies the model of vertically integrated cross-promotion that draws television audiences (*Siempre en Domingo*) to movie theaters and record stores. As far as I know, other *cine familiar* producers like the Galindos only participated in filmmaking, but the strategic multimedia overlap between popular music and cinema was still present. The first Galindo family film, *La niña de la mochila azul* (Rubén Galindo, 1979), was accompanied by Pedrito Fernández's debut album, *La de la mochila azul* (1978), released by Columbia Records.

Finally, a critical aspect of double appeal consistently utilized across *cine familiar* is the casting of established, veteran actors in the roles of the family members of the young protagonists.[54] These actors are distinguished from other secondary castmates in the opening credits with the denotation of *actuación especial* [special appearance]. Oftentimes these are Mexican comedians, Golden Age cinematic icons, and telenovela or television stars. The presence of these actors is specifically aimed at appealing to adult spectators who recognize them from other media spaces. While youth stars are nearly always top-billed on promotional materials, the veterans' names are the second largest. Comedian Adalberto "Resortes" Martínez appears as young Amy's (María Rebeca) drunk uncle in *La niña de la mochila azul* and its sequel, and as Chambitas, the kind taxi driver who looks out for Paquito

(Paquito Cuevas) in *Mamá, soy Paquito* (Sergio Véjar, 1984), both Galindo family films. Chili Western star Mario Almada even breaks from his usual genre to appear in *La mugrosita* (Rubén Galindo, 1982), less successful than *La niña de la mochila azul* but with much of the same cast, and *Un corazón para dos* as the loving grandfather. Other noteworthy special performances include Pedro Armendáriz Jr. in *Mamá solita* (Miguel M. Delgado, 1980) and *Los dos carnales* (Enrique Gómez Vadillo, 1983), Julissa in *Los dos carnales*, Blanca Guerra in *Mamá, soy Paquito*, Joaquín Cordero and Maricruz Olivier in *La niña de los hoyitos*, and David Reynoso in *Había una vez una estrella* (Sergio Véjar, 1989). Perhaps the actor with the most *cine familiar* credits is telenovela star José Elías Moreno [*Coqueta, Delincuente, Niño pobre, niño rico, Un corazón para dos, Había una vez una estrella*], who is frequently cast as older brother, tutor, friend, mentor (and one time, a priest) in order to model behavior and advise the young protagonists.

## Escaping Crisis, Restoring the Family, Absolving the State, and Other Narrative Tropes

The prevailing industrial and critical assumption in the 1980s that commercial cinema was ideologically empty and only for entertainment purposes was both good and bad for family films. On one hand, Rohrer notes that this attitude allowed commercial films like the *La India María* franchise (but also *cine familiar*), to evade practices of censorship.[55] On the other hand, this meant that records about these films were rarely archived, leaving a lacuna in Mexican commercial cinema history. Additionally, most critical reviews of *cine familiar* at the time take a snide, dismissive tone, utilizing every chance to deride the films. Tomás Pérez Turrent's review of *Coqueta* in *El Universal* drips with sarcasm: "La niña está por desgracia enferma del corazón y muere, pero no se asusten, mientras tanto nos echamos un buen número de canciones. Debuta aquí un futuro Premio Nobel de guión: Kiki Galindo Ripoll" [Unfortunately, the girl has heart problems and dies, but have no fear, in the meantime we'll sing a bunch of songs. Making her debut here, a future Nobel Prize–winner for scriptwriting: Kiki Galindo Ripoll].[56]

Critics' embittered feelings toward *cine familiar* (and the state of the film industry in the 1980s at large) prevent them from recognizing its ideological potency and how this widely seen cinema shaped the Mexican imaginary.

Miguel Pitti's response to *Ya nunca más* [*Never Again*](Abel Salazar, 1984), entitled "Nuestro minusválido cine" [Our Disabled Cinema], denies the film a review: "*Ya nunca más* es un anzuelo barato, una película cuya reseña sería inútil y ociosa, solo un ejemplo del cine que estimuló Margarita López Portillo y que ahora se sigue haciendo, nada más porque conviene y porque quién se va a quejar, si es inocuo" [*Ya nunca más* is cheap bait, a film whose review would be useless and inane, nothing more than an example of the cinema encouraged by Margarita López Portillo that now they continue making for no other reason than because it's convenient and who's going to complain, if it's innocuous].[57] Pitti is correct that youth star sensation Luis Miguel functions as spectator-bait for *Ya nunca más,* yet fails to see the implications of the film's messaging, which is far from innocuous.

The eighth most-seen Mexican film in Mexico in 1984, raking in 48,649,505 pesos at the box office, *Ya nunca más* promotes the value of obedience.[58] After his father expressly forbids him from riding motorcycles, Luis (Luis Miguel) has a terrible accident that necessitates the amputation of his leg. He spends the majority of the film writhing helplessly and wailing from his hospital bed. A parallel situation occurs in *Coqueta* when Rocío (Lucerito), ignoring her mother, goes roller-skating and later dies from the overactivity to her heart defect. By equating disobedience with tragedy, these drastic parables underscore the importance of children's obedience to their parents and, by extension, the paternal Mexican state. Zolov writes that "the idealized family of the post-revolutionary order was one in which the father was stern in his benevolence, the mother saintly in her maternity, and the children loyal in their obedience."[59] *Ya nunca más* and *cine familiar* tend toward upholding values and the traditional family dynamics that consolidate PRI power.

Just as the Hollywood family film was a response to the discursive presence of "family" in 1980s US politics, my close readings of *cine familiar* contextualize the films within 1980s Mexican society and consider their implicit commentary on the relationship between the Mexican family and the state.[60] The 1980s were a relatively turbulent decade for Mexico both economically and politically. As a result of skyrocketing inflation, the year 1982 witnessed significant cuts to public spending in Mexico, which in turn led to falling salaries and rising unemployment.[61] Luis Aboites Aguilar notes that "muchas familias comprendieron que tenían que vérselas por sí mismas" [many families understood that they had to take care of themselves], resulting in augmented self-employment as well as family separation when some men opted to migrate for better economic opportunities in the US.[62]

*Cine familiar* responded to these crises in two escapist ways. First, some *cine familiar* functioned as an escape valve, allowing tensions regarding state abandonment of the Mexican family to be rehearsed, released, and resolved on the big screen. The social critiques within *cine familiar* are oblique, especially when compared with its acerbic and confrontational contemporary, *¿Cómo ves?* (Paul Leduc, 1986), which unflinchingly confronts viewers with Mexican poverty and inequality. With *cine familiar*, villainous individuals tend to take the blame for state failures. In *Los dos carnales*, the stand-in villains take the form of malicious landlord, Don Rodolfo (Carlos Bravo y Fernández), and construction boss, Don Cristóbal (Pedro Armendáriz Jr.), who denies his workers the right to join a union. Don Cristóbal exercises a surprising amount of oppressive force against his striking workers—including young Pablo (Pedrito Fernández)—but the issue is reshaped when Pablo falls into a hole on the construction site. Don Cristóbal (who is secretly Pablo's father) and the disgruntled workers come together harmoniously to rescue him. After a grueling eight-hour excavation, Pablo is saved, Don Cristóbal reveals his identity, reunites with Pablo's mother, Susana (Julissa), and the film ends with a performance by Pedrito, who saccharinely croons, "Eres mi Dios, papá" [You are my God, daddy]. That Don Cristóbal is an "actuación especial," a recognizable and beloved actor, is of utmost important to making him a redeemable figure for spectators. *Los dos carnales* curbs the workers' collective political struggle and the state's failure to protect the right to unionization by overshadowing it with a heartwarming tale of family reunification, a paradigm I explore later.

Another way that *cine familiar* absolves the state of its failures is by proposing collective, popular solidarity as the solution to social crisis, *not* greater state intervention. As the title suggests, *Niño pobre, niño rico* explicitly compares the suffering of the rich and poor through the friendship of two young boys, Pepe (Paquito Cuevas) and Mario (Pedrito Fernández). Pepe, his family, and the other members of the tenements where he lives openly discuss poverty, rising rent prices, and the devaluation of the peso. One of Pepe's neighbors, unable to pay rent because her husband is on strike, is on the brink of eviction by a faceless landlord and his ruthless lawyers. Anger toward the state's abandonment is funneled to the villainous landlord and lawyers. Rather than state action, the neighbors' collective efforts save the woman from eviction and shortly thereafter, the labor union wins the strike. Economic disparities are downplayed; the film shows sympathy to the wealthy, who are presented as suffering in their own ways. When his business ventures abroad go awry, Mario's father (Armando Silvestre) nearly has a stroke. Through the young boys, the rich and poor families come together to form a cross-class alliance, exemplified by Pepe's carpenter father (Tony Bravo) donating blood to Mario's father.[63]

Important to note is that *Niño pobre* screened in December 1985, just months after the devastating 8.1 earthquake in Mexico City. The mega-earthquake was an event that brought to the fore state abandonment of its citizens, given the lack of timely disaster response. Carlos Monsiváis points to this moment as the birth of "la *sociedad civil*, que encabeza, convoca, distribuye la solidaridad" [*civil society*, which leads, summons, distributes solidarity] in the face of governmental inefficiency and bureaucracy.[64] As *Niño pobre* was written and filmed prior to September 1985, I am not suggesting the film somehow responds to the earthquake, but rather that its release date indicates it was not viewed by the PRI nor the industry as ideologically threatening during a moment of heightened political vulnerability. *Niño pobre* successfully redirects audiences' feelings of desertion by the state to instead celebrate the triumph of cross-class citizen-led collective action and solidarity.

The second way that *cine familiar* reacted to the 1970s–1980s economic downturn and peso crisis was through escapist fantasies. The light pleasure of musical numbers that populated *cine familiar* offered temporary reprieve from harsh, uncomfortable realities and unpredictable futures. *Escápate conmigo* (René Cardona Jr., 1989) quite literally invites viewers to join Lucerito on a *Wizard of Oz*–like adventure as she escapes the oppressive confines of a rural orphanage to the idealized (Emerald) Mexico City. Lucerito's *Fiebre de amor* is filled with teenage daydreams about Luis Miguel (who plays himself) that turn into reality. While not all *cine familiar* is quite so idyllic, the vast majority presents solvable problems with neat endings. The endings are not all happy, but *cine familiar* always gives resolution. This quality divides Mexican family films and Hollywood, where Allen points to "ambivalence and indeterminacy" as "the distinguishing formal qualities of texts."[65]

Grave health conditions are a favored plot conflict in *cine familiar*. Sickness provides structure to these emotionally driven narratives, where long-awaited surgeries or the intensification of terminal conditions make for good climaxes and the eventual death or curing of the individual delivers a resolute, closed ending. Some of the films are pedantic cautionary tales, like *Mamá, soy Paquito,* where Paquito's mother (Blanca Guerra) dies from typhus and Paquito nearly does as well. A doctor advises Chambitas (Resortes) to remove Paquito immediately from his home because the disease originates "en los lugares con suciedad, falta de aseo, se transmite por las pulgas de las ratas, los piojos" [in places of filth that lack toilets, transmitted by the fleas on rats and lice]. Emphasizing the gravity of the situation, the doctor urges, "Hay que llevarlo a un hospital, allí se podrá atender mejor" [You must take him to a hospital, they can better care for him there], adding instructively that "el hospital es absolutamente gratuito" [the hospital is completely free], resolving Chambitas's concern about paying for the treatment. Focusing on free healthcare paints the state as savior and shifts attention away from the state's failures in public health, that is, ensuring hygienic, safe living conditions for its citizens. Another example is *Amigo,* a production that directly collaborated with the Secretaría de Salubridad y Asistencia [Secretariat of Health and Assistance] (the former name for Mexico's Secretariat of Health), where we see Poncho (Pedrito Fernández) and other children in an orphanage getting vaccinated. In both films, state institutions are portrayed as benevolent forces that care for the well-being of orphans and the poor.

At the heart of *cine familiar* is a politics of restoration, the desire to reincorporate members of society back into the state's grasp. Family reconciliation or unification becomes a vehicle for describing parallel, idealized citizen-state relations. Children show love and unwavering forgiveness toward the parents or grandparents who temporarily abandoned their familial duties and obligations. Likewise, alienated family members (youth and others) are welcomed back with open arms into the family and, thereby, symbolically back into the nation. A redemptive return to the family structure is always possible.

## *Cine familiar*'s YouTube Afterlife

To the chagrin of Daniel Galindo (I), *cine familiar* began to die out between the late 1980s and the early 1990s. Galindo sought to engender support for the films in 1989 when he told *El Heraldo* that "las películas familiares son la mejor alternativa para dignificar nuestro cine" [family films are the best alternative to dignify our cinema].⁶⁶ By September 1990, Alejandro Salazar Hernández reported, "Ni el público ni las autoridades apoyan el cine familiar de Galindo. Por lo tanto, Daniel, hijo, se abstendrá" [Neither the public nor the authorities support Galindo's *cine familiar*. Therefore, Daniel Jr., will abstain].⁶⁷ I speculate that *cine familiar* declined around 1988 with the rise of neoliberalism and its emphasis on individualism as opposed to the familial kinship structures central to the welfare state. Neoliberal cinema's posh tales of the middle-class publicist, *Sólo con tu pareja* [*Love in the Time of Hysteria*] (Alfonso Cuarón, 1991), reflected Mexican audiences' new preferences.⁶⁸ Despite these shifts in taste as well as industrial structure, the story of *cine familiar* does not end in the 1990s.

While TV has long been a site of post-theatrical life for film, YouTube now takes on that role, creating a space of thriving afterlife for *cine familiar* and the vast majority of films treated in *The Lost Cinema of Mexico*.⁶⁹ Unlike closely monitored Hollywood films, older Mexican films are not often removed from YouTube for copyright violations. The number of views for *cine familiar* available on YouTube is stunning. A copy of *La niña de la mochila azul* uploaded in June 2012 had 4.7 million views by May 2019. *La niña de los hoyitos* accrued 7.8 million views from January 2014 to May 2019; one million of those views occurred from September 2018 to May 2019. Even more fascinating is that the success of a film uploaded to YouTube does not always correlate to its initial box office receipts. Both *Escápate conmigo* (the highest grossing film of 1989) and *La niña de los hoyitos* lasted six weeks in Mexico City theaters at the time of their release, but the *La niña* receives significantly more annual views than *Escápate,* which averages approximately 20,000 per year. A more in-depth study of this YouTube afterlife might explore why certain family films age better than others, perhaps accounting for the aforementioned qualities of *cine familiar* like multiplatform youth stars, popular music, special performances by veteran actors, and common narrative tropes. Future scholarship might also try to determine the demographics (age, sex, location) of typical viewers, especially because *cine familiar* had wide appeal across Latin America, not just in Mexico. We can assume that most spectators, if not all, are Spanish speakers because not a single film from the *cine familiar* corpus is available (on YouTube nor DVD releases) with English subtitles and most of the video comments are written in Spanish.

Perhaps the most interesting aspect of *cine familiar*'s YouTube afterlife is the community it fosters among uploaders and viewers. Commenters seem to find pleasure in affirming that they are not alone in watching these old films in the twenty-first century. Comments such as "Like si ahora lo ves en el 2019" [Like if you're watching this in 2019] or "Like si opines [sic] que estas películas son de las mejores *2018" [Like if you think that these movies are the best *2018] abound.[70] Maybe this is the digital equivalent to sharing the cinematic experience with strangers in a theater. Other viewers post comments requesting that the uploader find and upload different films. Many spectators comment on the content of the films and how the movie relates to their lives today. But nearly every *cine familiar* upload has a version of the same comment: "Estas sí son películas buenas y sanas, sin nada obsceno, ni sangre, ni muertes, ni sexo ni nada . . . todo como aquellos tiempos muy chido y lindo" [These films are good and clean, with nothing obscene, no blood, no murders, no sex or anything . . . just like back then, everything is cool and sweet]. This 2016 comment by Romeo Mendoza on *La niña de los hoyitos* received 205 thumbs-up from other viewers. *Cine familiar* draws spectators who seek to nostalgically reminisce about happier times, embracing romanticized memories to mourn the loss of a time that never existed as they recall it. Mendoza's comment evinces the effectiveness of *cine familiar* at manufacturing a space from which to escape the crises and chaos of the 1980s.

This chapter underscores not only methodological roadblocks but also new avenues of study for the field of Mexican cinema. One such challenge is the ephemerality of information regarding the business of 1980s filmmaking. Defining key players, determining ownership of production companies to even attaining more basic knowledge about budgets, length of shoots, and distribution practices would require significant digging—assuming that such documents even exist—but more likely would necessitate interviewing those who participated at various stages. The laissez-faire attitude from the industry that allowed *cine familiar* to bypass censorship also facilitated its erasure; why preserve materials for films that were only for entertainment purposes? And yet, while *cine familiar* was institutionally lost, I do not believe it was ever popularly forgotten.

The continued circulation and the remarkable number of views of *cine familiar* on YouTube is part of the impetus for the recovery and study of the filmic phenomenon. Given the richness of viewing practices of family films in Mexico, the US, Latin America, and perhaps elsewhere, there is a larger story to be told in terms of exhibition, distribution, and spectatorship, both in the 1980s (theatrical release, then VHS) and today (television, YouTube, DVD collections). *Cine familiar* points to new trajectories and dimensions of transnational film flows as it reverses the traditional paradigm of an elite transnational art cinema; here, lowbrow, critically dismissed commercial cinema won big with audiences across borders. Thus, the 1980s Mexican family film provides an important missing piece in the genealogies of commercial and transnational Mexican cinemas, a history especially relevant today as Mexico's domestic box office is again dominated by Hollywood and by privately funded, commercial Mexican films.

## Notes

1. This and all other translations are my own, unless otherwise noted. Emilio García Riera, *Historia del Cine Mexicano* (Mexico City: SEP, 1986), 325.

2. Tomás Pérez Turrent, "Crises and Renovations (1965–91)," *Mexican Cinema*, ed. Paulo Antonio Paranaguá, trans. Ana M. López (Mexico City: BFI and IMCINE, 1995), 105.

3. The media conglomerate Televisa, which has its roots in radio dating back to the early twentieth century, was founded and has been run by a number of Azcárragas; see Claudia Fernández and Andrew Paxman, *El Tigre: Emilio Azcárraga y su imperio Televisa* (Mexico: Grijalbo, 2013). The Agrasánchez family held a number of production companies including: Producciones Fílmicas Agrasánchez and Cinematográfica Grovas. The Calderóns are a bit of an outlier because they began to make films in the Golden Age (late 1930s) and went on to "invent" the genre of the *fichera*. For more, see Viviana García Besné's documentary *Perdida* (2015) and Silvana Flores, "Las producciones Calderón y su efecto en la región latinoamericana: un caso de intercambio transnacional," *AURA. Revista de Historia y Teoría del Arte* no. 3 (June 2015): 3–16.

4. García Riera, *Historia*, 323. This is later echoed by Carl Mora, Isis Saavedra Luna, Carmen Elisa Gómez and other scholars who rely upon García Riera's foundational narrative; many even repeat the word "disaster" or "disastrous."

5. Alejandro Pelayo, *La generación de la crisis. El cine independiente mexicano de los años ochenta* (Mexico City: IMCINE and CONACULTA, 2012), 94.

6. Colin Gunckel, "The Permanencia Voluntaria Archive and the Historical Study of Mexican Cinema," *Studies in Spanish & Latin American Cinemas* 16, no. 3 (2019): 384.

7. The rather extensive corpus of feature-length Mexican 1980s *cine familiar* includes: *La niña de la mochila azul* (Rubén Galindo, 1979), *Amigo* (Tito Davison, 1980), *El oreja rajada* (Rubén Galindo, 1980), *Mamá solita* (Miguel M. Delgado, 1980), *La niña de la mochila azul 2* (Rubén Galindo, 1981), *Allá en la plaza Garibaldi* (Miguel M. Delgado, 1981), *La mugrosita* (Rubén Galindo & Rubén Galindo Jr., 1982), *Los dos carnales* (Enrique Gómez Vadillo, 1982–1983), *Coqueta* (Sergio Véjar, 1983), *Ya nunca más* (Abel Salazar, 1983), *La niña de los hoyitos* (Rubén Galindo, 1984), *Delincuente* (Sergio Véjar, 1984), *Fiebre de amor* (René Cardona Jr., 1984), *Mamá soy paquito* (Sergio Véjar, 1984), *Niño pobre, niño rico* (Sergio Véjar, 1985), *Como si fuéramos novios* (Sergio Véjar, 1986), *El niño y el Papa* (Rodrigo Castaño, 1987), *Escápate conmigo* (René Cardona Jr., 1987), *Un sábado más* (Sergio Véjar, 1988), *Había una vez una estrella*

(Sergio Véjar, 1989), and *Un corazón para dos* (Sergio Véjar, 1990). If an official English title was not available, I chose to leave titles in Spanish rather than offer an unofficial translation.

8. Seraina Rohrer, *La India María: Mexploitation and the Films of María Elena Velasco* (Austin: University of Texas Press, 2017), 32.

9. Olivia Cosentino, "Televisa Born and Raised: Lucerito's Stardom in 1980s Mexican Media," *The Velvet Light Trap* no. 78 (Fall 2016): 39.

10. Mónica María González Saravia Peña, "Cine infantil: recopilación y análisis de largometrajes realizados en México (1939–2009)" (undergraduate thesis, Universidad Panamericana, 2010), 10.

11. González, "Cine infantil," 11.

12. González, "Cine infantil," 116.

13. Robert C. Allen, "Home Alone Together: Hollywood and the 'Family Film,'" in *Identifying Hollywood's Audiences: Cultural Identity and the Movies*, eds. Melvyn Stokes and Richard Maltby (London: BFI, 1999), 113.

14. Allen, "Home Alone," 114.

15. Although outside the scope of this chapter, Allen's description of the booming VHS industry in the US helps us understand *cine familiar*'s penetration into US markets. Current Ebay listings of VHS tapes of *cine familiar* films *Como si fuéramos novios*, *Un corazón para dos*, and *Mamá, soy Paquito* were all produced by Million Dollar Video Corp., an LA-based company that distributed Mexican films. One of the VHS tapes even has a "Hollywood Video" sticker, which confirms these tapes were available for rental in the US. The revenue from VHS sales/rentals in the US and how much this shaped the Mexican family film has yet to be explored.

16. Noel Brown and Bruce Babington, "Introduction: Children's Films and Family Films," in *Family Films in Global Cinema: The World Beyond Disney* (New York: I.B. Tauris, 2015), 15–6.

17. Brown and Babington, "Introduction," 18.

18. Brown and Babington, "Introduction," 14.

19. Brown and Babington, "Introduction," 25.

20. See the paradigmatic examples of Charles Ramírez Berg, *Cinema of Solitude* (Austin: University of Texas Press, 1992) and Carl Mora, *Mexican Cinema: Reflections of a Society, 1896–2004* (Jefferson, NC: McFarland & Company, 2005). For a discussion of the transnational as it relates to national specificity, see Dolores Tierney, *New Transnationalisms in Contemporary Latin American Cinema* (Edinburgh: Edinburgh University Press, 2018).

21. For more on the Mexican family in cinema, see Carmen Elisa Gómez, *Familia y estado: Visiones desde el cine mexicano* (Guadalajara: Universidad de Guadalajara, 2015).

22. "editorial," *fem* III, no. 7 (April–June 1978), 4.

23. Eric Zolov, *Refried Elvis: The Rise of Mexican Counterculture* (Berkeley: University of California Press, 1999), 51.

24. Rohrer, *La India María*, 62.

25. Andrew Paxman, "Who Killed the Mexican Film Industry? The Decline of the Golden Age, 1946- 1960," *E.I.A.L.* 29, no. 1 (2018): 11.

26. In my own Cosentino 2016, I misidentify *Delincuente* and *Coqueta* as Televisa productions, when Cinematográfica Tabasco was owned and run by the Galindo family.

27. When Pedro Fernández renewed his wedding vows in 2010, Daniel Galindo (I) and his wife served as "padrinos de velación," Joel O'Farrili, "¡Mega boda de Pedro Fernández!" *Tabasco HOY*, October 11, 2010, https://www.tabascohoy.com/nota/100665/iexcl-mega-boda-de-pedro-fernandez.

28. Norma Iglesias Prieto, *Entre yerba, polvo y plomo. Lo fronterizo visto por el cine mexicano* (Tijuana, Baja California: El Colegio de la Frontera Norte, 1991), 78.
29. Iglesias Prieto, *Entre yerba*, 74.
30. Iglesias Prieto, *Entre yerba*, 65.
31. Iglesias Prieto, *Entre yerba*, 64.
32. María Luisa Amador and Jorge Ayala Blanco, *Cartelera Cinematográfica 1980–1989* (Mexico: UNAM, 2006), 293.
33. Iglesias Prieto, *Entre yerba*, 63.
34. Iglesias Prieto, *Entre yerba*, 62.
35. Iglesias Prieto, *Entre yerba*, 78.
36. Rohrer, *La India María*, 61.
37. Information taken from the UNAM Filmoteca's online Filmografía mexicana database.
38. "Daniel Galindo Invirtió 35 Millones de Pesos en el Rodaje de "Delincuente," con Pedrito Fdez," *El Heraldo*, November 23, 1984, 3.
39. "Daniel Galindo," 3.
40. "Daniel Galindo," 3.
41. "Daniel Galindo," 3.
42. "Daniel Galindo," 3.
43. Rohrer, *La India María*, 75.
44. Raúl Trejo Delarbe, "La nueva política de masas de la derecha mexicana/Un vistazo a Televisa," in *Televisa el quinto poder* (Mexico City: Claves Latinoamericanos, 1985), 187.
45. Brown and Babington, "Introduction," 19.
46. "Entrevista a Pedrito Fernández," *Tele Guía* no. 1656 (5 Mayo–11 Mayo 1984): n.p.
47. "El conflicto de un adolescente enamorado; SPOT," Expediente A-01863, Centro de Documentación, Cineteca Nacional (Mexico).
48. González, "Cine infantíl," 168.
49. Brown and Babington, "Introduction," 16.
50. According to Allen, the most frequently cited Hollywood family film, *Home Alone*, features child/youth star Macaulay Culkin, who is not a singer.
51. Carlos Múnera, "La de los hoyitos," *Carlos Múnera–Somos Iguales* (blog), November 20, 2007, http://carlosmunera.blogspot.com.proxy.lib.ohio-state.edu/2007/11/la-de-los-hoyitos.html.
52. Laura Podalsky, "El cine, el rock, la televisión y las culturas juveniles en los 1960s en la Argentina," *Actas del V Congreso Internacional de AsAECA*, 2016, 1486.
53. Podalsky, "El cine," 1488.
54. This strategy is also employed by 1960s' youth rock and roll films. Emilio García Riera notes, "El blandísimo rock de los 'ídolos juveniles' hizo posible su ya apuntada coexistencia con los heroes maduros del melodrama convencional," pointing to Libertad Lamarque in *El cielo y la tierra* (1962) as an example. *Historia*, 261.
55. Rohrer, *La India María*, 52–54.
56. Tomás Pérez Turrent, "Cartelera dominical. Y Pedrito pierde a Lucerito en 'Coqueta,'" *El Universal*, February 18, 1985, 8.
57. Miguel Pitti, "Nuestro minusválido cine," *Novedades*, February 3, 1984, 3.
58. "La Quimera del Oro," *Dicine* no. 11 (May 1985): n.p.
59. Zolov, *Refried Elvis*, 4–5.
60. Allen, "Home Alone," 114–5.

61. Luis Aboites Aguilar, "El último tramo, 1929–2000," in *Nueva historia mínima de México* (Mexico City: El Colegio de México, 2004), 292.

62. Aboites Aguilar, "El último," 292.

63. This could be an allusion to Pedro Infante's iconic carpenter character Pepe el Toro, an archetype of the noble, urban working class, in the Golden Age staple *Nosotros los pobres* (Ismael Rodríguez, 1948).

64. Carlos Monsiváis, *"No sin nosotros" Los días del terremoto: 1985–2005* (Mexico City: Ediciones Era, 2005), 9.

65. Allen, "Home Alone," 125.

66. Alejandro Salazar Hernández, "Las Películas Familiares son la Mejor Alternativa Para Dignificar Nuestro Cine. Dicenos Daniel Galindo que Estan Filmando Una," *El Heraldo de México*, Espectáculos, May 9, 1989, 1.

67. Alejandro Salazar Hernández, "Ni el público ni las autoridades apoyan el cine familiar de Galindo," *El Heraldo de México*, September 29, 1990, 3.

68. For more on the effects of neoliberalism on the Mexican film industry, see Ignacio M. Sánchez Prado, *Screening Neoliberalism: Transforming Mexican Cinema, 1988–2012* (Nashville: Vanderbilt University Press, 2014).

69. This is not to undercut *cine familiar*'s televisual afterlife. Mexican pay-channel *De película* and, on weekends, free-to-air channels often air older Mexican cinema. Many YouTube uploads contain the "De película" logo in the corner.

70. Fabian Meraz, "pelicula la niña de los hoyitos pedrito fernandez," YouTube video, January 2014, https://youtu.be/cdhfAQ9l2DU.

## Bibliography

Aboites Aguilar, Luis. "El último tramo, 1929–2000." In *Nueva historia mínima de México*, 262–302. Mexico City: El Colegio de México, 2004.

Allen, Robert C. "Home Alone Together: Hollywood and the 'Family Film.'" In *Identifying Hollywood's Audiences: Cultural Identity and the Movies*, edited by Melvyn Stokes and Richard Maltby, 109–34. London: BFI, 1999.

Amador, María Luisa, and Jorge Ayala Blanco. *Cartelera Cinematográfica 1980–1989*. Mexico City: UNAM, 2006.

Brown, Noel, and Bruce Babington. "Introduction: Children's Films and Family Films." In *Family Films in Global Cinema: The World Beyond Disney*, edited by Noel Brown and Bruce Babington, 14–25. New York: I.B. Tauris, 2015.

"El conflicto de un adolescente enamorado; SPOT." Publicity materials for *Delincuente*. Expediente A-01863. Centro de Documentación, Cineteca Nacional, Mexico City, Mexico.

Cosentino, Olivia. "Televisa Born and Raised: Lucerito's Stardom in 1980s Mexican Media." *The Velvet Light Trap*, no. 38 (Fall 2016): 38–52.

"Daniel Galindo Invirtió 35 Millones de Pesos en el Rodaje de "Delincuente," con Pedrito Fdez." *El Heraldo*, November 23, 1984, 3.

"editorial." *fem* III, no. 7 (April–June 1978): 3–4.

"Entrevista a Pedrito Fernández." *Tele Guía* no. 1656 (5 Mayo–11 Mayo 1984): n.p.

Flores, Silvana. "Las producciones Calderón y su efecto en la región latinoamericana: un caso de intercambio transnacional." *AURA. Revista de Historia y Teoría del Arte*, no. 3 (June 2015): 3–16.

García Riera, Emilio. *Historia del Cine Mexicano.* Mexico City: Secretaría de Educación Pública, 1985.
Gómez, Carmen Elisa. *Familia y estado: Visiones desde el cine mexicano.* Guadalajara: Universidad de Guadalajara, 2015.
González Saravia Peña, Mónica María. "*Cine infantil: recopilación y análisis de largometrajes realizados en México (1939–2009).*" Undergraduate thesis, Universidad Panamericana, 2010.
Gunckel, Colin. "The Permanencia Voluntaria archive and the Historical Study of Mexican cinema." *Studies in Spanish & Latin American Cinemas* 16, no. 3 (2019): 383–401.
Iglesias Prieto, Norma. *Entre yerba, polvo y plomo. Lo fronterizo visto por el cine mexicano.* Tijuana, Baja California: El Colegio de la Frontera Norte, 1991.
Meraz, Fabian. "pelicula la niña de los hoyitos pedrito fernandez." YouTube video, posted January 2014, https://youtu.be/cdhfAQ9l2DU.
Monsiváis, Carlos. *"No sin nosotros" Los días del terremoto: 1985–2005.* Mexico City: Ediciones Era, 2005.
Mora, Carl. *Mexican Cinema: Reflections of a Society, 1896–2004.* Jefferson, NC: McFarland & Company, 2005.
Múnera, Carlos. "La de los hoyitos." *Carlos Múnera–Somos Iguales* (blog). November 20, 2007. http://carlosmunera.blogspot.com.proxy.lib.ohio-state.edu/2007/11/la-de-los-hoyitos.html.
O'Farrili, Joel. "¡Mega boda de Pedro Fernández!" *Tabasco HOY,* October 11, 2010, https://www.tabascohoy.com/nota/100665/iexcl-mega-boda-de-pedro-fernandez.
Paxman, Andrew. "Who Killed the Mexican Film Industry? The Decline of the Golden Age, 1946–1960." *E.I.A.L.* 29, no. 1 (2018): 9–33.
Paxman, Andrew, and Claudia Fernández. *El tigre: Emilio Azcárraga y su imperio Televisa.* Barcelona: Grijalbo, 2013.
Pelayo, Alejandro. *La generación de la crisis: El cine independiente mexicano de los ochenta.* Mexico City: IMCINE & Conaculta, 2012.
Pérez Turrent, Tomás. "Cartelera dominical. Y Pedrito pierde a Lucerito en 'Coqueta.'" *El Universal,* February 18, 1985, 8.
———. "Crises and Renovations (1965–91)." *Mexican Cinema* edited by Paulo Antonio Paranaguá, translated by Ana M. López, 94–115. Mexico City: BFI and IMCINE, 1995.
Pitti, Miguel. "Nuestro minusválido cine." *Novedades,* February 3, 1984, 3.
Podalsky, Laura. "El cine, el rock, la television y las culturas juveniles en los 1960s en la Argentina." *Actas del V Congreso Internacional de AsAECA* (2016): 1482–91.
"La Quimera del Oro." *Dicine* no. 11 (May 1985): n.p.
Ramírez Berg, Charles. *Cinema of Solitude: A Critical Study of Mexican Film, 1967–1983.* Austin: University of Texas Press, 1991.
Rohrer, Seraina. *La India María: Mexploitation and the Films of María Elena Velasco.* Austin: University of Texas Press, 2017.
Salazar Hernández, Alejandro. "Ni el público ni las autoridades apoyan el cine familiar de Galindo." *El Heraldo de México,* September 29, 1990, 3.
———. "Las Películas Familiares son la Mejor Alternativa Para Dignificar Nuestro Cine. Dicenos Daniel Galindo que Estan Filmando Una." *El Heraldo de México,* Espectáculos, May 9, 1989, 1.
Sánchez Prado, Ignacio M. *Screening Neoliberalism: Transforming Mexican Cinema, 1988–2012.* Nashville, TN: Vanderbilt University Press, 2014.

Tierney, Dolores. *New Transnationalisms in Contemporary Latin American Cinema*. Edinburgh: Edinburgh University Press, 2018.

Trejo Delarbe, Raúl. "La nueva política de masas de la derecha mexicana / Un vistazo a Televisa." In *Televisa el quinto poder*, edited by Raúl Trejo Delarbe, 180–96. Mexico City: Claves Latinoamericanos, 1985.

Zolov, Eric. *Refried Elvis: The Rise of Mexican Counterculture*. Berkeley: University of California Press, 1999.

# 7

## FELIPE CAZALS

The Question of the Film Auteur
in the Age of Cinematic Crisis

IGNACIO M. SÁNCHEZ PRADO

The Criterion Collection's recent release of Felipe Cazals's 1975 masterpiece *Canoa* constitutes a belated but welcome transnational recognition of one of Mexico's two major film auteurs of the 1970s (the other being Arturo Ripstein, now subject of a collective academic volume).[1] Championed by Alfonso Cuarón and Guillermo del Toro, who contributed special features to the box set, *Canoa* was at the time a brave political film, focused on the lynching of university employees stranded in a small town in Puebla, elicited by a priest who branded them as Communists. *Canoa* was also one of the rare feature films to make indirect reference to the 1968 massacre of students in Tlatelolco, by showing, as far as censors from the time would allow, references to the general climate of anti-student sentiment, while also showing, in striking sequences, protests by civil society and the persistence of authoritarian local structures in rural areas. *Canoa* was in part the result of a paradoxical boom in Mexican art cinema fostered by the nationalization of production in the early 1970s. After the collapse of the Golden Age in the late 1950s and the crisis elicited in the 1960s by the industry's inability to withstand competition from Hollywood, President Luis Echeverría (1970–1976) used the film industry as part of a larger strategy to appease left-wing intellectuals in the wake of the 1968 and 1971 massacres of students, of which he is widely considered to be responsible. His brother Rodolfo, a well-known actor, was appointed as director of the National Cinematography Bank, which in turn evolved into a major film institute that would reorganize cinema by having the state protect the industry from economic crisis. Although this effort never quite restored the domestic market, its efforts in producing an authorial cinema aligned to both the transnational film circuits of the time, as well as to the populist agenda of the Echeverría administration, fostered the emergence of some of Mexico's greater auteurs, including Alfonso Arau, Ripstein, whose masterpiece *El lugar sin límites* (1974) is the only challenger to *Canoa* as best Mexican film of the 1970s, or Jorge Fons. All of these directors remain very much active and influential, showing the impact of this period in Mexican cinema.[2]

Cazals's early cinema was very much part of this process and could be described as a form of sociopolitical auteurship in between two models of the film author. On the one hand, he was clearly subject to the socially engagé practices from European directors, mostly shaped in relation to Italian neorealists like Vittorio De Sica and Roberto Rossellini, as well as the left-wing efforts of Jean-Luc Godard and the Dziga Vertov collective. On the other, he belonged tangentially to the different strains of Latin American third cinema, which place Cazals in connection to figures like Glauber Rocha or Fernando Solanas. The key point here though is that these models were by and large oppositional in their political contexts, while Cazals and his contemporaries lived in a paradox between being political filmmakers critical of life in Mexico under the ruling party while functioning within an industry rendered possible by the investment of that same state infrastructure. The vulnerability of this structure became visible in 1976, when President López Portillo appointed his sister Margarita to replace Rodolfo Echeverría and began what is generally considered a dark period for art filmmakers. The period became characterized by policies such as the reshifting of state funding to exploitation cinema and a tragic event: the burning of the Mexican Cineteca in 1982, in which 99 percent of the institution's film patrimony burned to the ground.[3] Mexican filmmakers also faced production restrictions and had to compete with foreign productions over national studio resources.[4] While I do not think that the cinema produced under the López Portillo regime was all catastrophic, as often believed, the policies led to strange situations. Major national directors like Emilio Fernández, the great auteur of the Golden Age, finished their careers directing sexually-charged exploitation films like *Zona Roja* (1976) to make a living, while the state spared no expense in funding foreign coproductions like *Campanas rojas* [*Mexico in Flames*] (1982), a series of two films on John Reed, directed by Soviet master Sergei Bondarchuk and starring Spaghetti Western superstar Franco Nero. It was clear however that the authorial cinema of the previous administration would not last. Critic and screenwriter Francisco Sánchez, one of the figures from the press who pushed back against *lópezportillismo*, tellingly calls this a moment of "authorial castration."[5]

This is the type of historical juncture in national cinemas that requires a new approach to studying directors as auteurs. Mexican cinema of the 1980s challenges two important axioms in the understanding of the relationship between cinematic value and authorship. The first one has to do with the idea that the most important cinema in a national tradition is that of the auteur, particularly if that tradition is in the Global South. In Mexican and Mexicanist scholarship, the 1980s are often referred as the "generation of crisis," a term coined by Alejandro Pelayo, a filmmaker and twice director of the Mexican Cineteca.[6] Pelayo's book is a valuable intervention in rescuing Mexican independent cinema of the decade, but it is constructed under the presumption that the center of Mexican cinema in the 1980s is independent film, sidestepping the commercial cinema of the time. One finds versions of this narrative in scholars like Isis Saavedra Luna, who narrates the dismantling of the *echeverrista* infrastructure in the late 1980s as the "end of the Mexican film industry," notwithstanding the fact that the period in which she bases her study actually gave rise to directors like Alfonso Cuarón and Guillermo del Toro.[7] The only major work to balance authorial and popular cinema in the period is Charles Ramírez Berg's study *Cinema of Solitude*, but his work does suffer from its framing on the idea of "Mexicanness," which misses the complex transnational and domestic processes of the period.[8] The collection for which I write the present chapter might be the first serious scholarly consideration of these materials, following recent work like coeditor Olivia Cosentino's work on Televisa films, as well as recent evaluations of genres like exploitation in Latin American film studies.[9] The second axiom is related to the ways in which we use the notion of the film auteur as designed by a debate centered on European and US cinema, from Truffaut to Kael and Sarris and later expands it into forms of global filmmaking with more importance in transnational circuits than in local markets. A full conceptual revision of theories of film authorship would come too much at the expense of the study of Cazals here. One could point to John Caughie's landmark collection *Theories of Authorship* from 1981, which includes the perspective of *Cahiers du cinema* and Sarris, as well as structuralist and post-structuralist discussions prevalent in the late 1970s. This collection is useful to consider because it encompasses the theories of authorship active at the time of Cazals's own work and shows the inadequacy of these theories by the mere fact that the book wholly sidesteps authors not coming from Europe and the United States.[10] Yet, a similar problem plagues a more recent and exhaustive collection, Barry Keith Grant's *Auteurs and Authorship*, which is very US-centric and altogether ignores global film authors, even as many of them were active or visible in Hollywood at the time of publication.[11] Similar appraisals can easily be leveled against other collections in landmark series, like the AFI Film Reader *Authorship and Film*, edited by David Gertsner and Janet Staiger, which shyly moves into Latinx and Asian American film, or the Rutgers Depth of Field Collection *Film and Authorship*, edited by Virginia Wright Wexman, which does include a very good essay on Latin American transnational authors, but nothing that would allow us to think of directors working wholly within Latin American national scenes.[12] My point here is that the notion of the auteur operative in film studies at large eclipses the material cultural practices, as well as forms of aesthetics and craft, developed by directors who do not work under the socioeconomic and institutional conditions that allow for authorship in the United States and Europe. This is why, in approaching Cazals, I prefer to discuss his authorship from a detailed discussion of his work, rather than applying existing theories of the auteur. Cazals and directors like him, whose work is firmly grounded in national traditions of the Global South (or the Third World, or Third Cinema, or whichever non-hegemonic paradigm one privileges), need a new framework that allows for conceptualizing factors such as precarity, local tradition, historically specific notions of art, and political cinema and other questions.

Felipe Cazals's ordeals in the late 1970s and early 1980s offer a significant example to rethink the notion of authorship and the question of artistic and cinematic value within institutionally unstable national traditions. Economic precarity is a feature of cinematic production everywhere, and in systems with heavy reliance on state financing, like the Mexican industry, cycles of boom and bust are directly tied to concrete factuals such as the politics of the national film organizations, the size of the economic investments, the balance between public and private producers, and the effect that censorship has on production. It is telling that both Mexican presidents of the 1970s, Luis Echeverría (1970–1976) and José López Portillo (1976–1982) handed the directorship of the national film institute to their siblings, Rodolfo and Margarita respectively. That kind of appointment indicates an interest in keeping cinema production close to the state but can also be interpreted as a certain level of disregard for the industry. The effects, indeed, were quite different in each administration. Rodolfo Echeverría (himself a film actor under the name Rodolfo Landa), created major institutions of Mexican cinema, including the Cineteca and the Centro de Capacitación Cinematográfica (CCC), which, to this day, remains one of the two main film schools in the country. The institution that Echeverría directed was called the Banco Cinematográfico, and it was basically designed to provide financial backing to private production. As the financial crisis of cinema in the 1960s undermined private investment, Echeverría began shifting the Banco's money from collaboration with private entities to the full capitalization of films by the state. In numbers cited by Carl Mora, one can see two trends.[13] First, the aforementioned shift is noticeable between 1971, when sixty-three films were done in collaboration of the Banco and private investments, against five films fully funded by the state and seven fully private films, and 1976, when Banco collaborations disappeared completely, allowing the state to fully fund thirty-seven films, against only five from private producers. The second trend is also clear: production went from seventy-five in 1971 to forty-two in 1976. By freeing up filmmakers from market pressures, the *echeverrista* state-centered model fostered a new generation of authorial filmmakers like Cazals, while making cinema deeply dependent on state funding.

This factor, which proved to be a positive way to foster cinema until 1976, becomes the main reason why the following administration, under Margarita López Portillo, completely undermined the *echeverrista* model. As Pelayo documents, José López Portillo not only appointed his sister, but he also replaced the Banco Cinematográfico in 1977 with a large bureaucratic entity called Radio, Televisión y Cinematografía (RTC), which subsumed the main film institute, Conacine, into a more complex multimedia structure. The RTC itself was placed under the control of the ministry of government, charged with the political management of the country's internal affairs, thus tying cinematography to the politics of the state and creating a new basis for censorship. Unlike Rodolfo Echeverría, who came from the industry, Margarita López Portillo was a member of the intellectual class but not of the cinematographic guild, which impacted the early days of her administration, in which some films greenlighted under the Echeverría model still went through, but no new projects were visible.[14] In the end, López Portillo would push Mexican cinema back into precarious structures of private production (which in part led to the rise of Televisa as the lead producer of the 1980s, as well as to a rebirth of exploitation film and other popular genres) and grant state resources to coproductions featuring major world directors like Soviet Sergei Bondarchuk, Spanish Carlos Saura, and French Costa-Gavras, as well as to foreign producers like Dino de Laurentiis, who shot major commercial films like *Conan the Barbarian* (John Millius, 1982) and *Dune* (David Lynch, 1983) with major support from the Mexican state.[15] One has to say in the context of a scholarly discussion, though, that even though producers, critics and scholars are (understandably) near unanimous in reading *lópezportillismo* as a dark period, part of the reason why this is the case is that the popular Televisa films, as well as the exploitation cinema of the era, are seen as garbage because they are not authorial. It is equally important to remember, although not the purpose of this article to document this, that many of the films in the López Portillo era enjoyed significant success within working classes (in fact, one of the arguments for the shift was that the state had to produce films that people actually watched). One has to be very careful not to reify art cinema as inherently superior or to accept the accounts of filmmakers in the period at face value. It was also a period in which the crisis of exhibition fostered by economic crisis, and the later infrastructure crisis following the 1985 earthquake in Mexico City, created seismic shifts in film attendance that would account for the rise of home video as replacement structure.[16]

The shift between the *echeverrista* and *lópezportillista* models sets the stage for the complexities of the 1980s, and it is very clear that Cazals is one of the most important directors impacted by the fluctuations in funding. Under Echeverría, Cazals received support of the state beginning with his film *El jardín de la tía Isabel* (1972) and went on to produce one of the most notable series of works by any Mexican filmmaker, including a historical film on Maximilian of Habsburg, *Aquellos años* (1972), and his two political masterpieces, *Canoa* and *El apando* (1975).[17] His final film of the 1970s, *El año de la peste* (1978), based on a screenplay by Gabriel García Márquez, was one of the last works financed under *echeverrista* premises and became plagued by funding and labor issues.[18] Cazals's career in the 1970s seems to follow the script of what an auteur within a nationalist framework is expected to produce. Within the possibilities of the state's practices of semi-soft censorship (which would include review by the RTC and pressure on filmmakers but not outright bans or persecution, as experienced in dictatorial contexts), Cazals developed a significant work of *cinema engagé* that constantly sought to be attuned to Mexico's sociopolitical concerns, even if it did not challenge state authority directly. Yet, as Berg points out, while filmmakers had more thematic leeway under Echeverría, many political filmmakers were frequently marginalized during the López Portillo era by delaying release for two or three years, or by pushing them into the commercial and exploitation industries.[19] In contrast, Cazals's run under the Echeverría model placed him in a peculiar position in which he pointed to issues such as the anti-student climate post-1968 in *Canoa*, the exploitation of women in *Las poquianchis* (1975), and the brutal conditions of political imprisonment in *El apando*, adapting in this particular case the novella by José Revueltas, Mexico's most important Communist writer.

Yet, watching Cazals's output in the 1970s, one can also note that a fundamental feature of auteur cinema is missing: an identifiable consistent style. In this, he is different from contemporaries like Alejandro Jodorowsky, whose radical avant-gardism is visible in every film, or Ripstein, whose work generally has recognizable elements in his visual language as well as in his appeals to the canons of melodrama. In contrast, Cazals's ability to develop such a style varies greatly within the decade. The precarious beauty of *Aquellos años* develops a costume drama in which he visually contrasts the pastel and bright colors of Maximilian of Habsburg's court to the predominance of black and gray in the halls of Benito Juárez and his fellow Republicans. In *Canoa*, the growing darkness of the rural town creates counterpoints with the light of the city. In turn, *Canoa*'s experimental narrative style, famously carried by the nameless narrator that embodies and represents the view of the community at large, is quite distinct from the gritty realism of *Las poquianchis* or *El apando*. One of the reasons behind these inconsistencies in style is in the ways in which film crews and casts are assembled. In the 1970s, the two unions of film workers—the Sindicato de Trabajadores de la Industria Cinematográfica (STIC) and the Sindicato de Trabajadores de la Producción Cinematográfica (STPC)—had significant control in hiring everyone, from low-rank technicians to cinematographers and directors. These unions were in bitter conflict with each other, due to issues dating back decades, and were able to make or break productions.[20]

Cazals and his generation were able to rise out of this because the nationalization fostered by Echeverría ultimately opened spaces that broke union rank for the director, but this was not always the case for other members of production crews. Cazals's cinematographer in *Aquellos años*, for example, was Jorge Stahl Jr., who began shooting in 1941, at the heyday of the Golden Age. Stahl was, generally speaking, an experienced studio hand who was well-versed in traditional forms of Mexican cinema, and this is clear in the austere and clean style of *Aquellos años*, as it is in another historical film helmed by Cazals, *El jardín de la tía Isabel*. In contrast, *Canoa* and *El apando* were shot by Alex Phillips Jr., who begins his career in the 1960s, after the Golden Age, and develops his repertoire in exploitation films that never participated in the classical style in which Stahl Jr. was trained. Thus, in the films he shoots for Cazals, a grittier and more austere style is notable, one that is more indebted to the cinema of 1960s auteurs like Luis Buñuel than to the Figueroa-Fernández style of the midcentury. The same differences become clear when one compares the scripts of Tomás Pérez Turrent, which are very organic to Cazals's political style, to the odd fit of working with García Márquez, who at the time provided screenplays to Mexican directors to support them in the emerging crisis of the period and whose literary style overwhelmed Cazals.[21]

As the restrictions placed on authorship during the López Portillo period began to hit filmmakers like Cazals, Mexican cinema moved toward a process of re-privatization that would have deep effects on everything from funding to aesthetics. As mentioned before, directors (like Cazals himself) often remember this period as a dark moment in which left-oriented film was censored and authorial cinema was starved of resources, but underlying factors in the industry show a more complex picture. Various historians of the period note that the rationale behind López Portillo's policies had to do with the early adoption of what would become protoneoliberal free-market reforms (as Eduardo de la Vega Alfaro asserts) and, as Carl Mora writes, an attempt to shake what was thought to be an excessive dependence of filmmakers on the state bureaucracy.[22] This in turn yielded clear results. Even though the López Portillo economy would lead to the 1982 crisis, the period saw Televisa emerge as a major player in the market, the production would find an audience in the previously unexploited Mexican-American market, and both production and receipts of the industry would in fact be higher than in the Echeverría period.[23] Raúl Miranda notes that the key underlying phenomenon was the rise of television as the medium that would define the national, and, as such, moviegoers would, to the chagrin of critics and intellectuals, follow television stars to the big screen.[24] The economic changes allowed for private cinema to emerge as profitable because Televisa's mighty media empire would take advantage not only of the name recognition of stars but also of emerging technologies like a nascent home video market. Most of the available texts narrate this process as a calamity (Miranda compiles a few of them), which is certainly the case if one considers art cinema to be the most important part of cinematography. Yet the López Portillo period did set the stage, for better or for worse, for a popular cinema that reconnected with popular audiences that had either been lost or rendered invisible by authorial film. This cinema would rule domestic and theatrical screens until the neoliberal reforms of the late 1980s. As more nuanced accounts of this cinema are emerging, like Seraina Rohrer's exceptional study of one of the key figures of the period, María Elena Velasco better known as "La India María," we now see that popular production oftentimes worked around censorship to deliver its exploitational renderings of sexuality and of the working classes, and even as critics like Jorge Ayala Blanco forged their careers panning these works, their unquestionable success remains a very uncomfortable subject of study for most film scholars.[25] And, as noted by critics like Sergio de la Mora and Vinodh Venkatesh, *fichera* films of the period register phenomena like the public recognition of homosexuality or the increasing sexualization of the female body in media and become essential in creating what the latter calls "a method of viewership" and "an association with the erotics of the moving image" that will open paths for post-1988 filmmakers.[26]

Cazals's first two films in this process revolve around popular *cumbia* singer Rigo Tovar: *Rigo es amor* (1980) and *El gran triunfo* (1981). Cazals came to these productions after two and a half years of unemployment, as directors like him were acutely suffering the consequences of the López Portillo industrial realignments. Since shooting them, Cazals has always disavowed these two films as something he was forced to do to make a living and to eat, and he does not consider them representative of anything beyond a job. He famously pans the films as a bad melodrama and considers them to be antithetical to his own cinema.[27] Yet, a proper reconsideration of these films requires us to read Cazals's work against the grain of his assertions and memories. *Rigo es amor* and *El gran triunfo* are part of one of the most successful genres in Mexican cinema of the late 1970s and early 1980s: the star vehicle. Fueled in part by Televisa's near-monopoly in popular music and the rise of genres such as the romantic ballad and Northern Mexican *cumbia*, these films brought to the big screen the success of composers, youth stars, and crooners, creating a multimedia network of popular affect that was at the base of the social contract between cinema and popular classes in the period. Cazals was far from being the only auteur working in these films. Popular queer singer Juan Gabriel's trilogy of very successful films—*Del otro lado del puente* (1980), *El Noa Noa* (1981), and *Es mi vida* (1982)—were directed by Gonzalo Martínez Ortega, a filmmaker trained in the Soviet Union who worked with Igor Talankin and Jorge Fons, and whose best film was an adaptation of Anton Chekhov's *The Cherry Orchard* (1978). Crooner José José's biopic, *Gavilán o paloma* (1985), was directed by Alfredo Gurrola, whose political noirs like *Llámenme Mike* (1979) or *Días de combate* (1982) faced censorship and delayed release. Televisa films were not the exception: pop singer Luis Miguel's film debut *Ya nunca más* (1984), was directed by Abel Salazar, a major actor from the Golden Age who would spend the last years of his career directing films for Televisa.

The unexceptional nature of Cazals's work in the Rigo Tovar films and other exploitation works is essential to the questions raised by the idea of authorship in Mexico. It is not at all unusual for directors to work in studio systems, sometimes surrendering significant control of their style, without those works being disavowed by them. One can think of mainstream cases like Steven Soderbergh's work in the Danny Ocean trilogy or Christopher Nolan's foray into the world of Batman.[28] Even back in the 1980s, before the reification of the American auteur in the Sundance system, David Lynch was chosen to helm the mega-production of *Dune* (shot in Mexico no less).[29] Exploitation is also a film genre in which many directors (think, for example, Dario Argento and Abel Ferrara) worked with freedoms that the mainstream system would not allow. Even some Mexican exploitation directors like Juan López Moctezuma (who, incidentally, was *Canoa*'s off-screen narrator) would reach cult status with highly sexual films like his vampire classic *Alucarda* (1977). But even if one sticks to the musical genre, it is hard to deny that popular music, including nightlife genres like *rumba*, developed over time a central role and prestige in the formation of Mexican cinema at large.[30] The use of musical genres like *cumbia,* pop, and the romantic ballad reflected, much like the music of the Golden Age, experiences of popular modernization. About the ballad, for example, Alejandro Madrid has noted that singers like José José performed "a new genre of love song [that] borrowed musical features from the newest United States and European fads but retained the romantic sensibility that had made the *bolero* a favorite among Latin American audiences through the 1960s."[31] It is precisely this capturing of forms of working-class cosmopolitanism that turns the *balada* into one of the key genres in Televisa's musical repertoire and, by extension, into one of the most successful themes for private cinema in the 1980s.[32]

*Rigo es amor* and *El gran triunfo* fictionalize Tovar's musical career for dramatic purposes. This was a departure from his film debut, *Vivir para amar* (Rafael Villaseñor Kuri, 1980), in which he played a fictional character named Tony. Harnessing Tovar's success (in the same way as José José played himself in his own biopic), the films utilized his off-screen persona to mobilize the affects of audiences familiarized with his music and his performances. Tovar's music was part of a larger modernization of the Latin American *cumbia* genre, basically fostered by the incorporation of electric musical instruments (primarily the synthesizer keyboard and the guitar) and of the aesthetics and styles of rock and roll (Tovar's attire is midway between the styles of the 1960s tropical orchestras and Elvis Presley). As a border artist based primarily in the city of Matamoros, Tovar became hugely popular both in Latin America and with the Hispanic community of the southwest United States. That his success even happened in spite of the general rejection of his work as basic and vulgar by musicians and critics was itself, as Madrid suggests, part of an emerging mediascape in which marginal working-class cultural productions began to break the prejudices of middle and upper classes.[33] Although his shortened career, interrupted by blindness, did not allow him to become an icon comparable to contemporaries like Juan Gabriel and José José, he remains widely influential and remembered as a precursor of the *grupero* music that has ruled the charts in the US-Mexico borderlands ever since, and was even the subject of a tribute by a group of literary writers in 2013, a symbol of his cult status.[34] Tovar came to Cazals in the wake of breaking a major attendance record in Monterrey in 1979, gathering over four hundred thousand people and beating the attendance of Pope John Paul II's visit to the country. His eclectic style and taste included nods to metal bands like Black Sabbath and even *cumbia* adaptations of works by classical composers like Joseph Haydn.[35] Besides Cazals's films and the aforementioned fictional film, Tovar was also the subject of the highest-grossing documentary of the López Portillo era, *Rigo, una confesión total* (Víctor Vío, 1979), which captures him at the height of his fame.

The reception of Rigo's music as vulgar and simple is very much parallel to the objections that film critics raised to popular cinema of the time. In his valuation of Cazals's films of the period, Jorge Ayala Blanco underscores his three political films of the 1970s (*Canoa*, *El apando*, and *Las poquianchis*) as well as his 1983 political masterwork *Bajo la metralla* (which I will discuss at the end of this essay).[36] While the films are noticeably outside of Cazals's comfort zone, full of stock footage and a style that Ayala Blanco funnily describes as "masochistic long takes," there are notable elements that distinguish them from other films.[37] *Vivir para amar*, for example, utilizes significant amounts of outdoor shots and a bright photography that sticks close to television aesthetics. In contrast, Cazals harnesses the dark visuals of the historical cabaret genre in Mexican cinema as well as the gritty representation of urban spaces aesthetically kindred to his work with Alex Phillips Jr. to present Tovar's life. *El gran triunfo*, in particular, benefits from the excellent work of Daniel López, who worked for many years as the lighting technician for Gabriel Figueroa. Cazals recounts that, thanks to López's experience and the attraction they both felt for Amparo Muñoz, the famous Spanish singer who plays Tovar's love interest in the film, they worked with lenses to play between the focus in the actors on stage and the less-defined environment, a technique Cazals extended to scenes with

Tovar due to the vivacious colors of his attire.[38] Using this recourse (which he would later adapt to films like *Bajo la metralla*), Cazals shows exactly how authorship works in tension with the precarity of cinematic and industrial conditions in places like Mexico, not by heroically imposing a style or by claiming ownership on the totality of the industrial product. Rather, Cazals is able to produce in *Rigo es amor* and, in particular, *El gran triunfo*, innovative entries in formulaic genres by intervening in the technical and aesthetic limits of this work. Unlike Vío's documentary or *Vivir para amar*, Cazals's films begrudgingly but decisively develop a sense of modernity and a seductive aesthetic of the night that problematize the trite melodramatic plot of the screenplays. In their visual focus on Muñoz, for example, the film clearly undermines the familial dynamic of the plot, in which Rigo becomes preoccupied with his terminally ill child. If the narratives of the films focus on family life as an antidote to the alcoholism and sexual excess of Rigo's nightworld, Cazals's long shots, López's work with lighting, and their collaborative representation of the sensoriality of the night raise the film from a run-of-the-mill melodrama to a significant entry in Mexican musical cinema.

In the opening sequence of *Rigo es amor*, Cazals harnesses a series of resources that range from national traditions of cinema, from the opening shots of Mexico City as a cue to the narratives of modernity (one can refer for instance to the well-known opening sequence of Julio Bracho's *Distinto amanecer* [1943]) transitioning to the opening musical performance that was as much a feature of the Golden Age as it was to 1960s countercultural films (for instance, Angélica María's performance in *Cinco de chocolate y uno de fresa* [Carlos Velo, 1968]). Tovar's musical performances, the focus of the opening and closing sequences of both films, are variations within a cinematic theme focused on iconicity and presence as key cinematic languages. The difference between Tovar's vehicles and the much-celebrated works centered around Pedro Infante or Angélica María are a mere matter of taste, a historiographical construct in which the popular tied to the national state or to the counterculture of rock is regarded as valuable, while the popular engaged with the social undergrounds is seen, as Cazals himself calls it, as mere garbage. Despite Cazals's objection, and in honor to his work, his authorial presence is at its best not when the infrastructure is favorable or when he can direct a classic but when he can't, when the mastery of the popular manifests itself despite the director's ideologies about himself. In this, *Rigo es amor* and *El gran triunfo*, which force Cazals to engage with a canon against which the main line of his work is constructed, becomes essential to understand his style.

Cazals would return a few times to exploitation genres in the face of economic and employment crises of the industry. This is the case of *Las siete cucas* (1981), the third film that Cazals shot (along with the Rigo Tovar movies) for producer Fernando Pérez Gavilán. I won't go in depth on *Las siete cucas*, but a few things are worth nothing. The film is an excellent example of the complexities of exploitation cinema in the 1980s. A variation of the *fichera* film, it tells the story of a mother and her six virginal daughters who open a brothel in retaliation for the effects of town men's lust, including the death of Cuco, their patriarch. The female cast is helmed by Isela Vega, the most important actress in the genre and a figure in which the sexual politics of Mexican low cinema are embodied.[39] The cast is further propped by various stars in the sexploitation world, from divas like Angélica Chain and Merle Uribe to comedians like Alberto Rojas "El Caballo" and Eduardo de la Peña "Lalo el Mimo." The film, however, is internally tensioned by high-culture elements. It is in fact an adaptation of a homonymous novel by Spanish writer Eugenio Noel, originally published in 1927.[40] A work known probably only to literary specialists, the novel is a quite complex work of literature with very significant regional elements and tied to the critique of Spanish morality and clericalism. The work translates well into exploitation because it balances the same use of sexuality and ambiguous social mores that characterizes cinema at the time. Carmen Elisa Gómez Gómez has pointed out that, in the López Portillo era, many films broke with the historical representations of the family to highlight Mexico's sexual discrepancies.[41] Although Gómez Gómez mentions headier work by Ripstein and Jaime Humberto Hermosillo, the rejection of both virginity and sexuality is at the core of *Las siete cucas*. The film is quite surprising: in between its nods to exploitation, it is a very well-constructed drama with intelligent engagements of the source materials and a better use of Cazals's cinematic technique. In Cazals's account, he was limited by the production, since his attempts to delve deeper into the girls' psyche were rejected.[42] Yet, even as he regrets his inability to turn the film into an "excellent comedy in the Italian style," his directorial marks are present. The film has many religious processions that openly refer to *Canoa* and the ending, in which a music band of the town's men walk naked, is a much smarter ending in its allegorical and non-explanatory touch than one would expect in a film of the time. Although Cazals also disavows this film as garbage, his work—in terms of narrative structure, cinematography, and acting direction—turns the film into one of the underappreciated jewels of exploitation cinema.

After this trio of films, one can see a significant transformation in Cazals's political cinema, as his films internalize many of the aesthetic challenges of his cinematic crisis. This is the case of one of his most iconic films, *Bajo la metralla*, a dynamic political thriller focused on an urban guerrilla cell that goes into a safe house after the kidnapping of a businessman. Shot on a shoestring budget, *Bajo la metralla* was a brave political intervention, representing forms of political violence and riot that never got much media attention and that remain unknown to many Mexicans today. Casting major figures of both cinema and television, Cazals's film is notable due to his transition from the technically supported modes of filmmaking in the *echeverrista* era, which allowed the use of various locations, and the collaboration of the industry's unionized labor, to a strategy of minimalistic guerrilla filmmaking that brought him closer to the clandestine forms of filmmaking of authors in Southern Cone dictatorial contexts, like Raymundo Gleyzer, who famously shot his *México, la revolución congelada* (1971), a scathing critique of Luis Echeverría, by clandestinely posing as a pro-government crew.[43] Just as *Canoa* was one of the first cinematic representations of the anti-student climate post-1968, *Bajo la metralla* is a compelling representation of the Mexican Dirty War, a period that refers to the rise of radicalized left-wing groups, including both peasant and urban guerillas, in the wake of the 1968 movement and Echeverría's brutal persecution and repression of these groups. This Dirty War is still widely unknown, even among Mexicans, and only very recently has scholarly history begun to discuss it in depth.[44] It is thus notable that Cazals went forward with such a theme, and the film, per Ayala Blanco's account, was subject to veiled censorship, including a release delay of nearly two years.[45] Cazals recalls that even though he shot the film under the López Portillo administration, the following administration, of President Miguel de la Madrid, and the director of the newly created Instituto Mexicano de Cinematografía [Mexican Film Institute] (IMCINE), Alberto Isaac, regarded such a politically charged film to be "a bomb" inherited by the previous bureaucracy, and suggests that the film was set up to fail commercially.⁴⁶ Regardless, the film won four Ariels (Mexico's Academy Awards) in 1984, including Best Film, Best Director (for Cazals), Best Editing (for Rafael Ceballos), and Best Actor (for Humberto Zurita). As Ayala Blanco (who was generally very critical of Cazals but strongly supported *Bajo la metralla*) also noted, the paradox of censoring a film to later give it major industrial recognition was one of the absurdities of the time.

Notwithstanding these issues, *Bajo la metralla* takes Cazals's political cinema into new ideological and aesthetic territory. Instead of focusing on political repression or social conservatism as the core of the film, *Bajo la metralla* illuminates the contradictions and conflicts within political resistance and insurgency by dealing with topics (such as the kidnapping of major businessmen, a somewhat common occurrence in 1970s Mexico) uncomfortable not only to the state but also to the political Left. Unlike the innocent university workers lynched by a mob in *Canoa*, the protagonists of *Bajo la metralla* are trapped within their own ideological contradictions. The film was possible because the main filmmaking venue in Mexico City, Estudios Churubusco, housed the production of Damiano Damiani's *Amityville II: The Possession* (1982), one of the many films by producer Dino de Laurentiis shot there as part of an agreement with López Portillo's administration. As Tomás Pérez Turrent (now a researcher but in the 1970s also the screenwriter of *Canoa*) narrates in the official chronicle of Estudios Churubusco, of the ninety-three films shot in 1982, only fifteen could use the facilities, because most of the facilities were occupied by the production of David Lynch's *Dune*, while further resources were taken by Damiani's crew and other foreign productions.⁴⁷ The fact that mega-productions from the United States were made in Churubusco while Mexican directors were shut out of the government-owned facilities was a very clear example of the ways in which the precarization created by López Portillo's privatization desires, as well as the soft censorship on producers, operated. The window that allowed Cazals to shoot *Bajo la metralla* was nothing short of serendipitous. In his own telling, a few months before the end of the López Portillo administration, Cazals complained in the left-oriented magazine *Proceso* that he had been forced to work on undesirable films, which led him to a bad personal situation. This prompted Benito Alazraki, director of the Corporación Nacional Cinematográfica (CONACINE), the film branch of RTC, to call him in and provide him with resources to make a film, probably knowing that the distribution of it would fall in the next administration.[48]

Though resources were scarce, Cazals learned that Damiano Damiani's production left the house built for *Amityville II* intact in Churubusco and contacted Xavier Robles—a left-leaning screenwriter who cowrote *Las poquianchis* with Pérez Turrent—to develop a screenplay based on a famous moment of the Dirty War: the actions of the radical group known as "Enfermos" out of the University of Sinaloa in the early 1970s.[49] Robles, who would later become one of Mexico's most important screenwriters, took up the challenge and developed a screenplay that works the story of a guerrilla cell in the wake of a failed attack on a government official. Robles would bring the story of this type of operation from the radical 1970s and fold it with elements of Albert Camus's play *The Just Assassins* (1949), which explores the ethics of murder and terrorism in the context of the revolutionary group who assassinated the Grand Duke Sergei Alexandrovich of Russia in 1905.[50] Camus's sparse theatrical style was a very intelligent fit to work within the resources provided by Conacine and Churubusco, as Cazals basically had to constrain himself to a small group of actors (seven, including a cast of rising stars of the time like Humberto Zurita, Alejandro Camacho, and María Rojo), a single outdoors scene to be filmed in the backlot, and a film that had to be shot in a very short period of time (around five weeks) inside the house left by the *Amityville II* production.[51]

*Bajo la metralla*'s opening sequence, the only one outside the house, is a low-budget action scene depicting the guerrilla cell's attempt to kill or kidnap a government official. The scene is completely locatable within the paradigm of B-films produced by De Laurentiis and Roger Corman, which often were shot across Latin America, as a way in which these industries survived economically in response to contexts like the dictatorships or the 1982 debt crises. One can remember here that besides *Amityville*, De Laurentiis produced films in Mexico as varied as *Conan the Barbarian* and *Dune*, and that Peruvian director Luis Llosa spent a good amount of time working on low-budget political thrillers in the late 1980s.[52] It is also worth remembering that the revered Greek-French film director Costa-Gavras shot his political thriller *Missing* (1982), about the kidnapping of an American businessman, in Churubusco, even though the film takes place in Pinochet's Chile.[53] The point is that *Bajo la metralla*, in terms of production, is aligned to forms of low-budget action cinema of the 1980s that survived in a market below Hollywood's main productions and were often shot in global settings. This is the type of film that the López Portillo administration brings to Churubusco when producers like De Laurentiis, directors like Damiani or Costa-Gavras, or even franchises like *Conan the Barbarian* or *Rambo* engage in coproductions with film industries like Mexico. Even recognizing that Cazals was subject to censorship and marginalization (an unquestionable fact), his cinema morphed in fundamental and fascinating ways as he navigated the challenges of political restriction and economic precarity.

In these terms, *Bajo la metralla* is not a better film than *Rigo es amor* nor a worse film than *Canoa* but, rather, is the product of a displacement in the available languages of cinematic narrative to a director consistently working within the quickly shifting production infrastructures. *Bajo la metralla*, production-wise, is not much different than, say, Luis Llosa's *Hour of the Assassin* (1987), a political thriller starring Erick Estrada and produced under Roger Corman's empire, the type of film that thrived in the privatized, low-budget, direct-to-video environment that the López Portillo administration fostered in Mexico, or that allowed the existence of low-budget film industries in the United States and elsewhere.[54] *Bajo la metralla* is readable in the context of Global South–centered productions that dialogued with peripheral Global North cinemas in the creation of alternative industries that countered Hollywood with significant success in the 1980s and 1990s, building markets through genres like the Spaghetti Western and the B-film and venues like the midnight theaters of the United States or the barrio theaters of Los Angeles and Mexico City. The only substantive difference here is the political aim that Cazals infuses into the film, turning him into the rare kind of director who would work in these genres in the 1980s against the grain of their commercialism.

It is not surprising that, unlike the Rigo Tovar films, *Bajo la metralla* is subject to comparison to authorial action cinema by critics. Leonardo García Tsao, in his interview about the film, argues that the opening sequence is a Peckinpah-style violent film that then gives way to Bresson-like austerity and depuration.[55] A bit less generously, Ayala Blanco compares the violence in the first and last scenes to the work of Brian de Palma and argues, following an idea developed at the time by critic Richard Corliss in his oft-cited review of *Blade Runner* (Ridley Scott, 1982), that the film could be considered part of a tradition where the pleasure of the film is in its texture rather than its text.[56] Beyond the hyperbole used by these critics to prop up the film, the comparisons illuminate an important fact for my purposes: without the precarious conditions and the work in the three films that he now disavows, Cazals would have not evolved into a full-fledged auteur aligned to the global cinema of the 1980s. A case in point is his account of *Bajo la metralla*'s cinematographic challenges. Cazals notes that the set required significant use of the long lens as well as filtered natural light and he even improvised with ultra-cheap resources like covering light bulbs with newspaper.[57] Just like in *El gran triunfo,* Cazals and López build the film's affective and aesthetic structures by engaging with the limits in resources head-on. This is to the benefit of Cazals's craft in the long run.

Moving forward, Cazals would have a very productive career, and the elements that he picked up during this period are clear all throughout his work. His 1985 masterpiece *Los motivos de Luz,* a true-crime story of a woman accused of killing her four children that was adapted to the screen by Xavier Robles, revisits the motherhood theme explored in *Las siete cucas,* developing the sexual contradictions of Mexico into a more radical reflection of the tensions between justice and gender. The film was in the center of controversy, since the woman represented in the film, Luz Cruz, successfully sued the production arguing that the negative portrayal of her would harm her chances of a fair trial.[58] Beyond this, though, when seen as a fictional film, the virtuoso performances of Patricia Reyes Espíndola and other female actors can be read as highbrow versions of the ways in which exploitation actors like Isela Vega challenged gender mores. An even more surprising entry, and one that is often not remembered, is Cazals's 1986 nunsploitation film *Las inocentes.*[59] Written by Robles in the theatrical style of *Bajo la metralla* and with clear echoes of *Las siete cucas* in its representation of women in cloisters, *Las inocentes* tells the story of four nuns who are kept under strict control after being raped by a mob of lepers and becoming pregnant. As Tamao Nakahara discusses in a classic essay on the subject, nunsploitation thrived in Italy as a genre in between the sexual revolutions in European cinema during the sixties (including Scandinavian exploitation and even the work of directors like Bernardo Bertolucci), the weakening of religious censorship in the wake of the Second Vatican Council, and the rise of cult genres like the Spaghetti Western and the *giallo* in Italy.[60]

Unlike the homegrown *fichera* flicks, this type of exploitation genre allows Cazals to claim more cultural pedigree. In fact, the film is an adaptation of a story by Nobel Prize winner Luigi Pirandello, and this type of religious representation had entered the canon of Western cinema particularly since Pasolini's *Decameron* (1971).[61] Yet, the theme of the film is the same as *Las poquianchis* and *Las siete cucas:* women trapped in societal mechanisms of control. As García Tsao puts it, prostitutes in Cazals's films are "trapped in vice" while nuns "are trapped in virtue."[62]

One could continue listing and discussing Cazals films as I have done in this article, but it is essential to notice the conceptual opening they provide. Filmmakers like Cazals require us to challenge the reification of Eurocentric and US-centric models of film authorship and recognize the rocky but generative trajectories of filmmakers in industries like Mexico's. Even if Cazals participates in the ideology of the auteur, formative during his rise in the 1970s and 1980s, a closer look at his trajectory provides a different account. His films have both significant thematic and stylistic continuities from the 1960s to the 2010s, but they also have very visible stylistic departures. Indeed, people used to his grittiness in *Canoa* or to his work in closed spaces discussed here would be surprised to see a historical film like *Ciudadano Buelna* (2013), shot in the most stylized cinematography in his career (Martín Boege, the cinematographer, is well known within the canons of neoliberal cinema). Accounting for Cazals requires understanding authorship not as a signature style, nor as a director-centered aesthetic wager, but rather as a rhizomatic and constantly-evolving tensional engagement with the unstable aesthetics and economics of precarious industries. In the very good conditions provided by the *echeverrista* model, *Canoa* was unquestionably a peak in his work. But, in my view, it requires more talent to muster elegant night films out of commercial fare like *El gran triunfo* or to nearly improvise a major political film on a shoestring budget, as he does in *Bajo la metralla*. Cazals's recent visibilization in the Criterion Collection, alongside national authors who worked in parallel conditions (including the great Philippine director Lino Brocka, who also faced censorship and navigated the commercial and the art industries of his country with mastery), create an opportunity to rethink this type of authorship, generally caught in the blind spot between critical paradigms devoted to art and commercial cinema.[63] This kind of director, I would say, the film author in the time of cinematic crisis, is the one that truly defines national cinemas beyond the rarefied worlds of film festivals and of Hollywood's global hegemony.

As Cazals has more or less retired since 2013 and has expressed reluctance in making a new film after turning eighty years old, it is possible to see retrospectively how important his commercial forays were to the continuation of his work. Indeed, *Las siete cucas* was not at all the last film in his exploitation commercial career. In 1991, he was hired to shoot two films meant as vehicles for a then-emergent sex symbol, Lorena Herrera: *Burbujas de amor* (1991) and *Desvestidas y alborotadas* (1991). Both films were clearly tied to popular culture referentiality: the first one is named after a hugely successful *bachata* song by Dominican singer Juan Luis Guerra, while the second one parodies the popular 1968 film *Vestidas y alborotadas*. The films are late *fichera* works of the most canonical kind. *Burbujas de amor* is built on a tension between two prostitutes and a virginal woman and the desire that men feel toward all of them, much in the same vein of *Las siete cucas*. The second one includes a tension between the oversexualization of women and the visibilization of a trans woman, with a nice detail for the age of NAFTA: the presence of a woman seeking to escape her Texan boyfriend. In the interview that closes his conversations with García Tsao, Cazals reflects on these films in interesting ways. He recognizes that they were shot at the same time, for eight days each, with no suggestion or intervention on his part. Yet this regime makes him nostalgic for the Rigo films, which he describes as having "some craft in them."[64] Yet, Cazals also recognizes that Alex Phillips Jr., his cinematographer from *Canoa* notable to the point that the film was shot in Mexico City, but realistically depicts its action as if it had been shot in the coastal city of Puerto Vallarta, where only a few shots were made.[65] To García Tsao's argument that the Lorena Herrera films lasted a short time in theaters and thus were failures, Cazals retorts that they in fact made a lot of money in the videohome market and concludes that privatization was leading cinema to the abyss.[66] These films nonetheless are less trivial in Cazals's career than they sound. As an economic proposition, they allowed him to bridge the moment in which Mexican state institutions collapsed and the neoliberal structures were still rising. In the neoliberal period, Cazals would fully turn to historical cinema, beginning with *Kino* (1993), a wonderful epic film on a Jesuit priest, Eusebio Kino, who established various missions and explored the Baja California Peninsula. From this film forward, the skills of shooting outdoors seen in the Lorena Herrera films become a clear feature of his historical works. The stylized neoliberal visuals of *Ciudadano Buelna,* mentioned above, appear in Cazals's cinema for the first time in *Burbujas de amor.* An authorship theory that cannot recognize facts like this is of little use to trace the trajectory of the majority of important directors: not those who are simple studio hands, not those who live in the world of festivals and art cinema, but the ones that constitute the backbone of national industries and that are rendered invisible by esoteric notions of the auteur.

## Notes

1. Manuel Gutiérrez Silva and Luis Duno Gottberg, eds., *Arturo Ripstein. The Sinister Gaze on the World* (New York: Palgrave, 2019).

2. On the infrastructural issues surrounding the *echeverrista* period, see Eduardo de la Vega Alfaro, "Del neopopulismo a los prolegómenos del neoliberalismo. La política cinematográfica y el 'nuevo cine mexicano' durante el periodo 1971–1982," in *El estado y la imagen en movimiento. Reflexiones sobre las políticas públicas y el cine mexicano,* ed. Cuauhtémoc Carmona Álvarez and Carlos Sánchez Sánchez (Mexico: IMCINE/Conaculta, 2012), pp. 227–69. See also Alejandro Pelayo, "Una nueva política cinematográfica durante el régimen de Luis Echeverría Álvarez (1970–1976)," in *Miradas al cine mexicano vol. 2,* coord. Aurelio de los Reyes García-Rojas (Mexico: Secretaría de Cultura, 2016), 317–38. On the aesthetics and politics of *echeverrista* cinema, see Ignacio M. Sánchez Prado, "Alegorías sin pueblo. El cine echeverrista y la crisis del contrato social de la cultura mexicana," *Chasqui* 44, no. 2 (2015), 50–67.

3. Ericka Montaño Garfias, "Dos décadas del incendio en la Cineteca; efemérides de un crimen cultural," *La Jornada,* March 23, 2002.

4. De la Vega Alfaro, "Del neopopulismo a los prolegómenos," 248–60.

5. Francisco Sánchez, *Luz en la oscuridad. Crónica del cine mexicano 1968-2002* (Mexico: Conaculta/Juan Pablos, 2002), 179–82.

6. Alejandro Pelayo, *La generación de la crisis. El cine independiente mexicano de los años ochenta* (Mexico: Conaculta/IMCINE, 2012).

7. Isis Saavedra Luna, *Entre la ficción y la realidad. Fin de la industria cinematográfica mexicana 1989-1994* (Mexico: Universidad Autónoma Metropolitana-Xochimilco, 2007).

8. Charles Ramírez Berg, *Cinema of Solitude. A Critical Study of Mexican Cinema, 1967–1983* (Austin: University of Texas Press, 1992).

9. See Olivia Cosentino "Televisa Born and Raised. Lucerito's Stardom in 1980s Mexican Media," *The Velvet Light Trap* 78 (2016): 38–52; Victoria Ruétalo and Dolores Tierney, *Latsploitation, Exploitation Cinemas and Latin America* (London: Routledge, 2009). See also Seraina Rohrer, *La India María. Mexploitation and the Films of María Elena Velasco* (Austin: University of Texas Press, 2017).

10. John Caughie, ed., *Theories of Authorship. A Reader* (London: Routledge, 1981).

11. Barry Keith Grant, ed. *Auteurs and Authorship. A Reader* (London: Wiley-Blackwell, 2008).

12. David Gertsner and Janet Staiger, eds. *Authorship and Film,* (London: Routledge, 2002); Virginia Wright Wexman, ed., *Film and Authorship.* (New Brunswick: Rutgers University Press, 2003). The article included in the latter is Marvin D'Lugo, "Transnational Film Authors and the State of National Cinema," 112–30, which is one of the few very good essays on authorship in Latin American cinema out there.

13. Carl J. Mora, *Mexican Cinema. Reflections of a Society* (Jefferson: McFarland, 2012), 122.

14. Pelayo, "Una nueva política," 333.

15. *La fábrica de sueños. Estudios Churubusco 1945–2015,* 2 vols. (Mexico: Secretaría de Educación Pública/Consejo Nacional para la Cultura y las Artes/Estudios Churubusco, 2017).

16. On the changes in film attendance in the period, see Ana Rosas Mantecón, *Ir al cine. Antropología de los públicos, la ciudad y las pantallas* (Mexico: Universidad Autónoma Metropolitana-Iztapalapa, 2017), 190–202. Of particular importance here is her discussion of the disappearance of the *cines de barrio,* the main venues for commercial Mexican film.

17. Cazals himself speaks positively of Echeverría's support after facing the withdrawal of private funding. See Leonardo García Tsao, *Felipe Cazals habla de su cine* (Guadalajara: Universidad de Guadalajara, 1994), 84.

18. García Tsao, *Felipe Cazals habla de su cine,* 197–205.

19. Berg, *Cinema of Solitude,* 52.

20. Mora, *Mexican Cinema,* 139. It is not surprising that the rise of authorial cinema in the 1990s is tied to the decline of these unions. See Saavedra Luna, *Entre la ficción y la realidad,* 151–64.

21. On García Márquez and *El año de la peste,* see Alessandro Rocco, *Gabriel García Márquez and the Cinema. Life and Works* (Woodbridge, UK: Tamesis, 2004), 31–33 and 75–69. For Cazals's comment on the heavy literariness of García Márquez's style, see Gonzalo Restrepo Sánchez, *Gabriel García Márquez y el cine. ¿Una buena amistad?* (Santa Marta: Universidad del Magdalena, 2019), 123.

22. De la Vega Alfaro, "Del neopopulismo a los prolegómenos," 265–67; Mora, *Mexican Cinema,* 140–41.

23. Mora, *Mexican cinema,* 142–44.

24. Raúl Miranda López, *Del quinto poder al séptimo arte* (Mexico: Conaculta/Cineteca Nacional, 2006), 28–42.

25. See Rohrer, *La India María.*

26. Sergio de la Mora, *Cinemachismo. Masculinities and Sexuality in Mexican Film* (Austin: University of Texas Press, 2006), 109–14; Vinodh Venkatesh, *New Maricón Cinema. Outing Mexican Film* (Austin: University of Texas Press, 2016), 28–32.

27. The most well-known version of these remarks can be found in García Tsao, *Felipe Cazals habla de su cine,* 207–16.

28. In the case of Soderbergh, there is excellent work that problematizes the idea of authorship as antithetical to industrial cinema. See Mark Gallagher, *Another Soderbergh Experience. Authorship and Contemporary Hollywood* (Austin: University of Texas Press, 2013). Similar arguments have been made related to Nolan and his work with videogames, IMAX, and commercial structures. See Jacqueline Furby and Stuart Joy, eds, *The Cinema of Christopher Nolan: Imagining the Impossible* (London: Wallflower, 2015).

29. On the ways *Dune* relates to Lynch's figure as an author, see Antony Todd, *Authorship and the Films of David Lynch* (London: I.B. Tauris, 2012), 38–63.

30. On the importance of music in the Golden Age, see Jacqueline Avila, *Cinesonidos. Film Music and National Identity during Mexico's Época de Oro* (Oxford: Oxford University Press, 2019).

31. Alejandro L. Madrid, *Music in Mexico. Experiencing Music, Experiencing Culture* (Oxford: Oxford University Press, 2013), 57.

32. On the ballad and Televisa see Madrid, *Music in Mexico*, 59.

33. For a comprehensive study of Tovar's music and his historical importance see Alejandro L. Madrid, "Rigo Tovar, Cumbia and the Transnational Grupero Boom," in *Cumbia! Scenes of a Migrant Latin American Music Genre*, eds. Héctor Fernández L'Hoeste and Pablo Vila (Durham: Duke University Press, 2013), 105–18.

34. Cristina Rivera Garza, coord., *Rigo es amor. Una rocola a dieciséis voces* (Mexico: Tusquets, 2013).

35. See "Rigo Tovar. Un rockstar de la música tropical," *Reporte Índigo*, March 29, 2017, https://www.reporteindigo.com/piensa/rigo-tovar-rockstar-musica-tropical-abbey-road-rock-musica-clasica/; Betto Arcos, "Rigo Tovar. An Appreciation of a Mexican Popstar," *PRI: The World with Marco Werman*, Minneapolis: Public Radio International, August 29, 2013, https://www.pri.org/stories/2013-08-29/rigo-tovar-appreciation-mexican-pop-star; Betto Arcos, "Recordando a mi hermano con las canciones de Rigo Tovar," in Rivera Garza, *Rigo es amor*," 33–47.

36. Jorge Ayala Blanco, *La condición del cine mexicano* (Mexico: Universidad Nacional Autónoma de México, 2018), ebook without page numbers. This book collects Ayala Blanco's writings about films between 1973 and 1985 and is structured first as a critique of popular genres and then as a study of the notable film authors of the time.

37. Ayala Blanco, *La condición del cine mexicano*, 137.

38. García Tsao, *Felipe Cazals habla de su cine*, 250.

39. On Isela Vega, see Sergio de la Mora, "'Tus pinches leyes yo me las paso por los huevos.' Isela Vega and Mexican Dirty Movies," in Ruétalo and Tierney, *Latsploitation*, 245–57.

40. Eugenio Noel, *Las siete cucas. Una mancebía en Castilla*, ed. José Esteban (Madrid: Cátedra, 1992).

41. Carmen Elisa Gómez Gómez, *Familia y Estado. Visiones desde el cine mexicano* (Guadalajara: Universidad de Guadalajara, 2015), 106.

42. García Tsao, *Felipe Cazals habla de su cine*, 224.

43. For a detailed study of Gleyzer's *México. La revolución congelada*, a good point of comparison with Cazals's own guerrilla filmmaking in *Bajo la metralla*, see Adela Pineda Franco, *The Mexican Revolution on the World Stage. Intellectuals and Film in the Twentieth Century* (Albany: State University of New York Press, 2019), 125–61.

44. There is a considerable number of recent entries in the bibliography on the Mexican Dirty War, so I will not provide an exhaustive list. For the emergence of the radical left-wing groups like the one represented in *Bajo la metralla*, see Louise E. Walker, *Waking from the Dream. Mexico's Middle Classes after 1968* (Stanford: Stanford University Press, 2013), 23–44. Two collections offer a wide-ranging view both of the insurgencies and the repression: Fernando Herrera Calderón and Adela Cedillo, eds., *Challenging Authoritarianism in Mexico. Revolutionary Struggles and the Dirty War 1964-1982* (London: Routledge, 2011) and Jaime M. Pensado and Enrique Ochoa, eds., *Mexico beyond 1968. Revolutionaries, Radicals and Repression during the Global Sixties and the Subversive Seventies* (Tucson: University of Arizona Press, 2018).

45. Ayala Blanco, *La condición del cine mexicano,* n.p.

46. García Tsao, *Felipe Cazals habla de su cine,* 229–30.

47. Tomás Pérez Turrent, "La década de los setenta y lo que sigue," in *La fábrica de sueños,* n.p. Pelayo does note that this was due to the cheaper costs because of currency devaluations and that these productions were welcome by the unions, as they compensated for the scarcity of publicly funded productions at the time. Pelayo, *La generación de la crisis,* 79.

48. García Tsao, *Felipe Cazals habla de su cine,* 229.

49. García Tsao, *Felipe Cazals habla de su cine,* 230. On the "Enfermos" of Sinaloa, the radical group whose story inspires the film, see Sergio Arturo Sánchez Parra, *Estudiantes en armas. Una historia política y cultural del movimiento estudiantil de los enfermos (1972–1978)* (Culiacán: Universidad Autónoma de Sinaloa, 2012).

50. Robles deserves additional mention here, noting that, after writing Cazals's major films of the late 1980s (*Los motivos de Luz* and *El tres de copas*), he would also pen the great landmark political film of the 1980s, Jorge Fons's *Rojo amanecer* (1989), the first major film on the 1968 massacre in mainstream fiction cinema. He also wrote and directed in recent years a major documentary on the forty-three missing students of Iguala, Mexico, *Ayotzinapa. Crónica de un crimen de Estado* (2014). His book *La oruga y la mariposa. Géneros dramáticos en el cine* (Mexico: Universidad Nacional Autónoma de México, 2010) is the most widely read book on the theory of the screenplay in Mexico.

51. While working on the revisions to this article, a scholarly study of the influence of Camus on *Bajo la metralla* and a testimony on the Mexican guerila was published. See Juan Tomás Martínez Gutiérrez, "Los justos de Albert Camus como clave interpretativa en dos obras sobre la guerrilla urbana post-68 en México," *Alter/nativas* 9 (2018), https://alternativas.osu.edu/assets/files/issue9/ensayos/martinez-final.pdf.

52. De Laurentiis himself recalls the time in which Mexico became a "mecca" for Hollywood due to low-cost, high-quality resources and particularly recounts shooting Lynch's *Dune* in Churubusco. See Tulio Kezich, *Dino. The Life and Film of Dino de Laurentiis,* trans. James Marcus (New York: Miramax/Hyperion, 2004), 278–80.

53. On *Missing* and the Latin America-based political thriller of the 1980s, see William J. Palmer, *The Films of the Eighties. A Social History* (Edwardsville: Southern Illinois University Press, 1993), 141–43.

54. On the Llosa/Corman films, see Jeffrey Middents, "Roger Corman Dis/covers Peru: National Cinema and Luis Llosa's *Hour of the Assassin/Misión en los Andes,*" in Ruétalo and Tierney, *Latsploitation,* 55–69.

55. García Tsao, *Felipe Cazals habla de su cine,* 233.

56. Ayala Blanco, *La condición del cine mexicano,* n.p.; Richard Corliss, "The Pleasures of Texture," *Time,* July 12, 1982, 68.

57. García Tsao, *Felipe Cazals habla de su cine,* 232–33.

58. For a study of the film based on the judicial case, see Isabel Arredondo, *Motherhood in Mexican Cinema 1941–1991. The Transformation of Femininity on Screen* (Jefferson: McFarland, 2014). Unfortunately, Arredondo misses *Las siete cucas.* It would have been interesting to see how it would have fit in her otherwise excellent history of motherhood in Mexican cinema.

59. Perhaps one should note here that a reason behind this oblivion is that Cazals himself does not know where the master copy is and, as García Tsao notes, many have seen it only in private shows. García Tsao, *Felipe Cazals habla de su cine,* 273. Nonetheless, a VHS edition released in Spain does circulate.

60. Tamao Nakahama, "Barred Nuns. Italian Nunsploitation Films," in *Alternative Europe. Eurotrash and Exploitation Cinema since 1945*, ed. Ernest Mathijs and Xavier Mendik (London: Wallflower, 2004), 124–33.

61. See Patrick Rumble, *Allegories of Contamination. Pier Paolo Pasolini's Trilogy of Life* (Toronto: University of Toronto Press, 1996), 100–34.

62. García Tsao, *Felipe Cazals habla de su cine*, 275.

63. On Brocka's tensions between politics and popular cinema, see José B. Capino, *Martial Law Melodrama. Lino Brocka's Cinema Politics* (Berkeley: University of California Press, 2020).

64. García Tsao, *Felipe Cazals habla de su cine*, 291.

65. García Tsao, *Felipe Cazals habla de su cine*, 291.

66. García Tsao, *Felipe Cazals habla de su cine*, 292–93.

## Bibliography

Alfaro, Eduardo de la Vega. "Del neopopulismo a los prolegómenos del neoliberalismo. La política cinematográfica y el 'nuevo cine mexicano' durante el periodo 1971–1982." In *El estado y la imagen en movimiento. Reflexiones sobre las políticas públicas y el cine mexicano*, edited by Cuauhtémoc Carmona Álvarez and Carlos Sánchez Sánchez, 228–69. Mexico City: IMCINE/ Conaculta, 2012.

Arcos, Betto. "Rigo Tovar. An Appreciation of a Mexican Popstar." *PRI: The World with Marco Werman*. Minneapolis: Public Radio International, August 29, 2013. https://www.pri.org/stories/2013-08-29/rigo-tovar-appreciation-mexican-pop-star.

———. "Recordando a mi hermano con las canciones de Rigo Tovar." In *Rigo es amor. Una rocola a dieciséis voces*, edited by Cristina Rivera Garza, 33–47. Mexico City: Tusquets, 2013.

Arredondo, Isabel. *Motherhood in Mexican Cinema 1941–1991. The Transformation of Femininity on Screen*. Jefferson, NC: McFarland, 2014.

Avila, Jacqueline. *Cinesonidos. Film Music and National Identity during Mexico's Época de Oro*. Oxford: Oxford University Press, 2019.

Ayala Blanco, Jorge. *La condición del cine mexicano*. Mexico: Universidad Nacional Autónoma de México, 2018.

Capino, José B. *Martial Law Melodrama. Lino Brocka's Cinema Politics*. Berkeley: University of California Press, 2020.

Caughie, John, ed. *Theories of Authorship. A Reader*. London: Routledge, 1981.

Corliss, Richard. "The Pleasures of Texture." *Time*, July 12, 1982.

Cosentino, Olivia. "Televisa Born and Raised. Lucerito's Stardom in 1980s Mexican Media." *The Velvet Light Trap* 78 (2016): 38–52.

de la Mora, Sergio. *Cinemachismo. Masculinities and Sexuality in Mexican Film*. Austin: University of Texas Press, 2006.

———. "'Tus pinches leyes yo me las paso por los huevos.' Isela Vega and Mexican Dirty Movies." In *Latsploitation, Exploitation Cinemas and Latin America*, edited by Victoria Ruétalo and Dolores Tierney, 245–57. London: Routledge, 2009.

D'Lugo, Marvin. "Transnational Film Authors and the State of National Cinema." In *Film and Authorship*, edited by Virginia Wright Wexman, 112–130. New Brunswick: Rutgers University Press, 2003.

Furby, Jacqueline, and Stuart Joy, eds. *The Cinema of Christopher Nolan: Imagining the Impossible*. London: Wallflower, 2015.
Gallagher, Mark. *Another Soderbergh Experience. Authorship and Contemporary Hollywood*. Austin: University of Texas Press, 2013.
García Tsao, Leonardo. *Felipe Cazals habla de su cine*. Guadalajara: Universidad de Guadalajara, 1994.
Gertsner, David, and Janet Staiger, eds. *Authorship and Film*. London: Routledge, 2002.
Gómez Gómez, Carmen Elisa. *Familia y Estado. Visiones desde el cine mexicano*. Guadalajara: Universidad de Guadalajara, 2015.
Grant, Barry Keith, ed. *Auteurs and Authorship. A Reader*. London: Wiley-Blackwell, 2008.
Gutiérrez Silva, Manuel, and Luis Duno Gottberg, ed. *Arturo Ripstein. The Sinister Gaze on the World*. New York: Palgrave, 2019.
Herrera Calderón, Fernando, and Adela Cedillo, eds. *Challenging Authoritarianism in Mexico. Revolutionary Struggles and the Dirty War 1964-1982*. London: Routledge, 2011.
Madrid, Alejandro L. *Music in Mexico. Experiencing Music, Experiencing Culture*. Oxford: Oxford University Press, 2013.
———. "Rigo Tovar, *Cumbia* and the Transnational Grupero Boom." In *Cumbia! Scenes of a Migrant Latin American Music Genre*, edited by Héctor Fernández L'Hoeste and Pablo Vila, 105-18. Durham: Duke University Press, 2013.
Mantecón, Ana Rosas. *Ir al cine. Antropología de los públicos, la ciudad y las pantallas*. Mexico City: Universidad Autónoma Metropolitana-Iztapalapa, 2017.
Martínez Gutiérrez, Juan Tomás. "Los justos de Albert Camus como clave interpretativa en dos obras sobre la guerrilla urbana post-68 en México." *Alter/nativas* 9 (2018): 1-23. https://alternativas.osu.edu/assets/files/issue9/ensayos/martinez-final.pdf.
Middents, Jeffrey. "Roger Corman Dis/covers Peru: National Cinema and Luis Llosa's *Hour of the Assassin/ Misión en los Andes*." In *Latsploitation, Exploitation Cinemas and Latin America*, edited by Victoria Ruétalo and Dolores Tierney, 55-69. London: Routledge, 2009.
Miranda López, Raúl. *Del quinto poder al séptimo arte*. Mexico City: Conaculta/Cineteca Nacional, 2006.
Montaño Garfias, Ericka. "Dos décadas del incendio en la Cineteca; efemérides de un crimen cultural." *La Jornada*, March 23, 2002.
Mora, Carl J. *Mexican Cinema. Reflections of a Society*. Jefferson, NC: McFarland, 2012.
Nakahama, Tamao. "Barred Nuns. Italian Nunsploitation Films." In *Alternative Europe. Eurotrash and Exploitation Cinema since 1945*, edited by Ernest Mathijs and Xavier Mendik, 124-33. London: Wallflower, 2004.
Noel, Eugenio. *Las siete cucas. Una mancebía en Castilla*. Madrid: Cátedra, 1992.
Palmer, William J. *The Films of the Eighties. A Social History*, 141-43. Edwardsville: Southern Illinois University Press, 1993.
Pensado, Jaime M., and Enrique Ochoa, eds. *Mexico beyond 1968. Revolutionaries, Radicals and Repression during the Global Sixties and the Subversive Seventies*. Tucson: University of Arizona Press, 2018.
Pelayo, Alejandro. *La generación de la crisis. El cine independiente mexicano de los años ochenta*. Mexico City: Conaculta/IMCINE, 2012.
———. "Una nueva política cinematográfica durante el régimen de Luis Echeverría Álvarez (1970-1976)." In *Miradas al cine mexicano vol. 2*, edited by Aurelio de los Reyes García-Rojas, 317-38. Mexico City: Secretaría de Cultura, 2016.

Pérez Turrent, Tomás. "La década de los setenta y lo que sigue." In *La fábrica de sueños. Estudios Churubusco 1945–2015*, 2 vols., n.p. Mexico: Secretaría de Educación Pública/Consejo Nacional para la Cultura y las Artes/Estudios Churubusco, 2017.

Pineda Franco, Adela. *The Mexican Revolution on the World Stage. Intellectuals and Film in the Twentieth Century*. Albany: State University of New York Press, 2019.

Ramírez Berg, Charles. *Cinema of Solitude. A Critical Study of Mexican Cinema, 1967–1983*. Austin: University of Texas Press, 1992.

Restrepo Sánchez, Gonzalo. *Gabriel García Márquez y el cine. ¿Una buena amistad?* Santa Marta: Universidad del Magdalena, 2019.

"Rigo Tovar. Un rockstar de la música tropical." *Reporte Índigo*, March 29, 2017. https://www.reporteindigo.com/piensa/rigo-tovar-rockstar-musica-tropical-abbey-road-rock-musica-clasica/.

Rivera Garza, Cristina, ed. *Rigo es amor. Una rocola a dieciséis voces*. Mexico: Tusquets, 2013.

Robles, Xavier. *La oruga y la mariposa. Géneros dramáticos en el cine*. Mexico City: Universidad Nacional Autónoma de México, 2010.

Rocco, Alessandro. *Gabriel García Márquez and the Cinema. Life and Works*. Woodbridge, UK: Tamesis, 2004.

Rohrer, Seraina. *La India María. Mexploitation and the Films of María Elena Velasco*. Austin: University of Texas Press, 2017.

Rumble, Patrick. *Allegories of Contamination. Pier Paolo Pasolini's Trilogy of Life*. Toronto: University of Toronto Press, 1996.

Saavedra Luna, Isis. *Entre la ficción y la realidad. Fin de la industria cinematográfica mexicana 1989–1994*. Mexico: Universidad Autónoma Metropolitana-Xochimilco, 2007.

Sánchez, Francisco. *Luz en la oscuridad. Crónica del cine mexicano 1968–2002*. Mexico: Conaculta/Juan Pablos, 2002.

Sánchez Parra, Sergio Arturo. *Estudiantes en armas. Una historia política y cultural del movimiento estudiantil de los enfermos (1972–1978)*. Culiacán: Universidad Autónoma de Sinaloa, 2012.

Sánchez Prado, Ignacio M. "Alegorías sin pueblo. El cine echeverrista y la crisis del contrato social de la cultura mexicana." *Chasqui* 44.2 (2015): 50–67.

Todd, Antony. *Authorship and the Films of David Lynch*. London: I.B. Tauris, 2012.

Tulio Kezich, Dino. *The Life and Film of Dino de Laurentiis*. Translated by James Marcus. New York: Miramax/Hyperion, 2004.

Venkatesh, Vinodh. *New Maricón Cinema. Outing Mexican Film*. Austin: University of Texas Press, 2016.

Walker, Louise E. *Waking from the Dream. Mexico's Middle Classes after 1968*. Stanford: Stanford University Press, 2013.

# 8

## FINDING THE LOST CINEMA OF MEXICO

Critical Recovery, Rescue, and Reconceptualization

DOLORES TIERNEY

The essays in *The Lost Cinema of Mexico* make the case for a radical reconceptualization of Mexican film history to critically recover and rescue the commercial genres and other formats that have "slipped through the cracks" or been "maligned or misunderstood," "forgotten," and "writ[ten] out of" Anglo and Mexican cinema scholarship.[1] The book expansively addresses not only the lost genres (*cine familiar*, the Chili Western, the rock and roll film), the auteur exploitation films (of Felipe Cazals), the filmmaking dynasties (the Calderóns, the Galindos, the Agrasánchez), the stars (Lorena Velázquez), the racial melodramas, and forgotten formats (Super 8) but also the "lost" decades of the 1960s, 1970s, and 1980s themselves during which all of the above flourished.

The years 1960 to 1990 are often described in histories of Mexican cinema in terms of "decline," "crisis," and "collapse."[2] From a particular perspective, these years did represent a profound crisis for Mexican filmmaking on both institutional and ideological levels. After the Golden Age of classical filmmaking (1936–1954) when Mexican cinema achieved a huge level of domestic and region-wide success, as well as a negotiated reciprocity between the post-revolutionary state discourses and its audiences, in the course of the 1950s the industry and its ideological basis began to fall apart. Factors that precipitated and also signaled this breakdown included the shift to low-budget, rapidly made films exploiting certain profitable genres, the closure of several film studios, the loss of the Cuban market, and the suspension in 1958 of the Ariel Awards.[3] By the 1960s, Mexican cinema had entered a full-blown crisis. For the first time since 1950, in the first years of the 1960s, annual production declined and the decade was otherwise marked by a collapse of the classical filmmaking apparatus and a crisis of the state itself hastened by the massacre of students at the Plaza de Tres Culturas, Tlatelolco.[4] Substantial attempts were made to revive the film industry during the presidency of Luis Echeverría Álvarez (1970–1976), including "unprecedented financial and infrastructural" state backing in order to "promote Mexican cinema throughout the world."[5] Much of this backing was for projects by the Nuevo Cine directors, a group which had emerged in the early 1960s with a film journal (*Nuevo Cine*), and a series of low-budget independent films. As a sign that this approach was working, the Ariel was reintroduced in 1972. At the end of Echeverría's *sexenio,* however, the new president José López Portillo (1976–1982) withdrew many of the previous administration's initiatives to encourage quality Mexican cinema. He also named his sister, Margarita, director of a new organization the Dirección General de Radio, Televisión y Cinematografía (RTC). She made various disastrous decisions, undoing much of what had been achieved with Nuevo Cine in the preceding six years, including dismantling state production companies. Nuevo Cine directors now faced "lower budgets, stricter censorship, and tighter distribution policies."[6] A fire at the Cineteca Nacional in 1982 that destroyed films and archive materials is often portrayed as the final straw of Portillo-era disasters that irrevocably broke the film industry's back. The 1980s are characterized in these histories as an era when "socially relevant themes were discouraged, and pure entertainment was privileged."[7]

This history, as I have summarized it here, is the generally accepted narrative about the period from 1960 to 1990. However, as I and others have argued elsewhere, there's a greater complexity to these years that is often overlooked.[8] The authors of *The Lost Cinema of Mexico* untangle some of this period's complexity, piecing together a counter-history that offers an alternative account in essays that re-frame the period of supposed crisis as one of "unquestionable success."[9] These authors are revising and challenging the dominant narrative of Mexican cinema history, which has constructed the 1960s, 1970s, and

1980s from a Nuevo Cine perspective that considers them as decades "lost" to an industrial crisis and to "highly commercial" and "culturally disreputable" genres like *cine familiar,* the Chili Western, and the rock and roll film, which dominated in production numbers and at the box office. Of course, 1980s family films like as *Niño pobre, niño rico* (Sergio Véjar, 1983), starring Pedrito Fernández, and *Ya nunca más* (Abel Salazar, 1984), starring Luis Miguel, have never been really lost, not to the mass audiences that flocked to see them—nor, as Olivia Cosentino asserts in this volume—are they lost to contemporary audiences, whose enthusiasm for them on DVD and YouTube surpasses their initial theatrical runs.

This crisis narrative, which this volume challenges, is the product of what Andrew Higson might call a prescriptive national cinema model of film criticism that writes about what the national cinema *ought* to be, rather than describing the actual cinematic experience of popular audiences:

> The concept of a national cinema has almost invariably been mobilised as a strategy of cultural (and economic) resistance; a means of asserting national autonomy in the face of (usually) Hollywood international domination. . . . The discourses of "art," "culture" and "quality," and of "national identity" and "nationhood," have historically been mobilised against Hollywood's mass entertainment film, and used to justify various nationally specific economic systems of support and production.[10]

In the case of Mexico and Mexican film scholarship, national cinema concerns are pronounced in the framing of 1960s-to-1990s cinemas around discourses of auteur and art cinema (the Nuevo Cine), which struggled in the face of the aesthetic, economic, and ideological hegemony both of the Hollywood industry and the perceived-as-Hollywood-derived local commercial cinema through much of the period. It is not surprising, and even understandable, that "Mexican criticism" should have so wholeheartedly rejected the popular commercial cinemas in favor of the art and auteur cinemas, if we take into consideration the fact that its dominant critics of the 1970s–2000s (Emilio García Riera, Carlos Monsiváis, Jorge Ayala Blanco, Tomás Pérez Turrent, Felipe Cazals, and others) are themselves the same critics, filmmakers, screenwriters, and writers who, as young men in 1960s and 1970s, fought against the prevailing tide of commercial film for the chance to make a new and innovative (art) cinema. It is this set of critics (and filmmakers) cited and argued against throughout *The Lost Cinema* who "forged their careers panning [the specific] works" the essays in this book defend.[11]

However, in line with changing cultural and discipline-related imperatives, both in Mexican and Latin American film studies as they are carried out locally and in the Anglo-American academy, including in part the formative influence of the popular cultural studies approach of one of the original Nuevo Cine group, Monsiváis, and a new generation of critics who have a different perspective that sees greater value in popular/mass culture, the ways in which Mexican cinema is approached are changing.[12] Firstly, there's been a dramatic re-evaluation of the exploitation cinemas of the 1950s through the 2000s.[13] No longer outshone by the obvious nationalist, cultural, and political currency of the auteur cinemas produced during this period, Mexico's exploitation cinemas (increasingly delineated as "Mexploitation"[14]) have been re-examined to evidence their contributions to national cinema and the ways popular audiences relate and make use of them. The essays in *The Lost Cinema of Mexico*, which are focused mostly (but not all) on commercial cinema rather than strictly exploitation (although some would still fit within an expansive definition of the term), are an extension of this revisionist tendency in Mexican and Latin American film criticism. These essays challenge a "quality" and, in the case of the *superochero* films, a capital-based industrial-cinema-focused history of Mexican cinema from 1960 until 1990. They call attention to the "multiple positives" of the era, including an expansion of state support in the Echeverría period that "fostered the emergence of some of Mexico's greatest auteurs" and how its withdrawal in the López Portillo era actually set the stage "for a popular cinema that reconnected with popular audiences that had either been lost or rendered invisible by authorial film."[15] In this respect, the "lost" cinema of Mexico, identified as the impetus for this book, finds a point of contact with other national projects of cultural rescue, or *rescate*, across Latin America's film histories, such as the work of Juan Antonio García Borrero on Cuba's *cine sumergido*. García Borrero is referring here to a cinema submerged by the Instituto Cubano del Arte e Industria Cinematográfico [Cuban Institute of Cinematographic Art and Industry] (ICAIC)–centric post–1959 revolution history of Cuban cinema, which includes the country's pre-revolutionary commercial cinema, its amateur film clubs, the products of the San Antonio de los Baños film school, and the films produced by regional television companies.[16] Like García Borrero, *The Lost Cinema of Mexico* is picking up on the genres, films, and formats that have yet to surface on or be adequately acknowledged by the critical radar of Mexican film history.

The way forward, therefore, in Mexican film criticism according to the book's editors, Olivia Cosentino and Brian Price, and its essay authors, is to explore what cinemas remain "lost" to Mexico's dominant film histories and how these lost items can be recovered. Mexico's commercially very popular wrestling movies of the 1950s and 1960s and the *sexycomedias* of the 1980s are not included in the anthology and are not "lost" within the terms of the book. This is because they have, as Price notes in his chapter, "draw[n] occasional nods from the academy."[17] To this end, the authors both rehearse the reasons why these "lost" cinemas have been passed over and the reasons why they should be reclaimed. This doesn't mean however, that these films are being rehabilitated to be placed in some progressive pantheon for qualities that have gone previously unnoticed.[18] Several authors (Price, Fornoff, Cosentino) are clear on the essentially conservative and entrenched ideologies of these films. But still, they argue for their consideration and inclusion rather than straightforward disavowal in relation to Mexico's film history and for their value as cultural objects that are worthy of analysis.

Price, for instance, takes on the early rock and roll films made between the late 1950s and the end of the 1960s, suggesting that far from being "insignificant," as described by Ayala Blanco, films like *A ritmo del twist* (Benito Alazraki, 1962) played an "important role in promoting local musical talent" like Los Rebeldes del Rock and "domesticat[ing] foreign cultural influences" as well as offering youth audiences a "metaphor for cosmopolitan aspirations." Price suggests that although many rock and roll films were essentially conservative in their nature and, consequently, "became vehicles for criticizing and undermining the subversive countercultural gesture," the mere fact that they exist "attest[s] . . . to changes in Mexican society and filmmaking."

Cosentino explores *cine familiar*, arguing that the term delineates both a production category of films' intended content ("[about] families and their problems") and their intended audiences (families, including both "adults and children alike") *as well as* a mode of production in which, referring to the Calderóns, the Galindos, the Agrasánchez dynasties, "family members worked together as a team, taking on multiple roles and handling various stages of the film production process as a strategy for more cost-effective filmmaking." Suggesting that *cine familiar* has "slipped through the cracks" because of its pejorative association with the Margarita López Portillo era, Cosentino asserts the genre's "centrality" to 1980s Mexican cinema. Cosentino contends that the impetus for the recovery of these films is how they function "as an escape mechanism during the difficult 1970s and 1980s," helping families (some of who suffered the effects of the 1985 Mexico City earthquake) "envision a better tomorrow," particularly when confidence in the government after the earthquake was at an all-time low.

Ignacio M. Sánchez Prado offers a study of the disavowed exploitation films of Nuevo Cine auteur Felipe Cazals, suggesting that these films, like many produced during the Portillo era, are often seen as "garbage" because critics, including Cazals himself, are often led by art cinema concerns. Passing over the political films usually studied by scholars of Cazals's cinema in this period—*Canoa* (1976), *Las poquianchis* (1975), and *El apando* (1975)—Sánchez Prado explores Cazals's biopics of popular *cumbia* singer Rigo Tovar— *Rigo es amor* (1980) and *El gran triunfo* (1981)—arguing that these films are examples of one of the most successful genres of the 1970s and 1980s. Sánchez Prado also examines Cazals's *Bajo la metralla* (1983), a fictionalization of a real event that happened during Mexico's Dirty War, which he proposes is exploitation-like in terms of its rapid shooting schedule and other features but also highly political and contentious (the film suffered low-level censorship but also paradoxically received acclaim from the Mexican Academy in the form of four Ariels). Sánchez Prado writes that not only should these exploitation films be taken into consideration in terms of Cazals's oeuvre but that he would have been unlikely to develop further as the highbrow auteur he became in the 1980s without the technical lessons learned on these films. Sánchez Prado urges us to see how these commercial forays, including another film *Las siete cucas* (1981), are not just a necessary part of any director's career in a precarious and unevenly functioning film industry like Mexico's but also an essential part of Cazals's authorship, which should not be obscured by art cinema biases.

Iván Eusebio Aguirre Darancou focuses on the "cultural phenomenon of small-format film production," a fleeting production cycle of filmmakers using the Super 8mm film that arose in the wake of the 1968 "eruption of state violence in the Plaza de las Tres Culturas, Tlatelolco." Aguirre Darancou points out that the *superocheros* were seeking to shift the form of political engagement by using a format and aesthetics that were not compromised or assimilable by either Echeverría's authoritarian state institutions or the mass media. In this context, Aguirre Darancou argues, the Super 8 format offered "the possibility to imagine cinema as a space outside the overarching influence of both state and capitalist logics." Aguirre Darancou's chapter highlights how, although "forgotten" by film criticism for decades, the *superochero* movement is of particular historical, cultural, and filmic value in particular because the directors' "explorations set the basis for later cinema, video, musical, and artistic production of the century."

Carolyn Fornoff addresses the racial melodramas of the 1970s, suggesting their importance lies in the way they "centered on [issues to do with] Black subjectivity" including "discrimination, Black power, and Black beauty." At the same time Fornoff also notes how, by casting non-Mexican actors to play Black characters in racial melodramas like *El hombre de los hongos* (Roberto Gavaldón, 1976), the film industry continued "privileging [the] cultivation and promotion of whiteness" and reaffirmed the troubling assumption that "authentic" Blackness could only be found outside of Mexico, all while upholding the myth that "racial prejudice did not exist in Mexico" because of *mestizaje* (racial mixing of indigenous and Spanish ancestry).

David S. Dalton seeks to fill the gap left by an absence of attention to the stars of the era, particularly female stars of "Mexploitation" cinema. In his star study of Lorena Velázquez, also known as the "chica-Santo por excelencia" [Santo girl par excellence], he suggests that many of the films she starred in were essentially conservative in their depiction of women buoying the Virgin/Malinche paradigm. Nevertheless, there are aspects of Velázquez's performances and roles that extended to her a great deal of agency. Through her portrayals of "heroic" and "independent" women in *luchadora* films, Velázquez "laid the framework" for the "new wave of feminism."

Christopher Conway looks at the Chili Western, which, he argues, emerged and flourished in the wake of the 1968 Tlatelolco massacre with films like *Todo por nada* (Alberto Mariscal, 1968). Through the analysis of *Tunco Maclovio* (Mariscal, 1970), *La mula de Cullen Baker* (René Cardona Sr., 1971), and *La víboras cambian de piel* (René Cardona Jr., 1971), Conway suggests that the subgenre channels "a broader mood of disenchantment [with the Mexican state] and powerlessness" through its "portrayal of broken and symbolically castrated men." Like Sánchez Prado's essay, Conway is questioning demarcations between categories of film (i.e., the commercial film genre like the Chili Western and auteur cinema). Conway's is one of several essays in the anthology to acknowledge how the profound ideological crisis of the post-Tlatelolco massacre and post-1960s (the disruption of masculinity, the dissolution of the idea of the revolutionary family) could paradoxically contribute to a flourishing commercial and genre-based industry, which was as popular as the cinema of the pre-ideological crisis era.

The timely essays in *The Lost Cinema of Mexico* both fit within current vectors of Mexican and Latin American film scholarship and, at the same time, chart new directions and avenues for future research. The overall project of the book, in its interrogation of the classification of the film production period of the 1960s–1980s as a crisis era, squares with an ongoing "question[ing]" of "standard periodization[s]" of Latin American film cultures that doesn't "adequately reflect . . . the complexity of film culture" or "reduces film history to successive modes of production and stylistic change."[19] Specific essays such as Cosentino's are equally informed by current paradigms of scholarship such as Paul Julian Smith's work on multiplatform media and Ana M. López's work on intermediality.[20] Cosentino notes, for instance, how the success of *cine familiar* depends on the simultaneous recording and television careers of the child stars who started their careers on Televisa's variety show *Siempre en Domingo* and the intermedial dynamics of films where Luis Miguel, Pedrito Fernández, and Lucerito sing as many semi-diegetic musical numbers as possible, even at the expense of narrative coherence. Other essays, such as Sánchez Prado's, chart new directions. He advocates for a necessary shift in the model of auteur scholarship as it is currently conceived in relation to the stable and well-capitalized film industries of the Global North (to consider only "personal" projects part of the auteur's oeuvre), proposing that, for an auteur like Cazals working in the Global South, exploitation-like projects also need to be considered. Cosentino's essay, on the other hand, ends by suggesting that there's more work to be done in order to understand *cine familiar,* including further research on the industrial practices of private family dynasties of the Galindos, Calderóns and Agrasánchez by "defining key players, determining ownership of production companies to even attaining more basic knowledge about budgets, length of shoots, and distribution practices." Other essays figure the importance of external markets (the United States' Spanish-language circuit in the South, West, and East Coast metropolitan areas of New York and New Jersey) in the cinema of this era, both in terms of providing income and as a factor in determining subject matter. Fornoff, for instance, observes that the 1970s' racial dramas featuring Black characters and anti-racist narratives were likely made with material that would be interesting to Spanish speakers and permeated political conversations in the United States such as equality, the Civil Rights Movement, and the Black Power Movement.

Ultimately, a very significant contribution of this book is how, overall, it points to the ways the "lost" cinemas it examines actually anticipate and pave the way for subsequent eras of Mexican filmmaking, rather than exist as an aberration to the prosperous and "quality" Mexican cinema that came before and after. Sánchez Prado, for instance, urges the reconsideration of the López Portillo era and the popular cinema it gave rise to because the ways it publicly recognized homosexuality and increasingly sexualized the female body "opened paths for post 1988 filmmakers." Aguirre Darancou similarly affirms that the *superochero* movement, and, in particular, its "creative networks," broke the "centralization of culture so prevalent in Mexican arts and film" and, in this respect, "anticipated the video production networks of the 1990s and later." *The Lost Cinema of Mexico* is a solid contribution to the work of critical recovery, rescue, and reconceptualization of an era of Mexican cinema whose importance is only just beginning to emerge.

## Notes

1. See Cosentino, Price, and Aguirre Darancou in this volume.

2. Carl J. Mora, *Mexican Cinema: Reflections of a Society, 1896–1980* (University of California Press, 1982), 101; Alejandro Pelayo, *La generación de la crisis: El cine independiente mexicano de los años ochenta* (Mexico City: Conaculta, 2012); Charles Ramírez Berg, *Cinema of Solitude: A Critical Study of Mexican Film 1967–1983* (Austin: University of Texas Press, 1992), 37.

3. Like the US Academy Awards, the Ariels are the Mexican industry's own markers of esteem.

4. Berg, *Cinema of Solitude*, 29.

5. Berg, *Cinema of Solitude*, 29.

6. Emilio García Riera, *Breve historia del cine mexicano primer siglo 1897–1997* (Mexico City: Conaculta/IMCINE, 1998), 305; Berg, *Cinema of Solitude*, 51.

7. Berg, *Cinema of Solitude*, 54.

8. See Ana M. López, "Facing up to Hollywood," in *Reinventing Film Studies*, eds. Christine Gledhill and Linda Williams (London: Edward Arnold, 2000), 419–37; Dolores Tierney, *Emilio Fernández: Pictures in the Margins* (Manchester: Manchester University Press, 2008), viii, 13, 29, 45, 113, 169; Andrew Syder and Dolores Tierney, "Mexploitation/Exploitation: Or How a Crime-Fighting Vampire-Slaying Mexican Wrestler Almost Found Himself in a Sword

and Sandal Epic," in *Horror International*, eds. Stephen Jay Schneider and Tony Williams (Detroit: Wayne State University Press, 2005), 33–55.

9. See Ignacio M. Sánchez Prado, "Felipe Cazals," in this volume.

10. Andrew Higson, "The Concept of National Cinema," *Screen* 30, no. 4 (Autumn 1989): 37, 41.

11. Sánchez Prado, "Felipe Cazals," in this volume.

12. Although often disparaging of the quality of cinema in ways that reflect Adornian paradigms of an alienating mass culture, at the same time Monsiváis's work reflects the democratizing thrust of cultural studies in the way it addresses and implicitly values Mexico's heterogenous national culture including dance, mystic cults, pop stars, wrestling, comic books, and the Virgin of Guadalupe.

13. Among numerous examples see Syder and Tierney, "Mexploitation/Exploitation"; Colin Gunckel "El Signo de la muerte and the Birth of a Genre: Origins and Anatomy of the Aztec Horror Film," in *Sleaze Artists Cinema at the Margins of Taste, Style and Politics*, ed. Jeffrey Sconce (Durham: Duke University Press, 2007), 121–43; Seraina Rohrer, *La India Maria: Mexploitation and the Films of Maria Elena Velasco* (Austin: University of Texas Press, 2017). See Maricruz Castro Ricalde, "Popular Mexican Cinema and Undocumented Immigrants," *Discourse* 26, no. 1/2 (2004): 194–213. Raúl Criollo, Jose Xavier Navar, and Rafael Aviña, *Historia ilustrada del cine de luchadores* (Mexico City: Universidad Nacional Autónoma de México, 2011). See also essays by Adán Ávalos, Sergio de la Mora, Catherine Benamou, and Misha MacLaird in Victoria Ruétalo and Dolores Tierney's *Latsploitation, Exploitation Cinema and Latin America* (New York and London: Routledge, 2009).

14. See Doyle Green *Mexploitation: A Critical History of Mexican Vampire, Wrestling, Ape Man and Similar Films 1957–1977.* (Jefferson, NC: McFarland, 2005); Syder and Tierney, "Mexploitation/Exploitation," Rohrer, *La India María*.

15. Sánchez Prado, "Felipe Cazals," in this volume.

16. Juan Antonio García Borrero, *Guía Crítica de Cine Cubano de Ficción* (La Habana: Editorial Arte y Literatura, 2001), 19–20.

17. The ascent of these genres into scholarship or, to use Sconce's term, their "trashing [of] the academy" is potentially as a result of their accessibility via similar work by scholars (Eric Schaefer, Joan Hawkins, Jeffrey Sconce and others) writing on US exploitation and its adjacent genres of trash and paracinema in the late 1990s. Eric Schaefer, *Bold! Daring! Shocking! True!: A History of Exploitation Films 1919–1959* (Durham: Duke University Press, 1999); Joan Hawkins, *Cutting Edge: Art Horror and the Horrific Avant Garde* (Minneapolis: University of Minnesota Press, 2000); Jeff Sconce, "Trashing the Academy: Taste, Excess and an Emerging Politics of Cinematic Style," *Screen* 36, no. 4 (1995): 371–93. Although, it's worth noting many of these are still not fully institutionally credited in Mexico. See the introduction to this volume for an account of how exploitation star El Santo's films did not receive an homage for the centenary of the wrestler's birth at the Cineteca Nacional (but did receive a celebratory cycle at the Filmoteca de la UNAM). See also Dolores Tierney, "Latsploitation," in *Routledge Companion to Cult Cinemas*, eds. Ernest Mathijs and Jamie Sexton (London and New York: Routledge, 2019), 93 on why the arbiters of dominant film culture in Mexico and Latin America still do not embrace the exploitation cinemas.

18. Ana M. López, "Tears and Desire: Women and Melodrama in the 'Old' Mexican Cinema," in *Multiple Voices in Feminist Film Criticism*, eds. Diane Carson, Linda Dittmar and Janice R. Welsch (Minneapolis: University of Minnesota Press, 1994), 254–70.

19. Marvin D'Lugo, Ana M. López, and Laura Podalsky, eds., "Introduction: Troubling Histories," in *The Routledge Companion to Latin American Cinema* (London and New York: Routledge, 2017), 3.

20. Paul Julian Smith, *Multiplatform Media in Mexico: Change and Growth since 2010* (Cham: Palgrave Macmillan, 2019). Ana M. López, "Film and Radio Intermedialities in Early Latin American Sound Cinema," in *The Routledge Companion to Latin American Cinema*, eds. Marvin D'Lugo, Ana M. López and Laura Podalsky (London and New York: Routledge, 2017), 316–29.

## Bibliography

Castro Ricalde, Maricruz. "Popular Mexican Cinema and Undocumented Immigrants." *Discourse* 26 no. 1/2 (2004): 194–213.

Criollo, Raúl, Jose Xavier Navar, and Rafael Aviña. *Historia ilustrada del cine de luchadores*. Mexico City: Universidad Nacional Autónoma de México, 2011.

D'Lugo, Marvin, Ana M. López, and Laura Podalsky, eds., "Introduction: Troubling Histories." In *The Routledge Companion to Latin American Cinema*, 1–14. London and New York: Routledge, 2017.

García Borrero, Juan Antonio. *Guía Crítica de Cine Cubano de Ficción*. La Habana: Editorial Arte y Literatura, 2001.

García Riera, Emilio. *Breve historia del cine mexicano primer siglo 1897-1997.* Mexico: Conaculta/IMCINE, 1998.

Gunckel, Colin. "El Signo de la muerte and the Birth of a Genre: Origins and Anatomy of the Aztec Horror Film." In *Sleaze Artists Cinema at the Margins of Taste, Style and Politics*, edited by Jeffrey Sconce, 121–43. Durham: Duke University Press, 2007.

Hawkins, Joan. *Cutting Edge: Art Horror and the Horrific Avant Garde*. Minneapolis: University of Minnesota Press, 2000.

Higson, Andrew. "The Concept of National Cinema." *Screen* 30, no. 4 (Autumn 1989): 36–47.

López, Ana M. "Facing up to Hollywood." In *Reinventing Film Studies*, edited by Christine Gledhill and Linda Williams, 419–37. London: Edward Arnold, 2000.

———. "Film and Radio Intermedialities in Early Latin American Sound Cinema." In *The Routledge Companion to Latin American Cinema*, edited by Marvin D'Lugo, Ana M. López, and Laura Podalsky, 316–28. London and New York: Routledge, 2017.

———. "Tears and Desire: Women and Melodrama in the 'Old' Mexican Cinema." In *Multiple Voices in Feminist Film Criticism*, edited by Diane Carson, Linda Dittmar, and Janice R. Welsch, 254–70. Minneapolis: University of Minnesota Press, 1994.

Mora, Carl J. *Mexican Cinema: Reflections of a Society, 1896-1980*. Berkeley: University of California Press, 1982.

Pelayo, Alejandro. *La generación de la crisis: El cine independiente mexicano de los años ochenta*. Mexico City: Conaculta, 2012.

Ramírez Berg, Charles. *Cinema of Solitude: A Critical Study of Mexican Film 1967-1983*. Austin: University of Texas Press, 1992.

Rohrer, Seraina. *La India Maria: Mexploitation and the Films of Maria Elena Velasco*. Austin: University of Texas Press, 2017.

Ruétalo, Victoria, and Dolores Tierney. *Latsploitation, Exploitation Cinema and Latin America*. New York and London: Routledge, 2009.

Schaefer, Eric. *Bold! Daring! Shocking! True!: A History of Exploitation Films 1919–1959*. Durham: Duke University Press, 1999.

Sconce, Jeff. "Trashing the Academy: Taste, Excess and an Emerging Politics of Cinematic Style." *Screen* 36, no. 4 (1995): 371–93.

Smith, Paul Julian. *Multiplatform Media in Mexico: Change and Growth Since 2010*. Cham: Palgrave Macmillan, 2019.

Syder, Andrew, and Dolores Tierney. "Mexploitation/Exploitation: Or How a Crime-Fighting Vampire-Slaying Mexican Wrestler Almost Found Himself in a Sword and Sandal Epic." In *Horror International*, edited by Stephen Jay Schneider and Tony Williams, 33–55. Detroit: Wayne State University Press, 2005.

Tierney, Dolores. *Emilio Fernández: Pictures in the Margins*. Manchester: Manchester University Press, 2008.

# CONTRIBUTORS

IVÁN EUSEBIO AGUIRRE DARANCOU is assistant professor at University of California, Riverside. His major research project traces how a series of cultural artifacts—comics, music, performance, film, concerts, journalism, theatre—were used by citizens during the Mexican post-revolutionary period to generate alternative narratives of nation, consumption habits, and counterculture. Other research projects focus on female and lgbtttqi countercultural producers from the 1960s to the present as well as examine the ways in which humanimal subjectivities interact with ideologies of nationalism and gender. His fields of interest include Mexican literature and culture, critical theory, film and media studies, queer theory, ethics, and countercultural studies.

CHRISTOPHER CONWAY is professor of Spanish at the University of Texas at Arlington, where he teaches classes on Latin American literature and culture. His publications include *Heroes of the Borderlands: The Western in Mexican Film, Comics, and Music* and *Nineteenth-Century Spanish America: A Cultural History*. He has published numerous scholarly chapters and articles on gender studies, comics and visual culture, the Latin American cult of Bolívar, and Latin American fiction. His current research interests are in comparative literature and American popular culture, including Westerns, comics, pulp, and film.

OLIVIA COSENTINO is Zemurray-Stone Post-Doctoral Fellow at the Stone Center for Latin American Studies at Tulane University. Her research focuses on questions of affect, gender, stardom, and spectatorship in post–Golden

Age and contemporary Mexican cinema and culture. This work has been published in *The Velvet Light Trap, Journal of Cinema and Media Studies*, and *iMex*, as well as in edited collections, most recently *Domestic Labor in 21st Century Latin American Film*. She is currently developing her monograph, *Starscapes*, on the intersections of modernity, youth stardom, and media in twentieth-century Mexico.

DAVID S. DALTON is associate professor of Spanish at the University of North Carolina at Charlotte. He is the author of *Mestizo Modernity: Race, Technology, and the Body in Postrevolutoinary Mexico*. His next monograph, tentatively titled *Robo Sacer: Technology and Identity in the Post-NAFTA Mexican Nation(s)*, discusses the transnational ties between the United States and México and the racial hierarchies that these have produced. He is currently editing several books and special editions, including projects on *cine de luchadores*, Mexican animated cinema, and healthcare in Latin America.

CAROLYN FORNOFF is assistant professor of Latin American literatures and cultures at the University of Illinois at Urbana-Champaign. She is coeditor of two volumes: *Timescales: Thinking across Ecological Temporalities* and *Pushing Past the Human in Latin American Cinema*.

BRIAN PRICE is professor of Spanish at Brigham Young University. His research focuses on contemporary Mexican culture, literature, film, and music. He is the author of *Cult of Defeat in Mexico's Historical Novel: Failure, Trauma, and Loss*, editor of *Asaltos a la historia: Reimaginando la ficción histórica hispanoamericana*, and coeditor of *TransLatin Joyce: Global Transmissions in Ibero-American Literature*. He is currently completing two manuscripts, one on rock literature and another on rock film in Mexico.

IGNACIO M. SÁNCHEZ PRADO is Jarvis Thurston and Mona van Duyn Professor in the Humanities at Washington University in St. Louis. His work focuses on Mexican culture, with a particular focus on literature, cinema, and gastronomy. He is the author of seven books and over one hundred articles and the editor of fourteen scholarly collections. On film studies, he has published the book *Screening Neoliberalism. Transforming Mexican Cinema 1988–2012* and is currently completing two monographs: a polemic on transnational Mexican film of the 2010s and a study of popular cosmopolitanism in mid-twentieth-century cinema.

DOLORES TIERNEY is senior lecturer in film in the School of Media, Arts and Humanities at the University of Sussex. She has published widely on Latin American, transnational, and inter-American cinemas in numerous journals including *Screen, Cinema Journal*, and *Porn Studies* and is the author of *Emilio Fernandez* and *New Transnationalisms in Contemporary Latin American Cinemas* and co-editor of *Latsploitation, Exploitation Cinema and Latin America* and *The Transnational Fantasies of Guillermo del Toro*. She is currently working on the history of Mexican cinema personnel in Hollywood between 1927 and 1934, focusing on Emilio Fernández's time there as extra, bit-part player, and B-movie actor.

# INDEX

Academia Mexicana de Artes y Ciencias Cinematográficas (AMACC), 15
Actors: Black, 146–61, 226; veteran, 175, 178–79, 206; youth, 18, 52, 167, 177, 180, 188. *See also* Casting; Star studies
*Actuación especial*, 167, 178, 181
Afro-Mexican, 144–64
Agrasánchez family, 167, 171–74, 224
Aguilar, Antonio, 120, 136
Aguilar, Luis, 42, 45, 47
Agustín, José, 90, 104, 108
*Ah, verdá . . . ?* (1974), 106–9
Alazraki, Benito, 23, 34, 51, 57, 62, 66, 207
*Al compás del rock and roll* (1957), 40, 59
Alemán, Julio, 120, 124–25, 136
Alemán Valdés, Miguel, 12, 112, 120
*Alguien nos quiere matar* (1970), 104
*Allá en el Rancho Grande* (1936), 41, 178
Almada: brothers, 63, 121–23, 136; Mario, 125, 137
*Alucarda* (1977), 202
*Amigo* (1980), 183
*Amityville II: The Possession* (1982), 207–8
*Amor a ritmo de go go* (1966), 51, 54–55
*Amor de mis amores* (2013), 71
Angélica María, 51, 204
*Angelitos negros* (1948), 146
*Aquellos años* (1972), 198–99
*Aquí, allá, en todas partes* (1971), 113

Argentine cinema, 177
Ariel Awards, 15–16, 207, 221, 225, 228
*A ritmo de twist* (1962), 34, 51–53, 57
*Atacan las brujas* (1968), 69–72
Auteur films, 22, 192–213, 222–23, 227; critical preference for, 14–15; and politics, 192–93, 196–200, 206–9, 225. *See also* Auteur theory; Cazals, Felipe
Auteur theory, 195, 213, 227
Avándaro, music festival, 51
*Avándaro* (1972), 104, 112
Ayala Blanco, Jorge, 34, 200, 203, 222
Azcárraga family. *See* Televisa

*Bajo la metralla* (1983), 206–11, 225
Banco Nacional Cinematográfico, 11–13, 89, 122, 196
*Barbarella* (1968), 109
Beatles, The, 51, 96
B-films, 208–9. *See also* Exploitation, films
Bias: institutional, 1–18, 35, 171, 225; racial, 143, 152, 155
*Blackboard Jungle* (1955), 38–39
Blackface, 142, 146, 148, 158. *See also* Racism
Blackness, 142–64, 226, 228; beauty standards of, 145, 150, 156–57; and politics, 149–50; stereotypes of, 143–44, 148, 156; and transnational audiences, 149–50, 153. *See also* Afro-Mexican

Black Panther Movement, 150
Blaxploitation, 21, 153–56
Botellita de Jerez, 103, 110
Bracho, Julio, 2, 204
*Burbujas de amor* (1991), 212–13

*Cadena perpetua* (1979), 15
Calderón family, 6, 167, 171, 220, 224, 227. *See also* García-Besné, Viviana
*Campanas rojas* (1982), 194
Cannes Film Festival. *See* Festivals, film
*Canoa* (1975), 192, 198, 207, 211
Cantinflas, 14, 49
Capitalism, 89–90, 102–4, 110
Cardona, René, Jr., 117, 176, 182
Cardona, René, Sr., 23, 60, 70, 74, 76–79, 117, 127, 130–31, 153
Caribbean, 36, 142, 146–47, 149, 153
Carrasco Zanini, Eduardo, 90, 96–98
Casting, 40–41, 71, 73, 142–48, 153
Castration, 123, 126, 129–30. *See also* Freud, Sigmund; Psychoanalysis
Cazals, Felipe, 15, 22, 193–213, 225, 227
Celestinos, David, 90, 93–96, 98, 104, 109
*Cementerio del terror* (1985), 173
Censorship, 12, 17–18, 26, 179, 185, 196–97, 200, 201, 206–9, 221
Charro, 7, 102, 103, 104, 110, 118–19, 120, 137
*Charro Negro* films, 118–20. *See also* De Anda, Raúl
*Chica moderna,* 63–79, 81
Chili Westerns, 8, 122–38, 226–27; and family, 120–21, 135–36; masculinity in, 21, 117–23, 126–38, 226; and politics, 21, 118–23, 226, 136; psychoanalysis of, 123–31, 137
*Chin chin el teporocho* (1975), 98
*Chuchulucos y arrumacos para burgueses* (1974), 107–8
Churro, 36, 48, 50–56. *See also* Rock films
*Cinco de chocolate y uno de fresa* (1968), 35, 104, 204
*Cine de calidad,* 3–4, 7, 9. *See also* Quality, cinema
*Cine familiar,* 166–89, 222, 225, 227; and child-adult appeal, 175–79; as escapism, 171, 181–85, 225; industrial conditions of, 167, 171–75, 185, 224; and music, 169, 177–78; and politics, 169, 180–83; on YouTube, 184–87, 222
Cineteca Nacional de México, 2–5, 14–15
*Ciudadano Buelna* (2013), 211, 213
Civil Rights Movement, 146, 152
Colorblindness, 157–59
Colorism, 148
Columbia Records, 37
*Comedia ranchera,* 29, 40, 42–43, 48, 51, 53, 56, 118, 178
Commercial cinema, 2–8, 13–14, 16–17, 22–23, 36, 48, 63, 166–68, 179, 186, 194, 211, 222–27
*¿Cómo ves?* (1986), 181
*Conan the Barbarian* (1982), 197, 208–9
Cooperativa de Cine Marginal, 98–99
Coproduction, 11, 153, 194, 197
*Coqueta* (1983), 179–80
Corona Blake, Alfonso, 62, 67, 72, 76
Corporación Nacional Cinematográfica (CONACINE), 197, 207–8
Corpus Christi Massacre, 51, 88
Cosmic race, 144–45
Cosmopolitanism, 20, 56, 202, 224, 235
Counterculture, 56, 89–113; music of, 91, 96; and politics, 92–93; and rock music, 35, 43, 49, 51; and student activism, 95–96, 101
Crisis: film industry, 1–22, 192–94, 196–97, 200, 220–22; and masculinity, 123–35; auteur in, 194, 206, 211
Cuarón, Alfonso, 184, 194
Cuban cinema, 221, 223
*Cumbia,* 200–203, 225. *See also* Music: popular

Dance trends, 8, 20, 36, 42, 53–54
Davison, Tito, 110, 154
De Anda, Raúl, 118–20
De Anda, Rodolfo, 120, 123, 127
*Decameron* (1971), 211
De la Riva, Juan Antonio, 14–15

De Laurentiis, Dino, 208, 216
Delgado, Miguel M., 35, 49, 51, 54, 179
*Delincuente* (1984), 174, 176
Delinquency films, 38–41, 46–48
*Del otro lado del puente* (1980), 201
Del Toro, Guillermo, 192, 194
*Desvestidas y alborotadas* (1991), 212
*Días de combate* (1982), 201
Díaz Morales, José, 23, 39–43, 69, 72
Díaz Ordaz, Gustavo, 122
Dirty War, Mexican, 206, 208
*Distinto amanecer* (1943), 204
Distribution, cinema, 10–11, 149; and censorship, 70, 208, 221; and *cine familiar*, 167, 175, 185; and Hollywood, 38; *superocheros*, 90–91, 102
Domingo, Plácido, 52, 59
*Dos tipos de cuidado* (1953), 118
*Duelo en el desierto* (1964), 120
*Dune* (1983), 197, 202, 207, 216

Eastwood, Clint, 125
Echeverría, Rodolfo, 89, 122, 193, 196
Echeverría administration, 51, 122, 192–93, 196–98, 214, 221–23
*El año de la peste* (1978), 198
*El apando* (1975), 22
*El castillo de la pureza* (1973), 15, 170
*El derecho de los pobres* (1973), 153, 154, 162
*El derecho de nacer* (1966), 154
*El fin* (1970), 101–4
*El gran triunfo* (1981), 201–5, 211
*El grito* (1968), 89
*El hombre de los hongos* (1976), 147, 150
Elías Moreno, José, 179
*El jardín de la tía Isabel* (1972), 198–99
*El lugar sin límites* (1977), 2, 193
*El Noa Noa* (1981), 201
*El peñón de las ánimas* (1942), 119
*El poder negro* (1975), 148
*El principio* (1973), 15
*El rayo justiciero* (1955), 121
*El sabor de la venganza* (1971), 136
El Santo (Rodolfo Guzmán Huerta), 2–6, 20, 24, 65–73, 82. See also *Lucha libre* films

*El Sargento Capulina* (1983), 177
*El Silencioso* (1967), 121
*El solitario* (1964), 120–22
*El topo* (1969), 126
*El tunco Maclovio* (1970), 117, 124–27
*El vampiro y el sexo* (1969), 24, 70
*Enlatamiento*. See Distribution, cinema
*Escápate conmigo* (1989), 182, 184
*Es mi vida* (1982), 201
*Esperanza* (1988), 15, 114
Estudios Churubusco, 11, 38, 41, 207–9
Exploitation, films: auteur, 194, 197, 199–212, 225, 227; Latin American (Latsploitation), 12, 17, 22; Mexploitation, 13, 26, 62–63, 65–68, 123, 168, 171, 174, 193, 223; and teenpics, 38; and the Western, 136, 155. See also Blaxploitation; Sexploitation

Family dynasty. See Galindo family; Televisa
Family films, Hollywood, 168–69, 182, 188. See also *Cine familiar*
*Fando y Lis* (1968), 126
Fernández, Emilio, 8, 14–15, 41, 193–94, 199
Fernández, Pedrito, 172, 174, 176–78, 181, 183, 222, 227
Festival Internacional de Cine de Morelia (FICM), 2, 6
Festivals, film, 8–9, 13, 16, 109
*Fichera*, film, 13, 117, 147, 155, 200, 212
*Fiebre de amor* (1985), 176, 182
*Fiebre de primavera* (1965), 177
Figueroa, Gabriel, 14, 199, 203
Film critics, 1–15, 35, 57, 179, 200, 222–23
Fons, Jorge, 193, 201, 216
Foro Tlalpan, 89, 112. See also García Michel, Sergio
Fourth cinema, 90–92, 105
Freud, Sigmund, 123–24, 126, 129
*Fuego negro* (1979), 154

Galindo family, 167, 171–75, 178–79, 183–84
Gámez, Rubén, 89, 94–95
García-Besné, Viviana, 6–7
García Michel, Sergio, 21, 89–92, 101–13. See also Super 8 films

Index 239

García Riera, Emilio, 15, 49–50, 125, 222
García Tsao, Leonardo, 211–12
Garduño, Eduardo, 11
*Gavilán o paloma* (1985), 201
Gaze, 89, 92, 104, 106, 107; male, 55, 67, 74, 78, 133, 139, 157; and race, 155, 157
Gender roles, 41, 44–45, 78–79, 90, 118, 137
*Goitia, un dios para sí mismo* (1989), 15
Golden Age of Mexican cinema, 1–14, 25, 38, 89, 220; and Chili Westerns, 135; and *cine familiar*, 170; and gender, 118
Guacarrock, 103, 110
Gurrola, Alfredo, 104, 109, 201
Guzmán, Enrique, 51–52, 104
Guzmán Huerta, Rodolfo. *See* El Santo

*Había una vez una estrella* (1989), 179, 186
Halconazo. *See* Corpus Christi Massacre
Herrera, Lorena, 212–13
Homosociality, 77, 132–38. *See also* LGBTQ+
*Hour of the Assassin* (1987), 209

Independent cinema, 4, 10, 14–15, 20–21, 48, 194
India María, La (María Elena Velasco), 14, 18, 26, 168, 179, 200
Infante, Pedro, 12, 14
Instituto Mexicano de Cinematografía (IMCINE), 15, 206
Instituto Politécnico Nacional (IPN), 43–44
Interracial romance, 154–61
Isaac, Alberto, 15, 206

Jenkins, William, 10–11
*Jipiteca*, 104, 113
*Jodidismo*, 96–98
Jodorowsky, Alejandro, 126, 198
Julissa, 110, 179, 181
*Juventud desenfrenada* (1956), 39, 41, 47

Katzman, Sam, 48–49
*Kino* (1993), 212

*La amargura de mi raza* (1972), 151–53
Laboriel, Johnny, 53, 104

*La choca* (1974), 15
*La Diana cazadora* (1956), 110
*La fórmula secreta* (1965), 93–94
*La locura del rock 'n roll* (1957), 40, 43–45
Lamarque, Libertad, 150, 153, 159
*La mugrosita* (1982), 179, 186
*La mula de Cullen Baker* (1971), 117, 127–32
*La nave de los monstruos* (1960), 62
Landeta, Matilde, 23, 146
*La negra Angustias* (1950), 146, 149
*La negrada* (2018), 161
*La niña de la mochila azul* (1979), 178, 184
*La niña de los hoyitos* (1984), 184
*La otra virginidad* (1974), 15
Lara, Agustín, 42–43
*Las inocentes* (1986), 210
*Las lobas del ring* (1965), 74, 78–80
*Las luchadoras contra el médico asesino* (1963), 73–75
*Las luchadoras contra la momia* (1964), 75–78
*La sombra del caudillo* (1960), 2
*Las poquianchis* (1975), 198–99, 203, 208, 211, 225
*Las puertas del paraíso* (1971), 15
*Las siete cucas* (1981), 205, 210
*Las víboras cambian de piel* (1974), 117, 131–35
Leduc, Paul, 2, 181
LGBTQ+, 200, 212, 228; hints of, 68–71, 117–20. *See also* Homosociality
*Llámenme Mike* (1979), 201
Llosa, Luis, 208–9
*Lo blanco, lo rojo y lo negro* (1979), 155, 158
*Locos peligrosos* (1957), 40, 45–47
López Moctezuma, Juan, 202
López Portillo, Margarita, 166–67, 170, 173, 180, 193, 196–97, 221, 226
López Portillo administration, 166–67, 173, 193, 196–205, 221–23, 228
*Los caifanes* (1967), 110
*Los chiflados del rock 'n roll* (1957), 40–43, 45
*Los dos carnales* (1983), 181
*Los hermanos del Hierro* (1960), 120, 124
*Los marcados* (1971), 136

*Los motivos de Luz* (1986), 210
*Los olvidados* (1950), 38, 58
*Los tres García* (1947), 41
Lucerito, 168, 172, 174, 177–78, 180, 182, 227
Luchadora cinema, 72–79, 226. *See also* Women's wrestling
Lucha libre films, 2–6, 14, 20, 62–72, 148, 224
Luis Miguel, 177–78, 180, 182, 201, 222, 227
*Lux externa* (1973/2003/2008), 108
Lynch, David, 197, 201

Malinche. *See* Virgin of Guadalupe / La Malinche binary
*Mamá, soy Paquito* (1984), 183
*Mamá Dolores* (1970), 151, 154, 162
*Mamá solita* (1980), 179, 186
*Mandingo* (1975), 154
Manzanero, Armando, 102, 104
*María Candelaria* (1944), 8, 162–63
*Mariana, Mariana* (1987), 15
Mariscal, Alberto, 116–17, 121–24, 136, 155
Martínez Ortega, Gonzalo, 15, 201
*Materia nupcial* (1974), 109
*Mecánica nacional* (1972), 15, 170
Melodrama, 9, 12, 18, 35, 41, 117, 143, 146, 153, 155, 159, 198, 226
Mestizaje, 21, 91, 103–4, 112, 143–64, 226
Mexicanidad, 8–9, 13–14, 24, 169–70
Mexican Miracle, 18, 55, 112, 123
*México, la revolución congelada* (1971), 206, 215
*Mi casa de altos techos* (1970), 93–96
Migrant communities, 18, 29
Mil Máscaras, 20, 148, 153
*Missing* (1982), 208, 216
Modernity, 8–9, 36, 149, 204
Modernization, 14, 19, 88, 93, 123, 202. *See also* Mexican Miracle
Monsiváis, Carlos, 117, 123–24, 182, 222–23
Montero, Rafael, 90, 107–8
Moore, Juanita, 146
*Mulata* (1953), 146
Music: covers, 37, 39, 46, 53; foreign, 37, 53–54; popular, 8, 35, 201–4; rock, 19, 20, 36–38, 40, 42, 45, 50, 52–54, 57–58, 90–91, 96, 104, 109–12. *See also Refritos*; Rock films
Musicians, 22, 42, 52–53, 55, 110, 200–202

*Naufragio* (1977), 15
Negrete, Jorge, 12, 118–19
*Negro es un bello color* (1974), 150, 159
New Latin American Cinema (NLAC), 13, 16–17
*Niño pobre, niño rico* (1983), 173–74, 178, 181–82, 222
Nuevo Cine, 13, 24, 123, 221–25

*Otro país* (1972), 99–101

Paxman, Andrew, 10–11, 25
Paz, Octavio, 72, 107, 124, 137
Peckinpah, Sam, 131, 209
Pelayo, Alejandro, 2–6, 14–15, 167, 194, 196
Pérez Turrent, Tomás, 166, 179, 199, 207–8, 222
Permanencia Voluntaria. *See* García-Besné, Viviana
Phillips, Alex, Jr., 199, 203, 212
*Pistoleros de la frontera* (1967), 121
*Policía judicial federal*, 110, 114
Popular cinema. *See* Commercial cinema
Presley, Elvis, 41–42, 51, 53, 202
Psychoanalysis, 117, 123–24

Quality, cinema, 3, 7, 9, 11, 14, 18, 63, 221–23, 228

Racism: anti-Asian, 75–76, 84; anti-Black, 142–64, 226, 228; anti-brown, 152, 162
Radio, Televisión y Cinematografía (RTC), 166, 167, 196–98, 207, 221
Ramírez Berg, Charles, 2, 12, 14, 18, 35, 118, 123, 194
*Reed: México insurgente* (1970)
*Refritos*, 37, 39, 53–54. *See also* Music: covers
Retes, Gabriel, 98–99
*Rigo, una confesión total* (1979), 203
*Rigo es amor* (1980), 201–5

*Río Escondido* (1948), 41
Ripstein, Arturo, 2, 15, 121, 170, 192–93, 198
Robles, Xavier, 208, 210, 216
Rock films, 34–59, 171, 224; and counterculture, 20, 35–36, 51, 59; delinquency in, 38–40, 46–48, 58; and family values, 43, 47; transitional, 36–52
Rodríguez, Ismael, 14
Rohrer, Seraina, 12, 17, 168
*Rosas blancas para mi hermana negra* (1970), 153, 158–60
Rossel, Liza, 54
Ruiz, Edaena, 70–71
*Rumbo a Brasilia* (1961), 146

Salazar, Abel, 153, 180, 201
*Santa* (1932), 41
*Santo contra las mujeres vampiro* (1962), 67–69
*Santo contra los hombres infernales* (1961), 10
*Santo en la venganza de la momia* (1973), 6
*Santo vs. los zombies* (1962), 62, 66–67
Second cinema, 16–17, 27. See also Nuevo Cine
Sexploitation, 13, 22, 147, 155, 205. See also Fichera, film; *Sexycomedias*
Sexuality: Black, 155–57; female, 68–80, 90, 104–12, 155–57, 200–205, 212, 228; male, 70, 155
*Sexycomedias*, 13, 170, 224
*Shane* (1953), 116
*Simón del desierto* (1965), 49
*Sólo con tu pareja* (1991), 184
Stahl, Jorge, Jr., 199
Star studies, 12, 18, 23; system, 36, 51–52, 63, 65, 76
Star vehicle film, 36, 201
Student movement, 19, 51, 92–96, 99, 206
Super 8 films, 20, 59, 88–112, 225–26, 228; music in, 91–92, 96, 100, 110–11; and politics, 88–90, 97–107, 111–12, 225–26; poverty in, 94–101; youth in, 101–9
*Superocheros*, 8–9, 21, 23, 88–113. See also Super 8 films

Televisa, 168, 175–78, 186, 197, 200–202
Television, 13, 16, 51–52, 116, 177–78, 200, 227
*The Cherry Orchard* (1978), 201
*The Gunfighter* (1950), 120, 121–22
*The Just Assassins* (1949), 208
*The Searchers* (1957), 116
*The Wild Bunch* (1969), 131
Third Cinema, 16, 89, 92, 106, 193, 195
Thomas, Philip Michael, 147
*Tiempo de morir* (1966), 121
Tlatelolco Massacre, 19, 88, 93, 95, 102, 136, 192, 221, 225, 226–27
*Todo por nada* (1968), 116, 121–22, 136
Tovar, Rigo, 201–5, 209, 212, 225
Transnational: film genres, 8–9, 137; markets and audiences, 37, 143, 147, 149–54, 175, 186, 193–95
*Twist Around the Clock* (1961), 49

*Una larga experiencia* (1982), 109
*Un corazón para dos* (1989), 176, 179, 187
Universidad Nacional Autónoma de México (UNAM), 43–44, 91, 102
*Un Quijote sin mancha* (1969), 49
*Un toke de roc* (1988), 109–11

Valdés, Germán, 45, 59
Valdés, Ramón, 46, 59
Vargas, Pedro, 42
Vega, Isela, 205, 210
Véjar, Sergio, 173–74, 176, 179
Velázquez, Jesús "Murciélago," 78, 80
Velázquez, Lorena, 12, 20, 62–82, 226
Velázquez, Víctor, 76–77
*Veneno para las hadas* (1985), 15
*Vestidas y alborotadas* (1968), 212
*Víctor Ibarra Cruz* (1971), 96–97
Videohome, 5, 18, 168, 197, 200, 209, 212
*Vidita negra* (1973), 156–57
Violence: in delinquency films, 39; racial, 151, 154; state, 88–90, 92–93, 101, 103–4, 110, 120–22, 206, 209; in Westerns, 124, 127–28, 135–36
Virgin of Guadalupe / La Malinche binary, 62–81, 226

*Viva la juvented* (1956), 39
*Vivir para amar* (1980), 203

Welter, Ariadna, 46, 85
Western: Hollywood, 116, 118, 123; Spaghetti, 122–23, 131, 135–37, 194, 209–10. *See also* Chili Westerns
Women, 12–13, 20, 23, 55–56, 62–75; and the family, 79–81, 106, 170, 210; independent, 75, 106–10, 226; stereotypes, 79; submissive, 41–48, 76–80, 210–11
Women's wrestling, 74, 78, 80, 84–85. See also *Luchadora* cinema

Yanga, Gaspar, 147
*Ya nunca más* (1984), 180, 222
*Ya sé quién eres (te he estado observando)* (1971), 104
Youth: audiences, 35, 224; culture, 34–35, 37, 56, 92, 93, 105–6; films, 17–18; and rock and roll, 40–41, 43, 50, 104; as social subject, 9, 94, 102–3, 108–9, 171, 183; stars, 167–68, 177–78, 180, 201
YouTube, 16, 22, 222; afterlife, 183–86

*Zona roja* (1976), 194

Reframing Media, Technology, and Culture in Latin/o America

EDITED BY HÉCTOR FERNÁNDEZ L'HOESTE AND JUAN CARLOS RODRÍGUEZ

Reframing Media, Technology, and Culture in Latin/o America explores how Latin American and Latino audiovisual (film, television, digital), musical (radio, recordings, live performances, dancing), and graphic (comics, photography, advertising) cultural practices reframe and reconfigure social, economic, and political discourses at a local, national, and global level. In addition, it looks at how information networks reshape public and private policies, and the enactment of new identities in civil society. The series also covers how different technologies have allowed and continue to allow for the construction of new ethnic spaces. It not only contemplates the interaction between new and old technologies but also how the development of brand-new technologies redefines cultural production.

*Telling Migrant Stories: Latin American Diaspora in Documentary Film*, edited by Esteban E. Loustaunau and Lauren E. Shaw (2018)

*Mestizo Modernity: Race, Technology, and the Body in Postrevolutionary Mexico*, by David S. Dalton (2018)

*The Insubordination of Photography: Documentary Practices under Chile's Dictatorship*, by Ángeles Donoso Macaya (2020)

*Digital Humanities in Latin America*, edited by Héctor Fernández L'Hoeste and Juan Carlos Rodríguez (2020)

*Pablo Escobar and Colombian Narcoculture*, by Aldona Bialowas Pobutsky (2020)

*The New Brazilian Mediascape: Television Production in the Digital Streaming Age*, by Eli Lee Carter (2020)

*Univision, Telemundo, and the Rise of Spanish-Language Television in the United States*, by Craig Allen (2020)

*Cuba's Digital Revolution: Citizen Innovation and State Policy*, edited by Ted A. Henken and Sara Garcia Santamaria (2021)

*Afro-Latinx Digital Connections*, edited by Eduard Arriaga and Andrés Villar (2021)

*The Lost Cinema of Mexico: From Lucha Libre to Cine Familiar and Other Churros*, edited by Olivia Cosentino and Brian Price (2022)

www.ingramcontent.com/pod-product-compliance
Lightning Source LLC
Chambersburg PA
CBHW030824230426
43667CB00008B/1368